D1260953

Books by ANDREW SARRIS

THE FILMS OF JOSEF VON STERNBERG [1966]
INTERVIEWS WITH FILM DIRECTORS [1967]
THE FILM [1968]
THE AMERICAN CINEMA: DIRECTORS AND DIRECTIONS,
   1929–1968 [1969]
FILM 68/69, COEDITOR [1969]
CONFESSIONS OF A CULTIST: ON THE CINEMA,
   1955–1969 [1970]
THE PRIMAL SCREEN: ESSAYS ON FILM AND RELATED
   SUBJECTS [1972]

THE
PRIMAL
SCREEN

ESSAYS ON FILM AND RELATED SUBJECTS

ANDREW SARRIS

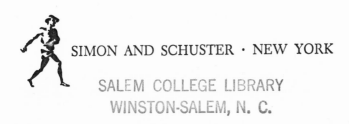

SIMON AND SCHUSTER · NEW YORK

SALEM COLLEGE LIBRARY
WINSTON-SALEM, N. C.

PN
1995
S354

COPYRIGHT © 1973 BY ANDREW SARRIS

ALL RIGHTS RESERVED INCLUDING THE RIGHT OF REPRODUCTION, IN WHOLE OR IN PART IN ANY FORM.

PUBLISHED BY SIMON AND SCHUSTER, ROCKEFELLER CENTER, 630 FIFTH AVENUE, NEW YORK, NEW YORK 10020

FIRST PRINTING

SBN 671-21341-5

LIBRARY OF CONGRESS CATALOG CARD NUMBER: 72-90401

DESIGNED BY EVE METZ

MANUFACTURED IN THE UNITED STATES OF AMERICA

For permission to reprint articles originally appearing in their publications the author gives grateful acknowledgment for the following:

FILM CULTURE for "The High Forties Revisited," "Notes on the Auteur Theory in 1962," and "The Man Who Shot Liberty Valance." Reprinted from *Film Culture* #24 (Spring 1962), #27 (Winter 1962/3) and Summer 62.

FILM COMMENT for "Notes on the Auteur Theory in 1970." Reprinted by permission from *Film Comment* Volume 6 Number 3, Fall 1970. Copyright © 1970 Film Comment Publishing Corporation.

THE NEW YORK TIMES for "Lola Montès," "Gawking at the Geeks," "Censorship: The Career of a Censor," "Josef von Sternberg," "Harold Lloyd," "Judy Garland," "The Dostoyevsky Game," "Richard Gilman," and "Jack Kerouac." Copyright © 1965/1967/1969/1970/1971 by The New York Times Company. Reprinted by permission.

PRINCETON ALUMNI WEEKLY for "James Stewart." Reprinted from *Princeton Alumni Weekly*, © 1971 Princeton University Press.

COLUMBIA UNIVERSITY FORUM for "Buster Keaton." Reprinted from *The Columbia Forum* Volume XII, No. 4 (Winter 1969). Copyright the Trustees of Columbia University in the City of New York.

MOVIEGOER for "Pop Go the Movies!" Reprinted from *Moviegoer* #2, Summer/Autumn 1964.

THE DRAMA REVIEW for "The Illusion of Naturalism." First published in *The Drama Review*, Volume XIII, Number 2 (T 42), Winter 1968. © 1968 by The Drama Review. Reprinted by permission. All rights reserved.

MID-CENTURY for "The Declining West," © The Mid-Century 1962.

ARTS MAGAZINE for "Role Playing and Parading." Reprinted from *Arts Magazine*, December 1966/January 1967, and "The Need for Film," reprinted from "The Museum World," Arts Yearbook #9, 1967.

SIGHT AND SOUND for "Censorship: A View from New York." Reprinted by permission from *Sight and Sound*, Autumn 1960.

and

THE VILLAGE VOICE for all others. Reprinted by permission of The Village Voice. Copyright by The Village Voice, Inc., 1964, 1965, 1966, 1967, 1969, 1970, 1971, and 1972.

This book is dedicated to
all the auteurists in Creation

CONTENTS

THE PRIMAL SCREEN: A FOREWORD

I have often wondered over the years why film critics seem to arouse so much controversy with so little effort. I am not referring now to the unseemly Senecan spectacle of warring critics in the process of dismembering each other. (See the battle records of Sarris–Kael, Sarris–Macdonald, and Sarris–Simon for some of the gruesome details.) Nor am I referring to the tedious misunderstandings between artists, their relatives, agents, promoters, and admirers on one side and the supposedly spiteful critics on the other. Film, after all, is hardly unique in its critical rivalries and in the anti-critical rhetoric of its art industry. And nothing is more human than a desire for praise coupled with an aversion to abuse. When my own writings are inadequately appreciated by some churlish book reviewer, I suddenly experience a twinge of remorse for all the victims of my judicial (and I hope judicious) sentences. Just a twinge, mind you, not a lasting pain, and with a glass or two of Vermouth Cassis I am back on the job again in a state of magisterial calm. Thus, I suppose, have critics through the ages coped with the banality of their emotional conflicts as they attempted to honor the sublime at the expense of the ridiculous. Not that critics should ever be too pompous in defining their role. Criticism is simply a job of work, and if one person doesn't do it, another will, and most of the hostility aroused by a critic's ego-crushing labors can be anticipated in advance.

Nonetheless, there does happen to be a complication unique to cinema in the curiously uneasy relationship between critic and audience. This unique complication I choose to designate as the Primal Screen, that factor of childhood reverie which forms a barrier between what we think about movies and what we feel about them. I have sensed this barrier as a critic, as a lecturer and as a teacher. Indeed, I have felt this barrier even within my own psyche. Just a touch of latent philistinism, I assured myself as I mopped my brow

SALEM COLLEGE LIBRARY
WINSTON-SALEM, N. C.

made feverish with nostalgia. But the fever never went away. And I wondered why. And then I stopped wondering for a time and resigned myself to periodic hot spells of enthusiasm. But I assumed professorial mannerisms all the same. I wrote and spoke of *mise-en-scène* and montage, of *auteurs* and *metteurs-en-scène*, of deep focus and jump cuts, and all the while I was aware of a psychic resistance all the more unnerving for being undefined.

As I look back on my own childhood in the Thirties, I can remember a time when movies were truly miraculous, a time when, like Buster Keaton in *Sherlock Jr.*, I could absorb the luminous forms and movements on the screen as personal fantasies without any intellectual interference whatsoever. Most moviegoers who grew up in the Thirties, Forties and Fifties (I can't really tell about the Sixties yet) experienced their first traumatic shock with the Primal Screen when they realized that those people up there were not really phantoms of their own infantile imaginings but instead flesh-and-blood careerists with vulgar existences off screen. This first step of emotional evolution—from fantasy to fandom—is often the last stop for a great many movie buffs. On the most naïve autograph-book level, stars are worshipped as the agents of their own destinies, the speakers of their own lines, the originators of their own movements and gestures, even the initiators of their own intrigues. Their very duplicity in existing apart from their roles becomes a divine duality. The love of the fan is increasingly diverted from the shadow to the substance, from the character to the actor, from the portrait to the model. In some ways, the step from fantasy to fandom is a step backward. What is gained in sophistication is lost in perception. The child who looks at the Primal Screen without any awareness of actors and actresses is more likely to appreciate images for their own sake. Once the child "recognizes" the faces on the screen, he begins neglecting the over-all spectacle. Hence, the compleat film critick must often return to the innocence of his earliest childhood to recapture an instinctive comprehension of *mise-en-scène*.

It is no accident that children of the television generation tend to prefer the kinetics of commercials to the relative stases of the regular programs. The unconceptualized eye is at the beginning and at the end of all visual appreciation. In between are the ideological distractions of psychology, sociology and applied aesthetics. Above all, there has been ever since the coming of the talkies the fatal distraction of the ear. From the Thirties onward, as we have gotten older we have tended to look at movies less and listen to them more. At least movies in the English language. The foreign art films have always been exempt from the tyranny of the ear. Our relative ignorance of foreign languages and alien folkways tended to return us to a state of innocence, a state in which we were more receptive to purely visual stimulation.

Not that I wish to argue the pre-eminence of the purely visual in cinema. I merely wish to suggest that if we had looked at American talkies as closely as we listened to them, much of the naïve overestimation of foreign-language films might have been avoided. I myself have contributed to this overestimation in the past simply because my eyes were glazed by sound. Of course, we are dealing here with precise historical coordinates. Film historians old enough to have witnessed the premiere of *Potemkin* never fully reconciled themselves to the demise of the silent film. Their feelings of loss and betrayal took curious forms. Evaluations in the early Thirties of the Marx Brothers, for example, tended to glorify mute Harpo at the expense of wise-cracking Groucho. The critical verdict nowadays is, of course, almost all Groucho. In fact, it is hard to remember that there was ever a time when we were solemnly told that comedians should be seen and not heard (*vide The Golden Age of Comedy* by James Agee). We cannot understand most of the film histories written between 1930 and 1950 if we do not take into account the Primal Screen in the Teens and Twenties, that period in which the late James Agee and his father experienced Charlie Chaplin for the first time. Indeed, there are people still alive who were born before there were any movies at all. Their autobiographies thus coincide with the archaeology of the cinema.

But until very recently the earliest moviegoing experiences, silent and sound both, were mercifully free of the stink of culture. There were no courses in the subject, no obligations and no imperatives. The voluptuous passivity with which we viewed movies took an ever increasing toll of cultural guilt. As we got older we began to develop a more defensive attitude toward this cultural vice to which we had become so hopelessly addicted. We began snickering at the love scenes and complaining excessively about those same old clichés.

The gap began to widen not so much between what we thought and what we felt as between what we really liked and what we dared admit we liked. The moviegoers who grew up to be culturally ambitious (and these are the great bulk of my readers, after all) assumed an ironic attitude toward the Primal Screen. Old movies could be regarded as childhood dreams, as occasions for spiritual communication with the vulgar masses, as invocations of a shared existence with the old folks. (I have always strongly suspected, without the slightest statistical verification, that the strongest manifestations of nostalgia for old movies are usually connected with dizzying, disorienting feelings of upward social and cultural mobility.)

Still, a curious paradox emerges out of our supposedly shared experiences with movies. Obviously a part of us recognizes that any given movie may have been seen by millions and millions of people, and yet in some ineffable way it must belong to each of us individually and uniquely, not really even to each of us but to the me, me, me alone in each of us. Often when I discuss a movie even casually with another person I suddenly have the feeling that we are gnawing at the movie like two dogs fighting over a bone for exclusive possession. It is not the usual taste-bud disagreement we might have over a book, a play, a painting or an opera. What is at stake is not so much which of us has judged it more accurately as which of us is more in tune with its dreamlike essence. It is a battle for spiritual custody. A great deal of the tension generated in even the most frivolous games of trivia arises from this unconscious desire to authenticate a collective experience as one's private property. Name the most obscure character actor in *Casablanca* you can think of, and there is at least some part of that cult movie that is more yours than anyone else's. (Even a violently iconoclastic critic like Manny Farber is not above playing a hip version of the trivia game by knowingly eulogizing Leonid Kinskey's performance in *Casablanca* when there are at least a dozen players more prominent and at least a score more memorable.)

The possessiveness engendered from earliest childhood by the Primal Screen undermines the authority of the film scholar and historian. Indeed, the film scholar is resented even more than the psychoanalyst if only because the psychoanalyst cannot interpret dreams without the collaboration of the patient-dreamer, and the film scholar can. It is the curse and glory of cinema that its visual-aural field is accessible to all viewers indiscriminately but is still emotionally intimate with each viewer individually. At least this has been true for that great mass of movies made for the darkness, movies that seem to dream us as much as we dream them. To be wakened from any dream can be psychically painful. To be wakened from movie dreams can be positively traumatic, especially when the alarm clock is an authority figure whose time has come historically if not emotionally.

When the neurotic becomes disengaged from his Pain, I believe he stops feeling in a complete way. The neurotic, until he really feels again, doesn't know that he isn't feeling. Thus, it is not possible to convince a neurotic that he is unfeeling. Feeling again seems to be the sole convincing factor. Until that happens, the neurotic might properly reply that he recently saw a tragic scene in a movie that moved him to tears. "Surely, that is feeling," he might say. But the person was not feeling his own personal sadness, and therefore, it would not be considered a full feeling. If he were to relate that movie scene to the exact conditions of his life, he might have a Primal right in the theater. Indeed, many Primals have begun when a patient discusses a movie scene that made him cry. However, the feeling in the theater and the subsequent feeling in the office are two disparate phenomena.

Tears in a movie are a fragment of the denied past of the neurotic. They are generally the result of the release of feeling rather than the expansion into total Primal feelings. The release process is what helps make the complete feeling unfelt. It vitiates and aborts the feeling and thus mitigates the hurt.

—ARTHUR JANOV, Ph.D., The Primal Scream, p. 71

Dr. Janov has kindly allowed me to make a pun on *The Primal Scream* with *The Primal Screen*, but my choice of title for both book and essay does not in itself imply a clinical concern with the medium. I am willing enough to accept Dr. Janov's thesis that movies are more a consolation than a cure for our neuroses. For the most part cinema is a halfway house between life and art, never quite one entirely, never quite the other entirely. This relatively indiscriminate intermingling of the real and the illusory tends to muddle the subject for the specialists. The clinical psychologist regards the compulsive moviegoer at best as a neurotic with an identity crisis and at worst as a hard-core voyeur. The high-brow aesthete finds the great mass of movies hopelessly vulgarized by merely representational elements and catchpenny illusionism. The sociologist interprets motion-picture history as a conspiracy of devious manipulators to condition the helpless masses with visual opiates. There is some validity to all the foregoing formulations and to many more equally invidious. If cinema is a halfway house, it is also an open house, veritably without walls, and it should not be necessary for defenders of film to shut off every draft. When I first became embroiled in the Hundred Years' War over the *auteur* theory, I was unduly sensitive to the charge that film enthusiasts like me were neurotic. As I have grown older I have come to realize that any form of enthusiasm involves the kind of psychic displacement that can be interpreted as a neurosis. Obviously, movies have long served many of our neurotic needs. No one who cries over Spencer Tracy's virile death scene in *Captains Courageous* can help mourning at the same time a father had, lost or wished for. The cynical dream merchants (and now political managers) who can spot an up-and-coming father figure a mile off have always had something to do with our tears and warm feelings, and a mixture of art, magic and carpentry have done the rest. But it would be a mistake to view the cinema in terms of unchanging archetypes. A curious sidelight on D. W. Griffith is instructive in this respect.

Griffith is relatively unique even among film pioneers in that he had become an adult before the advent of films. He was already forty when he began film history as we know it today with *Birth of a Nation* (1915), and thus to the conventional explanations of his decline we must add the simpler diagnosis of old age (*vide* The Marx Brothers, Mae West *et al.*). Much has been written of his Victorian heroines and their obsolescence in the supposedly roaring Twenties, but little if anything has been written on Griffith's physical intensity in treating family relationships, particularly the sibling attachments in *Dream Street* (brothers) and *Orphans of the Storm* (the sisters Gish no less). *Dream Street* came out in 1921 and *Or-*

phans of the Storm in 1922, and it is folly to speculate on the reactions of audiences a half century ago. Possibly they summed up
all their reactions in the convenient journalistic catch phrase "corny
and old-fashioned." No matter. What still seems strangely shocking
today is the full-mouthed kisses exchanged by the brothers in *Dream
Street* and by the sisters in *Orphans of the Storm*. Even allowing for
the fact that silent-screen acting was, of necessity, more physically
expressive than the more oblique acting styles in the talkies, Griffith's frankness and forthrightness in registering domestic emotions
still seem unusual to the point of embarrassment. That the behavioral
intensity of Griffith's family reunions and reconciliations far exceeded
the requirements of his scenarios indicates an especially personal
concern on his part. But he was not so much reproducing his own
emotional past (and no genuine artist ever attempts to do that) as
expressing remembered feelings through gestures of contact and
breakthrough. There is no reason to suppose that Griffith escaped
the emotional repressions and regrets of his White Protestant Border
State childhood. Nor the emotional release to be found in Victorian
melodrama. Unlike Chaplin, however, Griffith was never able to
find a consistently viable form with which to express his emotional
vulnerability. By the time of *The White Rose* (1923), the world
of his films was an open wound.

I suspect that where Griffith miscalculated, at least with his public,
was in not realizing that film itself had made audiences self-conscious
about the depiction of family feelings on the screen. Whereas Griffith
tended more and more to use the screen to project his emotional
memories, his audiences began to demand that the screen mirror
their own cooler fantasies. Thus we can chart probably the first
generation gap in the history of the medium. And what seemed like
decline (even to the late André Bazin) can be more properly and
more charitably described as a divergence between the memories of
the artist and the fantasies of the audience. No one's fault really.
Just part of the historical process connected with the Primal Screen.
However, historical process is as often cyclical as progressive, and
therefore no judgment is final. Taking Griffith as a case in point,
we find that his fevered vision has become more compelling in the
touch-scream-encounter-oriented Seventies than anyone would have
thought possible in the touch-and-go Twenties. As it is, historical

process has come very late to the Primal Screen. Through the Thirties, Forties and Fifties film revivals were extraordinarily infrequent due to the pressure of the "new product" coming off the assembly lines. Moviegoers were forced to construct their Primal Screen out of old memories, and they resented any effort to muck up these memories with scholarly footnotes. Most moviegoers would prefer to linger on the surface of the screen and not burst through beyond it. For beyond the screen lurks the very perplexing otherness from which the moviegoer is in full flight.

I am thus resigned to my role as professional spoilsport. How can you still enjoy movies, I am often asked more in sorrow than in anger, when you spend all your time analyzing them and researching them? All I can say in response is that I enjoy movies more than ever, but admittedly in a very different way from my very first excursions into the illuminated darkness. In the beginning the movies were miraculous manifestations of my own fantasies. Then came an awkward period of demystification with the cumbersome jargon of scenarios and camera angles, and it is this awkward period from which otherwise enlightened debunkers of film scholarship never quite recover. But at the end of this awkward period I have found a richer pleasure, less miraculous perhaps but certainly no less amazing than the first. Through the veils of magic I have perceived the essence of art. And what is amazing is that out of all the back-screen chaos and confusion and bickering and brawling there has emerged so much beauty and lucidity. Admittedly, the gods and goddesses and the spellbinders and sorcerers of the Primal Screen have been cut down to size. But that makes their achievements all the more admirable. And is it not more mature to view movies not as a mirror of our own dreams but as a window into the souls of others? Thus this book is dedicated not so much to the Primal Screen itself as to the historical process of which the Primal Screen is only a part.

I.

CRITICAL CREDOS AND CAUSES

THE HIGH FORTIES REVISITED

While reminiscing about "The High Forties" in the *Sight and Sound* of Autumn 1961, John Russell Taylor complains about the "sheer unavailability" of Forties films in Britain. The sheer unavailability of films everywhere is a recurring problem for aspiring scholars. It would be helpful if the various governments of the world appropriated funds for the preservation and systematic exhibition of all the feature films produced within their boundaries. (Something is wrong—and pleasantly absurd—when an American must visit Paris to see *Scarface*.) International exchanges could be arranged through the UN to acquaint critics in depth with a comprehensive world picture. Retrospective exhibitions of the complete output of key directors could be sent to every town and hamlet where any interest is indicated. Treatises, monographs and filmographies could be cleared and translated by an international agency for the propagation of cinematic information. Specialization in the backwaters of the cinema—e.g., *The History of Monogram*—might be encouraged by academic recognition in the form of honored chairs at burgeoning film academies.

Now that we have indulged the fantasies of film enthusiasts, let us return to grim reality. Anyone who wishes to check the verdicts of film historians must take what he can get when he can get it. Too often he will settle for faded, mutilated, even dismembered prints as alternatives to complete ignorance. If he is concerned primarily with texture and continuity, he will find American commercial-ridden television more visible than visual. In the course of his excavations he may become disheartened by the eerie loneliness of his calling and the low assay of gold to dross. Discovery may become an end in itself, and the deeper the excavations, the more pointless the attempt to communicate to the world on the surface level of comprehension. Instead of acquiring cultural respectability along the way, he will content himself with the grudging acknowledgments of kindred eccentrics. Yet, he will probably keep digging if only not to admit that a career has degenerated into an addiction.

Nonetheless, the cinema must justify itself at some point in the search. There is no purpose in crossing a desert if there are no mountain ranges beyond, and, consequently, if Hollywood in the Forties were not represented by the peaks of Chaplin, Welles, Ford, Hitchcock, Renoir, Ophuls, Hawks, Sternberg and others, the incidental absurdities of Veronica Lake and Maria Montez would not warrant much misplaced nostalgia. Fun is fun, but if the Forties are worth troubling about at all, they merit a degree of intellectual sincerity. Otherwise, too much time and work is involved. When Mr. Taylor expresses concern for young critics who have never seen *The Maltese Falcon* or *The Cat People*, he fails to convey the full dimensions of the vacuum. Over four thousand films were produced in Hollywood between 1940 and 1949. If young critics were permitted to see three films a day from this period at the British Film Institute, it would require almost four years to complete the course in the High Forties. Even if one restricted the curriculum to the 2,700-some-odd productions from the major studios, it would require almost three years to graduate. Considering the academic facilities available today, it is a bit unfair to chide the young for being unfamiliar with Val Lewton, an overrated cult property of the late James Agee. Besides, there is more to be gained by saving the Fifties and Sixties than mourning the unfortunate neglect of the Thirties and Forties, particularly when the older generation has failed thus far to produce an adequate critical history of the American sound film.

Despite his presumably good intentions, Mr. Taylor performs a disservice to the cause of revival when he observes: "But then with popular films it has always been, for the really dedicated regular at least, not so much what they are as who is in them which counts." The operative word here is "popular," an epithet which justifies a suspension of value judgments by removing Hollywood from the stream of serious film history. The same tone of condescending frivolity can then be applied to *Citizen Kane* and *Cobra Woman*, and the Forties can be defamed by an undiscriminating adoration, the

kiss, as it were, rather than the sword. Then also, as Louis Kronen-
berger has said of Oscar Wilde, "everything counts, and nothing
matters." However, what does matter in the Forties and in every
other period of the cinema is who is directing what and, subordi-
nately, with whom. The illusion that stars transcend their vehicles is
seldom sustained by retrospective judgment. Even the divine Garbo
has tough going in her wheezier projects, and would her image be
quite as lustrous today if it had not been for Cukor (*Camille*),
Lubitsch (*Ninotchka*) and Mamoulian (*Queen Christina*)? As for
Grierson's guerrillas, the Marx Brothers, it is not surprising that
their anarchic talents were best exploited by Leo McCarey in *Duck
Soup*.

It has been argued in the past by some critics that the American
cinema is a producer's rather than a director's cinema and that the
studio system standardizes the work of individual directors. Indeed,
the gist of Mr. Taylor's article implies an inability to distinguish (or
remember) individual films. Presumably, one can reach out at random and emerge with a typical film of the period with typical decor
and typical background music. There is one practical advantage to
such presumption, and that is prose relatively unencumbered by film
titles. Mr. Taylor roams through the period with twenty-five film
references, including the most casual citations and the captions for
stills. These include, in rough chronological order, *Rebecca* (1940),
The Lady Eve, *Citizen Kane*, *Suspicion* and *The Maltese Falcon*
(1941); *Bambi*, *Mrs. Miniver*, *Random Harvest* and *Cat People*
(1942); *Madame Curie* (1943); *The Curse of the Cat People*, *Miracle of Morgan's Creek*, *Double Indemnity*, *Cobra Woman* and
Dark Waters (1944); *To Have and Have Not*, *A Song to Remember*, *The Body Snatchers*, *Sudan* and *Scarlet Street* (1945); *The
Strange Love of Martha Ivers*, *The Dark Mirror* and *Strange
Woman* (1946); *Up in Central Park* and *Siren of Atlantis* (1948);
and *The Beautiful Blonde from Bashful Bend* (1949). Other references include two British films, *The Man in Grey* and *Gaslight*, if
the latter is the Dickinson rather than the Cukor version; the last
film of the Thirties, *Gone with the Wind*; two films of the Fifties,
The Asphalt Jungle and *Moulin Rouge* and Chabrol's *Les Bonnes
Femmes*, the last an invidious reference. On *Night of the Demon*,
Mr. Taylor has me. The only other person who has ever reported

seeing it is Bill Everson, and he has seen everything.

Apart from statistical inadequacy, the list of references is eclectic if not downright bizarre. At least we can be grateful for the omission of such socially conscious standbys as *The Ox-Bow Incident* and *Crossfire*, but they may have been omitted out of respect. It might also be noted in passing that Robert Siodmak's interview in *Sight and Sound* appears to have colored impressions of the period. The duration of the period is never firmly established in Mr. Taylor's article. "The Forties came in with the war and went out with the New Look," we are informed, but elsewhere in the article the Forties keep shrinking and expanding. Vincente Minnelli is treated as post-Forties although his first film was released in 1943, more than five years before Maria Montez impersonated the *Siren of Atlantis*. It is also difficult to understand why Judy Garland and Rita Hayworth are considered pre-Forties stars. Judy literally and figuratively grew up in the Forties, while Miss Hayworth, a contract vamp and second lead at Columbia in the late Thirties (*vide Only Angels Have Wings*), hit her stride in *Cover Girl* (1944) and *Gilda* (1946). One recalls the pin-up of her frolicsome pose in a negligee as one of the prominent artifacts of the war.

Almost every generalization Mr. Taylor makes can be refuted by a different selection of films and players, or even by unmentioned plot elements in the films he does mention. For example, according to Mr. Taylor: "The men—well, the men can be virtually ignored. Apart from one or two of the tough private eyes (Humphrey Bogart in the big pictures, Lloyd Nolan and Tom Conway in the series), they counted for little. Poor, weak, yielding creatures, lost in their shapeless, voluminous suits, they were trampled on by ruthless *femmes fatales* and sung at by high-powered feminine vocalists." Could Mr. Taylor have forgotten the startling number of betrayals and aggressions committed against the female of the species in the Forties? Bogart probably started it when he let Mary Astor "take the fall" in *The Maltese Falcon* even while she was embracing him. Alan Ladd delivered Veronica Lake (*Saigon*) and Gail Russell (*Calcutta*) to similar fates. Maureen O'Hara was John Garfield's pigeon in *Fallen Sparrow*, while Glenn Ford slapped Rita Hayworth out of a promising strip tease in *Gilda* before sending Janis Carter to the gallows in *Framed*. Dan Duryea rose to minor stardom by bashing Joan Bennett for Fritz Lang in *Woman in the Window* and *Scarlet Street*. The war of the sexes reached a stand-off in *Double Indemnity* and *Duel in the Sun*, where the lovers chose lethal revolvers to demonstrate their mutual passion through mutual perforations. Of course, one can prove everything and nothing with random plot citations. On this surface level, Hollywood has always had something for every taste except the very highest and the very lowest. The studio discouraged the former, the censors the latter, and the art of the cinema was probably retarded in the process. We shall never know, and it is a waste of time to speculate. Too many film histories have degenerated into a discussion of metacinema, the cinema which should or would have existed if governments, peoples, banks, studios and producers had been more enlightened.

If I have backed into the Forties through Mr. Taylor's stimulating article, it is only to demonstrate the hazards of not seeing the trees for the forest. Whether or not there is also a question of unfamiliarity breeding contempt, I cannot say. The temptation to generalize a subject with as many variables as the weather is understandable, and Mr. Taylor cannot be singled out for admittedly pre-adolescent fancies recollected without revaluation. What remains disturbing is the implication that Hollywood need not be taken too seriously in retrospect. Most American (and, I suppose, British) intellectuals have been conditioned to curl their lips ever so slightly at Hollywood for such a long time that admirers of the American cinema may become too strident in its defense. If the conception of the best Hollywood directors as full-fledged artists is to counter the image of an automated industry unconsciously purveying popular myths, articles on the Forties or any other arbitrary time span may do more harm than good. The chronological division of the cinema as one entity tends to perpetuate what may be called the pyramid fallacy of many film historians. This fallacy consists of viewing the history of cinema as a process by which approved artisans have deposited their slabs of celluloid on a single pyramid rising ultimately to a single apex, be it Realism, Humanism, Marxism, Journalism, Abstractionism or even Eroticism. Directors are valued primarily for their "contributions" to the evolution of a Utopian cinema efficiently adjusted to a Utopian society. Once a formal contribution has been made, subsequent refinements are downgraded. If Murnau disposed of camera movement, why should we honor Ophuls? Since most of the technical vocabulary, the zoom notwithstanding, was established by the end of the silent era, there has been a tendency to honor sound films almost exclusively for social content. The 1958 Brussels poll, which may have been the last gasp of the pyramid critics, cited only three sound films out of the top twelve, and of these three, *La Grande Illusion* and *The Bicycle Thief* were clearly content selections while *Citizen Kane* probably received mixed support from its formal and political partisans. (It might be noted that the recent *Sight and Sound* poll reflected the rising influence of the new French critics and film-makers.)

The patent system of the pyramid generally holds that silent directors invented forms while sound directors perfected styles, and in the pyramid histories, particularly those oriented to realism, stylists are the drones of the cinema. It might be uncharitable to suggest that stylists are harder to analyze than inventors and that it at least seems easier to define Eisenstein than to define Hitchcock. Actually, critics who are superficial about Hitchcock are usually superficial about Eisenstein as well.

One problem with the pyramid approach is that the base becomes rigid, and silent classics, especially, become encrusted with reverential moss. It is then almost as difficult to dislodge Pudovkin without disturbing Eisenstein as it is to move Stalin without compromising Lenin. Since new criticism is inevitably revolutionary, new critics may find it useful to smash the pyramid altogether and start with what they know first hand. Another hazard with the pyramid is that deviations from the apex are rejected even when acknowledged masters are involved. Indeed, what is most striking about pyramid histories is the number of directors who have allegedly declined, compromised, sold out, retreated from reality, evaded responsibility and otherwise gone astray. Some directors, of course, decline by any standards. It cannot be reasonably argued that René Clair in 1962 is equal to René Clair in 1932. What is tiresome about pyramid critics is their tone of moral outrage. In his *Sequence* attack on Hitchcock's Hollywood films, Lindsay Anderson seemed irritated even by the posh hotel Hitchcock patronized on his London visits. Perhaps the most remarkable pyramid denunciation of all time is Kracauer's criticism of German directors for being too esoteric for the masses.

What then is the alternative to the pyramid? I would suggest an inverted pyramid opening outward to accommodate the unpredictable range and diversity of individual directors. The time span of the cinema can then be divided into the career spans of its directors, each of whom is granted the options of a personal mystique apart from any collective mystique of the cinema as a whole. The inverted pyramid does not require a new manifesto. Critics and film-makers have been moving in that direction for the past decade. History as biography is reflected in the increasing frequency of director retrospectives and in the popularization of director cults. Television has siphoned off a great deal of the sociological criticism with which the cinema was once afflicted, and the new medium may eventually provide a permanent home for the documentary. Not that the era of high-brow promotion is without its drawbacks. In discovering the cinema, it may become even more fashionable to abandon the movies. It is one thing to enjoy an evening at Marienbad. It is quite another to spend the next ten years wandering through its interminable corridors without the slightest desire to see the new western down the street, particularly since Marienbad's redeeming humor is derived mainly from Hollywood.

When the Forties are revisited via the directors of the period, it becomes apparent that Hollywood has the capacity to ride off furiously in all directions and that generalizations about "trends" are usually derived from insufficient evidence. In retrospect, the major directors of 1940 by almost any standard except the most vulgar would include: Charles Chaplin (The Great Dictator), John Ford (The Grapes of Wrath, The Long Voyage Home), Alfred Hitchcock (Rebecca, Foreign Correspondent), Howard Hawks (His Girl Friday), Ernst Lubitsch (The Shop Around the Corner), George Cukor (The Philadelphia Story, Susan and God), Frank Borzage (The Mortal Storm, Strange Cargo, Flight Command), King Vidor (Northwest Passage, Comrade X), Fritz Lang (The Return of Frank James), Raoul Walsh (They Drive by Night, Dark Command), Preston Sturges (The Great McGinty, Christmas in July), Cecil B. De Mille (Northwest Mounted Police) and George Stevens (Vigil in the Night). One could stretch a point with Garson Kanin (My Favorite Wife, They Knew What They Wanted) and Gregory La Cava (Primrose Path), two likable directors with elusive personalities. Even more dubious are William Wyler (*The Letter*, *The Westerner*) and Lewis Milestone (*Of Mice and Men*, *The Night of Nights*, *Lucky Partners*), two overrated directors of the time with no personality at all. Although we have run through twenty-nine films, we have barely scratched the surface of Hollywood in 1940 from the point of view of the regular moviegoer.

The fun really begins down the line past the personalities and the stylists to the moderately competent and the expensively incompetent. The last step to the dregs is the inexpensively incompetent, and there only the most hardened movie addicts have ventured. (Their discoveries are often recorded in *Films in Review*, a publication which knows the credits of everything and the value of nothing.) Apart from such curiosities as George Abbott (*Too Many Girls*) and the one-shot team of Lee Garmes and Ben Hecht (*Angels Over Broadway*), Edward F. Cline, the directorial appendage of W. C. Fields (*My Little Chickadee*, *The Villain Still Pursued Her*, *The Bank Dick*), the lower middle range of directors include Busby Berkeley (*Strike Up the Band*, *Forty Little Mothers*), Clarence Brown (*Edison the Man*), John Cromwell (*Victory*), Michael Curtiz (*Virginia City*, *The Sea Hawk*, *Santa Fe Trail*), William Dieterle (*Dr. Ehrlich's Magic Bullet*, *A Dispatch from Reuters*), Allan Dwan (*Sailor's Lady*, *Young People*, *Trail of the Vigilantes*), Tay Garnett (*Slightly Honorable*, *Seven Sinners*), Edmund Goulding (*'Till We Meet Again*), Alexander Hall (*He Stayed For Breakfast*, *The Doctor Takes a Wife*), Henry Hathaway (*Johnny Apollo*, *Brigham Young*), Stuart Heisler (*The Biscuit Eater*), William K. Howard (*Money and the Woman*), Henry King (*Little Old New York*, *Maryland*, *Chad Hanna*), Henry Koster (*Spring Parade*), Rowland V. Lee (*The Son of Monte Cristo*), Mitchell Leisen (*Remember the Night*, *Arise My Love*), Robert Z. Leonard (*Pride and Prejudice*), Mervyn Le Roy (*Waterloo Bridge*, *Escape*), Anatole Litvak (*Castle on the Hudson*, *City for Conquest*, *All This and Heaven Too*), Rouben Mamoulian (*The Mark of Zorro*), George Marshall (*When the Daltons Rode*), Irving Pichel (*Earthbound*, *The Man I Married*, *Hudson's Bay*), Henry C. Potter (*Congo Maisie*, *Second Chorus*), Wesley Ruggles (*Arizona*, *Too Many Husbands*), Mark Sandrich (*Buck Benny Rides Again*, *Love Thy Neighbor*), Victor Schertzinger (*Road to Singapore*, *Rhythm on* the *River*), Vincent Sherman (*Saturday's Children*, *Flight from Destiny*), Robert Stevenson (*Tom Brown's School Days*), Andrew Stone (*The Great Victor Herbert*), Richard Thorpe (*The Earl of Chicago*), Jacques Tourneur (*Phantom Riders*), W. S. Van Dyke (*I Take This Woman, I Love You Again, Bittersweet*), Charles Vidor (*My Son, My Son, The Lady in Question*), James Whale (*Green Hell*) and Sam Wood (*Raffles, Our Town, Rangers of Fortune*). Now that we have approached the hundred film mark in 1940, we are considerably closer to the typical Hollywood film with which Mr. Taylor's article is concerned, but we cannot be sure even now that we have completed our preliminary research. If some bright new critic should awaken the world to the merits of Joseph Lewis in the near future, we will have to scramble back to his 1940 record: *Two-Fisted Rangers, Blazing Six-Shooter, Texas Stage Coach, The Man from Tumbleweeds, Boys of the City, Return of Wild Bill* and *That Gang of Mine*. Admittedly, in this direction lies madness.

The only way to manage the year and the period and the Hollywood cinema as a whole is to concentrate on the top people, accept occasional dividends from the "intermediates" and forget about the dregs. However, it is irresponsible to palm off a random sampling of the three levels as characteristic of the period. It is also a mistake to assume that strong star personalities can carry the day very often against vile direction. Anatole Litvak was given James Cagney for *City for Conquest*, John Garfield for *Castle on the Hudson*, Charles Boyer and Bette Davis for *All This and Heaven Too*, but all three films turned out heavy and turgid in the best Litvak tradition. On the other hand, Vivien Leigh and Conrad Veidt were well mounted by Mervyn Le Roy in *Waterloo Bridge* and *Escape* respectively, Marlene Dietrich salvaged *Seven Sinners* for Tay Garnett, Robert Montgomery made Richard Thorpe look adequate for *Earl of Chicago* and Judy Garland furnished Busby Berkeley and Mickey Rooney with some class in *Strike Up the Band*. This is the realm of happy accidents, studio policies and the autonomous elements of artless entertainment. Here the intellect must combat the outrageous responses of the nerve centers. I must admit that I prefer *Waterloo Bridge* to *The Return of Frank James* even though Mervyn Le Roy cannot begin to fit into Fritz Lang's shadow. There is at most one scene in the Lang which I can attribute to his personality, but the weakest Lang is still more interesting than the strongest Le Roy if only as a link in a longer and stronger chain of personal achievements. At least as far as movies are concerned, what we like is not always art. I suppose every critic has an unrecorded shame list of bad films he secretly enjoys along with a recorded pride list of serious films he secretly loathes. If the gap between what a critic really likes and what he officially admires is too great, he may overcompensate for his aesthetic guilt by exaggerating the gulf between art and entertainment in the cinema. Worse still, he may suggest to his readers that pleasure is a response to bad art.

Hollywood's vaunted dream apparatus has never worked with quite the efficiency attributed to it by serious critics. Its strength in the diversity of its genres can be misleading. An inept western or musical is not appreciably more enjoyable than a "serious" film. Only the most provincial audiences patronized the pulp westerns during the Thirties, and few people viewed Betty Grable and Dorothy Lamour as the embodiments of grace and beauty. When one talks about the "bread and butter" western, one is talking mainly about the westerns of Ford and Hawks and the post-*Duel in the Sun* Freudian westerns of King Vidor, Nicholas Ray, Raoul Walsh, Fritz Lang, Samuel Fuller, Budd Boetticher and Gerd Oswald. The Metro musical reached its flowering with Minnelli, Donen and Kelly and, on a lower level, Walters and Sidney. When one goes any lower, the Metro musicals become almost as much of an ordeal as the Fox and Warner atrocities. The mystiques of studio, producer, period and genre ultimately collapse before the mystique of the director, but the farther one gets from art, the harder it is to make distinctions. The consistently superior craftsmanship of a Leisen over a Leonard requires an incredibly esoteric analysis to prove the point. If the point is not necessarily worth making, it nevertheless confirms the validity of careful distinctions at every level of the cinema.

The intermediate directors did come up with occasional surprises in the Forties whenever stars, scripts and technicians suddenly clicked in an unexpected way. In addition to the ambitious sleepers of Arthur Ripley (*Voice in the Wind, The Chase*) and the overdiscovered Val Lewton horror classics directed by Jacques Tourneur,

Robert Wise and Mark Robson, there were more than fifty films which ran stronger than their directors. The bulk of these films were in the vehicle category, and the directors were usually specialists in dishing out the corn with a little flair. With actresses like Vivien Leigh, Margaret Sullavan, Bette Davis, Ida Lupino, Dorothy Mc-Guire, Jennifer Jones, Gail Russell, Laraine Day, a little corn went a long way, particularly with a score by Max Steiner, Victor Young or Frank Skinner. There were often good actors like Cary Grant, Robert Montgomery, Charles Boyer and John Garfield to balance things out.

If there is one intermediate masterpiece of the Forties, it is *Casablanca*, the happiest of happy accidents. Again Michael Curtiz is somewhat more moderately competent as a studio craftsman. Nevertheless, *Casablanca* emerges as a miracle of casting comparable to *The Maltese Falcon*. The idea of Humphrey Bogart, Ingrid Bergman, Paul Henreid, Claude Rains, Conrad Veidt, Sidney Greenstreet, Peter Lorre and Marcel Dalio acting together in a routine project suggests the incredible human resources of the period. The density of character acting in the Forties is so prodigious that the period is almost worth reviving just to see the various stock companies in action. Suddenly everyone seemed to be in Hollywood: Albert Basserman glaring at Maria Ouspenskaya past Walter Huston in Sternberg's *Shanghai Gesture*, the Mercury Players breaking into each other's lines, the festivals of bit players erupting in eight Preston Sturges films for Paramount in four years, the Warners night people, not to mention the return of Erich Von Stroheim, the arrivals of Peter Van Eyck, Alexander Granach and Carl Esmond, and the revivals of Judith Anderson, Ethel Barrymore and Francis Lederer. However, the waste of resources was equally prodigious. It was difficult to imagine then how absurd it would seem today to see Humphrey Bogart, Conrad Veidt and Judith Anderson cavorting in a tenth-rate espionage quickie like *All Through the Night*. We took such atrocities in stride because we had no idea that Hollywood was so close to sublimity and that one day we would remember with awe and futile regret. It is not entirely middle-aged nostalgia which prompts veterans of the period to recall the Forties as the Golden Age of the stars. The Thirties had filtered out the unadaptable silent players while the Fifties witnessed the abolition of the studio contract lists. Consequently, the Forties had the best of both eras. It is difficult to recall many Depression deities who did not at least work in the Forties; it is almost as difficult to cite many current stars who did not at least begin their careers in the Forties. If a specialist in actors were limited to films of the Forties, he would miss Jean Harlow, Marie Dressler, Helen Hayes, Louis Wolheim, Osgood Perkins, Ruth Chatterton, Helen Chandler and Phillips Holmes from the preceding decade, in most cases through untimely deaths. The few additions since 1949—Marlon Brando; James Dean; Grace Kelly; Audrey Hepburn, depending on the exact dates of her minor British credits; the male ingenues at Universal; the pallid blondes from Actors' Studio; the kooks and the curiously unattractive fashion models—have failed to keep pace with the needs of an aging star system. Hollywood's gradual hardening of the arteries is most conspicuously observed in this phase of the industry. It is perhaps more than a coincidence that on the directorial level as well, the older directors have continued to dominate the scene.

Even in 1940 the Hollywood cinema was aging at the top. Chaplin, Ford, Borzage, King Vidor, Walsh, De Mille and Dwan had directed their first films before 1920; Hitchcock, Hawks, Lubitsch, Lang, Wyler, Milestone and La Cava before sound; Cukor, Stevens, Kanin and Mamoulian after sound. Preston Sturges led off the writer-director movement in 1940, and there was a brief period of apparent rejuvenation. Orson Welles made his grand entrance in 1941 and was followed (at a considerable distance) by John Huston. Jean Renoir, René Clair and Robert Siodmak popped in from Europe, and Josef Von Sternberg and Frank Capra of the pre-sound generation extended their careers into the Forties. Billy Wilder, Albert Lewin, Anthony Mann, Jules Dassin and Fred Zinnemann hit the circuits in 1942; Leo McCarey, another pre-sound figure, resumed. Douglas Sirk and Vincente Minnelli led off 1943 followed by Norman Krasna, Mark Robson and Herman Shumlin. Otto Preminger resumed a career which had been marginal in the Thirties, and he was accompanied by ancient veteran John Stahl. Budd Boetticher, Clifford Odets and Phil Karlson were admitted in 1944; Elia Kazan and Robert Wise in 1945; Joseph L. Mankiewicz, Dudley Nichols and Robert Montgomery in 1946; Max Opuls (sic) and Joseph Losey in 1947; Abe Polonsky in 1948; Nicholas Ray and Samuel Fuller in 1949. When you add together the holdovers, the emigrés and the newcomers, Hollywood had enough directorial talent in the Forties to supply five golden ages. Even pioneers Griffith, Stroheim and Flaherty were available, Griffith and Stroheim as untouchables and Flaherty outside the industry. Hollywood was still close enough to its beginnings and far enough from television to look forward with some confidence, but everything seemed to go wrong at once. The anti-Communist drive expelled Chaplin, Losey and Polonsky, it now seems forever, and ironically all Hollywood could salvage after the storm had cleared were Edward Dmytryk, Carl Foreman and Robert Rossen. One by one, Renoir, Ophuls (sic), Lang, Siodmak and Clair returned to Europe. Ford and Hitchcock fell into disfavor with the critics and worked privately with "minor" genres, while Hollywood's man of all genres, Howard Hawks, continued to be anonymously successful. Welles and Sternberg joined Griffith and Stroheim in the ranks of the untouchables. Preston Sturges was exiled; Ernst Lubitsch, Gregory La Cava and John Stahl died. The superficial ugliness of neorealism gave Hollywood a bad case of artistic jitters, while British color fostered a professional neurosis. Above all, the critics went berserk on the pyramid of social significance. The wrong films and the wrong directors were honored. Propaganda was exalted above personality, as was verbal solemnity over visual style.

By 1948 Hollywood itself was so disgusted with its output that it nominated Hamlet and The Red Shoes for Academy Awards, with Hamlet winning. This was the year Opuls (Ophuls in less opulent Europe) was represented by Letter from an Unknown Woman, Welles by Lady from Shanghai, Ford by Fort Apache, Hitchcock by Rope, Hawks by Red River and Borzage by Moonrise, to mention just the most glaring omissions from chronicles of the period. The fact that all six of these films and their directors were underrated at the time suggests the area where reappraisal is most necessary. One advantage in following directors instead of the commercial trinity of stars, subjects and studios is the higher yield of lasting art. It is one thing to recollect the mediocre joys of one's youth. It is quite another to justify expenditures for the mere preservation of the past in a tangible form. If it were possible to save all the films of the period and then exhibit them in however haphazard an order, audiences could judge for themselves. It is quite likely, however, that a degree of selectivity will be required. After rummaging through hundreds of films of this period quite recently, I can find no sensible alternative to directors' retrospectives in organizing the period. The stars may be ageless, as Gloria Swanson reminds us in *Sunset Boulevard,* but they are not constant. Teresa Wright is scarcely bearable in Wyler's *Mrs. Miniver* and she is almost glorious in Hitchcock's *Shadow of a Doubt.* One could draw corresponding parallels for Montgomery Clift in Wyler's *The Heiress* and Hawks's *Red River,* for Zachary Scott and Betty Field in almost everything they did apart from Renoir's *The Southerner.* In retrospect, players who were wasted on bad directors lose ground to players who worked with the masters. Joan Fontaine (Ophuls, Hitchcock) finally triumphs over Olivia de Havilland (Wyler, Litvak). Anne Baxter (Renoir, Welles and later Hitchcock and Lang) and Joan Bennett (Renoir, Ophuls and Lang) are miraculously resurrected as directors' actresses, while Bette Davis and Ida Lupino have to be rescued from the footnotes to their vehicles.

The emphasis on subjects is even more hopeless. Where are the topical films of yesteryear, and who cares anymore about the burning social issues of that time? *Home of the Brave, Lost Boundaries, Pinky, Intruder in the Dust, Crossfire, Gentleman's Agreement, The Ox-Bow Incident, Watch on the Rhine, All the King's Men, None but the Lonely Heart, The Searching Wind* and even *The Best Years of Our Lives* date badly, so badly, in fact, that the old question arises: Are there major and minor subjects, or just major and minor artists? Very often it depends on whether cinema is considered analogous to painting or to literature, to abstraction or to representation. The alleged size of a screen subject is generally a function of the writing of the film, and unfortunately writing is and always has been Hollywood's weakest cog. Much of the apparent absurdity of the Forties can be traced to the superficial impact of scripts. For one thing, films were saturated with propaganda, some hung over from the Depression and the Spanish Civil War, some improvised after Pearl Harbor, less after the beginning of the Cold War because of box-office resistance. Hollywood propaganda is unlike propaganda anywhere else. Instead of boy meets tractor, we have boy meets long-legged or big-bosomed girl who talks about nothing but tractor. The idea of Gary Cooper posing as a ban-the-bomb atomic scientist in *Cloak and Dagger* should have appalled any intelligent scenarist, but the possibilities of subliminal, star-associated ideology always seemed irresistible to the commissars and gauleiters of the swimming pools. The proceedings of the House Un-American Activities Committee achieved their most hilarious effects in the analysis of individual films and sequences. It often came down to hack politicians arguing with hack writers about the content of commercials in the programming. Like all attempts at censorship, the political pressure on Hollywood was very silly and very harmful, but it is almost as silly to argue that Hollywood lost its soul as a consequence. After all, we still have the cinema of Stanley Kramer where no social issue is left to chance or central casting. A bigot in *Judgment at Nuremberg* must be played by the same unsavory character actor who mistreated a "One World" amputee in *The Best Years of Our Lives*.

However, even aside from the propaganda, Hollywood films have never read as well as they looked. The subterfuges to evade the censorship account for at least some of the ambiguities of the period. The spectacular mortality rate can be similarly attributed to the censor's insistence on some form of moral retribution, no matter how lurid. Hollywood still suffers from the Scribean script policy of the Thirties when each character was allotted one motivation and one motivation only. The relatively mysterious characterizations and moods of the Forties can be attributed in part to the vogue for psychoanalysis and in part to the stylistic revolution of *Citizen Kane*. Renoir's classic observation in *The Rules of the Game* that everyone has his reasons has become one of the premises of the modern cinema. Consequently, the gradual liberation of directors from the rigid moral allegories hammered out in studio-controlled script conferences give the films of the Forties a more personal quality than is found in comparable works of the Thirties. Nevertheless, only the top directors took full advantage of the period advantages.

It is now clear that Chaplin was moving into his deepest period in the Forties. As his public abandoned him, he revealed more and more of his personality. *The Great Dictator*, along with Renoir's *Diary of a Chambermaid* and Eisenstein's *Ivan the Terrible*, one of the few profoundly political films ever made, expressed the ambiguity of Chaplin's personality through a revealing comprehension of both Hitler and the barber. *Monsieur Verdoux* unmasked Chaplin even further, too far, in fact, for the public to accept. The increasing bitterness of Chaplin's art as he became older is, perhaps, a key to the American cinema as well. In their various ways, Welles, Ford, Hitchcock, Hawks and Sternberg became more confidential in their art, more indifferent to the critics and the public. Ford, for example, can now be traced more accurately from *Steamboat Around the Bend* through *Stagecoach* to the personal summit of his later westerns rather than from *The Informer* through *The Grapes of Wrath*. Hitchcock's parabola shows a steady rise from *Shadow of a Doubt* through *Notorious* and *Under Capricorn* all the way through to *Psycho*. His British period now looks like a primitive apprenticeship for the elaborate formality of the casuistic universe he was to create in Hollywood virtually unnoticed.

Some critics have attempted to organize the period and the American cinema as a whole in terms of studios, producers and technicians. Some of the more advanced visual critics have even started playing the photographer's game as an esoteric substitute for the director's game. There is just enough of a pattern in these areas to encourage a system, but research in depth, the relentless enemy of generalization, eventually wrecks the system. Subtract Gregg Toland from Welles and you still have a mountain; subtract Toland from Wyler and you have a molehill. Until 1945 Paramount had the fuzziest texture of any of the major studios. *Double Indemnity* looks particularly weak visually today vis-à-vis Fox's *Laura* and Metro's *Gaslight* that same year. Yet in 1945 the photography in Paramount's *Love Letters* and *The Lost Weekend* was superior to anything from the other studios. *Love Letters* can be explained by the temporary alliance of Lee Garmes and William Dieterle, but *The Lost Weekend* has no comparable variable. Studio identification was still meaningful in the Forties, but usually at the lower levels of production. The fact that Metro had the best lab work, Fox the best process shooting, Warners the best night quality is interesting but hardly crucial.

I am afraid it is impossible to generalize about a period represented by the polarities of Chaplin and Welles, Ford and Hitchcock, Hawks and Sternberg, Renoir and Ophuls, *The Southerner* and *Laura*, *My Darling Clementine* and *Notorious*, *Sergeant York* and *Shanghai Gesture*, *She Wore a Yellow Ribbon* and *Under Capricorn*, *Monsieur Verdoux* and *The Magnificent Ambersons*, *Swamp Water* and *The Exile*, *They Were Expendable* and *Lifeboat*, *High Sierra* and *Suspicion*, *The Air Force* and *Gaslight*, *They Live by Night* and *On the Town*. One advantage of the inverted pyramid is its sanction of alternatives. One need not be inconsistent to admire Chaplin and Renoir on the left, Ford and Hitchcock on the right and Sternberg in the erotic center. It is to be hoped also that one is not compelled to choose between the masculine code of Hawks and the boudoir sensibility of Ophuls. Instead of standing up to be counted, we might try sitting down to better concentrate on the great art in our midst. In the foreseeable future it will be difficult to prove that the continuity of a director's career is more interesting than the surfaces of individual films. The sheer unavailability of films will haunt us for some time to come, but once the principle of directorial continuity is accepted even in Hollywood, films can never look the same again. If there is ever an organized program for reviving the Forties, it should begin with all the films of all the directors who have the slightest factional support. After that, the period can be thrown open to the wildest actor, genre and studio cults. Of course, it would be even more desirable to go back to the beginning of each director's career and follow through to the end, letting the Forties intersect where they may. For all serious purposes, the High Forties were nothing more than ten years in the lives of a group of directors.

NOTES ON THE *AUTEUR* THEORY IN 1962

> *I call these sketches Shadowgraphs, partly by the designation to remind you at once that they derive from the darker side of life, partly because like other shadowgraphs they are not directly visible. When I take a shadowgraph in my hand, it makes no impression on me, and gives me no clear conception of it. Only when I hold it up opposite the wall, and now look not directly at it, but at that which appears on the wall, am I able to see it. So also with the picture which does not become perceptible until I see through the external. This external is perhaps quite unobtrusive but not until I look through it, do I discover that inner picture which I desire to show you, an inner picture too delicately drawn to be outwardly visible, woven as it is of the tenderest moods of the soul.*
>
> —*Søren Kierkegaard, Either/Or*

An exhibitor once asked me if an old film I had recommended was *really* good or good only according to the *auteur* theory. I appreciate the distinction. Like the alchemists of old, *auteur* critics are notorious for rationalizing leaden clinkers into golden nuggets. Their judgments are seldom vindicated because few spectators are conditioned to perceive in individual works the organic unity of a director's career. On a given evening, a film by John Ford must take its chances as if it were a film by Henry King. Am I implying that the weakest Ford is superior to the strongest King? Yes! This kind of unqualified affirmation seems to reduce the *auteur* theory to a game of aesthetic solitaire with all the cards turned face up. By *auteur* rules, the Fords will come up aces as invariably as the Kings will come up deuces. Presumably we can all go home as soon as the directorial signature is flashed on the screen. To those who linger, *The*

Gunfighter (King, 1950) may appear worthier than *Flesh* (Ford, 1932). (And how deeply one must burrow to undermine Ford!) No matter. The *auteur* theory is unyielding. If, by definition, Ford is invariably superior to King, any evidence to the contrary is merely an optical illusion. Now what could be sillier than this inflexible attitude? Let us abandon the absurdities of the *auteur* theory so that we may return to the chaos of common sense.

My labored performance as devil's advocate notwithstanding, I intend to praise the *auteur* theory, not to bury it. At the very least, I would like to grant the condemned system a hearing before its execution. The trial has dragged on for years, I know, and everyone is now bored by the abstract reasoning involved. I have little in the way of new evidence or new arguments, but I would like to change some of my previous testimony. What follows is consequently less a manifesto than a credo, a somewhat disorganized credo, to be sure, expressed in formless notes rather than in formal brief.

1. AIMEZ-VOUS BRAHMS?

Goethe? Shakespeare? Everything signed with their names is considered good, and one wracks one's brains to find beauty in their stupidities and failures, thus distorting the general taste. All these great talents, the Goethes, the Shakespeares, the Beethovens, the Michelangelos, created, side by side with their masterpieces, works not merely mediocre, but quite simply frightful.

—TOLSTOY, *Journal*, 1895–1899

The preceding quotation prefaces the late André Bazin's famous critique of *la politique des auteurs* which appeared in *Cahiers du Cinéma* of April 1957. Because no comparably lucid statement opposing the *politique* has appeared since that time, I would like to discuss some of Bazin's arguments with reference to the current situation. (I except, of course, Richard Roud's penetrating article "The French Line," which dealt mainly with the post-*nouvelle vague* situation when the *politique* had degenerated into McMahonism.)

As Tolstoy's observation indicates, *la politique des auteurs* ante-dates the cinema. For centuries, the Elizabethan *politique* has decreed the reading of every Shakespearean play before any encounter with the Jonsonian repertory. At some point between *Timon of Athens* and *Volpone*, this procedure is patently unfair to Jonson's reputation. But not really. On the most superficial level of artistic reputations, the *auteur* theory is merely a figure of speech. If the man in the street could not invoke Shakespeare's name as an identifiable cultural reference, he would probably have less contact with all things artistic. The Shakespearean scholar, by contrast, will always be driven to explore the surrounding terrain with the result that all the Elizabethan dramatists gain more rather than less recognition through the pre-eminence of one of their number. Therefore on balance, the *politique* as a figure of speech does more good than harm.

Occasionally some iconoclast will attempt to demonstrate the fallacy of this figure of speech. We will be solemnly informed that *The Gambler* was a potboiler for Dostoevski in the most literal sense of the word. In Jacques Rivette's *Paris Nous Appartient*, Jean-Claude Brialy asks Betty Schneider if she would still admire *Pericles* if it were not signed by Shakespeare. Zealous musicologists have played *Wellington's Victory* so often as an example of inferior Beethoven that I have grown fond of the piece, atrocious as it is. The trouble with such iconoclasm is that it presupposes an encyclopedic awareness of the *auteur* in question. If one is familiar with every Beethoven composition, *Wellington's Victory*, in itself, will hardly tip the scale toward Mozart, Bach or Schubert. Yet, that is the issue raised by the *auteur* theory. If not Beethoven, who? And why? Let us say that the *politique* for composers went Mozart, Beethoven, Bach and Schubert. Each composer would represent a task force of compositions, arrayed by type and quality, with mighty battleships and aircraft carriers flanked by flotillas of cruisers, destroyers and minesweepers. When the Mozart task force collides with the Beethoven task force, symphonies roar against symphonies, quartets maneuver against quartets, and it is simply no contest with the operas. As a single force, Beethoven's nine symphonies outgun any nine of Mozart's forty-one symphonies, both sets of quartets are almost on a par with Schubert's, but *The Magic Flute*, *The Marriage of Figaro* and

Don Giovanni will blow poor *Fidelio* out of the water. Then, of course, there is Bach, with an entirely different deployment of composition and instrumentation. The Haydn and Handel cultists are moored in their inlets ready to join the fray, and the moderns with their nuclear noises are still mobilizing their forces.

It can be argued that any exact ranking of artists is arbitrary and pointless. Arbitrary up to a point, perhaps, but pointless, no. Even Bazin concedes the polemical value of the *politique*. Many film critics would rather not commit themselves to specific rankings ostensibly because every film should be judged on its own merits. In many instances this reticence masks the critic's condescension to the medium. Since it has not been firmly established that the cinema is an art at all, it requires cultural audacity to establish a pantheon for film directors. Without such audacity I see little point in being a film critic. Anyway, is it possible to honor a work of art without honoring the artist involved? I think not. Of course, any idiot can erect a pantheon out of hearsay and gossip. Without specifying any work, the Saganesque seducer will ask quite cynically, *"Aimez-vous Brahms?"* The fact that Brahms is included in the pantheon of highbrow pick-ups does not invalidate the industrious criticism which justifies the composer as a figure of speech.

Unfortunately, some critics have embraced the *auteur* theory as a shortcut to scholarship. With a "you-see-it-or-you-don't" attitude toward the reader, the particularly lazy *auteur* critic can save himself the drudgery of communication and explanation. Indeed, at their worst, *auteur* critiques are less meaningful than the straightforward plot reviews which pass for criticism in America. Without the necessary research and analysis, the *auteur* theory can degenerate into the kind of snobbish racket which is associated with the merchandising of paintings.

It was largely against the inadequate theoretical formulation of *la politique des auteurs* that Bazin was reacting in his friendly critique. (Henceforth, I will abbreviate *la politique des auteurs* as the *auteur* theory to avoid confusion.) Bazin introduces his arguments within the context of a family quarrel over the editorial policies of *Cahiers.* He fears that by assigning reviews to admirers of given directors— notably Alfred Hitchcock, Jean Renoir, Roberto Rossellini, Fritz Lang, Howard Hawks and Nicholas Ray—every work, major and

minor, of these exalted figures is made to radiate the same beauties
of style and meaning. Specifically, Bazin notes a distortion when the
kindly indulgence accorded the imperfect work of a Minnelli is
coldly withheld from the imperfect work of a Huston. The inherent
bias of the auteur theory magnifies the gap between the two films.

I would make two points here. First, Bazin's greatness as a critic
(and I believe strongly that he was the greatest film critic who ever
lived) rested in his disinterested conception of the cinema as a universal entity. It follows that he would react against a theory which
cultivated what he felt were inaccurate judgments for the sake of
dramatic paradoxes. He was, if anything, generous to a fault, seeking
in every film some vestige of the cinematic art. That he would seek
justice for Huston vis-à-vis Minnelli on even the secondary levels of
creation indicates the scrupulousness of his critical personality.

However, my second point would seem to contradict my first.
Bazin was wrong in this instance insofar as any critic can be said to
be wrong in retrospect. We are dealing here with Minnelli in his
Lust for Life period and Huston in his Moby Dick period. Both
films can be considered failures on almost any level. The miscasting
alone is disastrous. The snarling force of Kirk Douglas as the tor-
mented Van Gogh, the brutish insensibility of Anthony Quinn as
Gauguin and the nervously scraping tension between these two absurdly limited actors deface Minnelli's meticulously objective decor,
itself inappropriate for the mood of its subject. The director's presentation of the paintings themselves is singularly unperceptive in the
repeated failure to maintain the proper optical distance from can-
vases which arouse the spectator less by their detailed draftsmanship
than by the shock of a Gestalt wholeness. As for Moby Dick, Gregory Peck's Ahab deliberates long enough to let all the demons flee
the Pequod, taking Melville's Learlike fantasies with them. Huston's
epic technique, with its casually shifting camera viewpoint, then
drifts on an intellectually becalmed sea toward a fitting rendezvous
with a rubber whale. These two films are neither the best nor the
worst of their time. The question is which deserves the harder review. And there's the rub. At the time, Huston's stock in America
was higher than Minnelli's. Most critics expected Huston to do
"big" things and, if they thought about it at all, expected Minnelli
to stick to "small" things like musicals. Although neither film was a

critical failure, audiences stayed away in large enough numbers to make the cultural respectability of the projects suspect. On the whole, *Lust for Life* was more successful with the audiences it did reach than was *Moby Dick*.

In retrospect, *Moby Dick* represents the turning downward of Huston as a director to be taken seriously. By contrast, *Lust for Life* is simply an isolated episode in the erratic career of an interesting stylist. The exact size of Minnelli's talent may inspire controversy, but he does represent something in the cinema today. Huston is virtually a forgotten man with a few actors' classics behind him surviving as the ruins of a once promising career. Both Eric Rohmer, who denigrated Huston in 1957, and Jean Domarchi, who was kind to Minnelli that same year, somehow saw the future more clearly on an *auteur* level than did Bazin. As Santayana has remarked: "It is a great advantage for a system of philosophy to be substantially true." If the *auteur* critics of the Fifties had not scored so many coups of clairvoyance, the *auteur* theory would not be worth discussing in the Sixties. I must add that, at the time, I would have agreed with Bazin on this and every other objection to the *auteur* theory, but subsequent history, that history about which Bazin was always so mystical, has substantially confirmed most of the principles of the *auteur* theory. Ironically, most of the original supporters of the *auteur* theory have now abandoned it. Some have discovered more useful *politiques* as directors and would-be directors. Others have succumbed to a European-oriented pragmatism where intention is now more nearly equal to talent in critical relevance. Luc Mollet's belated discovery that Samuel Fuller was, in fact, fifty years old signaled a reorientation of *Cahiers* away from the American cinema. (The handwriting was already on the wall when Truffaut remarked recently that where he and his colleagues had "discovered" *auteurs*, his successors have "invented" them.)

Bazin then explores the implications of Giraudoux' epigram: "There are no works; there are only authors." Truffaut has seized on this paradox as the battle cry of *la politique des auteurs*. Bazin casually demonstrates how the contrary can be argued with equal probability of truth or error. He subsequently dredges up the equivalents of *Wellington's Victory* for Voltaire, Beaumarchais, Flaubert and Gide to document his point. Bazin then yields some ground to

Rohmer's argument that the history of art does not confirm the decline with age of authentic genuises like Titian, Rembrandt, Beethoven or, nearer to us, Bonnard, Matisse and Stravinsky. Bazin agrees with Rohmer that it is inconsistent to attribute senility only to aging film directors while at the same time honoring the gnarled austerity of Rembrandt's later style. This is one of the crucial propositions of the *auteur* theory because it refutes the popular theory of decline for aging giants like Renoir and Chaplin and asserts instead that, as a director becomes older, he is likely to become more profoundly personal than most audiences and critics can appreciate. However, Bazin immediately retrieves his lost ground by arguing that whereas the senility of directors is no longer at issue, the evolution of an art form is. Where directors fail and fall is in the realm not of psychology but of history. If a director fails to keep pace with the development of his medium, his work will become obsolescent. What seems like senility is in reality a disharmony between the subjective inspiration of the director and the objective evolution of the medium. By making this distinction between the subjective capability of an *auteur* and the objective value of a work in film history, Bazin reinforces the popular impression that the Griffith of *Birth of a Nation* is superior to the Griffith of *Abraham Lincoln* in the perspective of timing which similarly distinguishes the Eisenstein of *Potemkin* from the Eisenstein of *Ivan the Terrible,* the Renoir of *La Grande Illusion* from the Renoir of *Picnic on the Grass* and the Welles of *Citizen Kane* from the Welles of *Mr. Arkadin.*

I have embroidered Bazin's actual examples for the sake of greater contact with the American scene. In fact, Bazin implicitly denies a decline in the later works of Chaplin and Renoir and never mentions Griffith. He suggests circuitously that Hawks's *Scarface* is clearly superior to Hawks's *Gentlemen Prefer Blondes* although the *auteur* theory would argue the contrary. Bazin is particularly critical of Rivette's circular reasoning on *Monkey Business* as the proof of Hawks's genius. "One sees the danger," Bazin warns, "which is an aesthetic cult of personality."

Bazin's taste, it should be noted, was far more discriminating than that of American film historians. Films Bazin cites as unquestionable classics are still quite debatable here in America. After all, *Citizen Kane* was originally panned by James Agee, Richard Griffith and

Otis Ferguson, and *Scarface* has never been regarded as one of the landmarks of the America cinema by native critics. I would say that the American public has been ahead of its critics on both *Kane* and *Scarface*. Thus to argue against the *auteur* theory in America is to assume that we have anyone of Bazin's sensibility and dedication to provide an alternative, and we simply don't.

Bazin finally concentrates on the American cinema, which invariably serves as the decisive battleground of the *auteur* theory, whether over *Monkey Business* or *Party Girl*. Unlike most "serious" American critics, Bazin likes Hollywood films, but not solely because of the talent of this or that director. For Bazin, the distinctively American comedy, western and gangster genres have their own mystiques apart from the personalities of the directors concerned. How can one review an Anthony Mann western, Bazin asks, if it were not an expression of the genre's conventions? Not that Bazin dislikes Anthony Mann's westerns. He is more concerned with otherwise admirable westerns which the *auteur* theory rejects because their directors happen to be unfashionable. Again, Bazin's critical generousity comes to the fore against the negative aspects of the *auteur* theory.

Some of Bazin's arguments tend to overlap each other as if to counter rebuttals from any direction. He argues in turn that the cinema is less individualistic an art than painting or literature, that Hollywood is less individualistic than other cinemas and that, even so, the *auteur* theory never really applies anywhere. In upholding historical determinism, Bazin goes far as to speculate that if Racine had lived in Voltaire's century, it is unlikely that Racine's tragedies would have been any more inspired than Voltaire's. Presumably the Age of Reason would have stifled Racine's Neoclassical impulses. Perhaps. Perhaps not. Bazin's hypothesis can hardly be argued to a verifiable conclusion, but I suspect somewhat greater reciprocity between an artist and his *Zeitgeist* than Bazin would allow. He mentions more than once, and in other contexts, capitalism's influence on the cinema. Without denying this influence, I still find it impossible to attribute X directors and Y films to any particular system or culture. Why should the Italian cinema be superior to the German cinema after one war when the reverse was true after the previous one? As for artists conforming to the spirit of their age, that spirit is often expressed in contradictions whether of Stravinsky and Sibelius, Fielding and Richardson, Picasso and Matisse, Chateaubriand and Stendhal. Even if the artist does not spring from the idealized head of Zeus, free of the embryonic stains of history, history itself is profoundly affected by his arrival. If we cannot imagine Griffith's *October* or Eisenstein's *Birth of a Nation* because we find it difficult to transpose one artist's unifying conceptions of Lee and Lincoln to the other's dialectical conceptions of Lenin and Kerensky, we are nevertheless compelled to recognize other differences in the personalities of these two pioneers beyond their respective cultural complexes. It is with these latter differences that the *auteur* theory is most deeply concerned. If directors and other artists cannot be wrenched from their historical environments, aesthetics is reduced to a subordinate branch of ethnography.

I have not done full justice to the subtlety of Bazin's reasoning and to the civilized skepticism with which he propounds his own arguments as slight probabilities rather than absolute certainties. Contemporary opponents of the *auteur* theory may feel that Bazin himself is suspect as a member of the *Cahiers* family. After all, Bazin does express qualified approval of the *auteur* theory as a relatively objective method of evaluating films apart from the subjective perils of impressionistic and ideological criticism. Better to analyze the director's personality than the critic's nerve centers or politics. Nevertheless, Bazin makes his stand clear by concluding: "This is not to deny the role of the author, but to restore to him the preposition without which the noun is only a limp concept." "Author," undoubtedly, but of what?

Bazin's syntactical flourish raises an interesting problem in English usage. The French preposition *de* serves many functions, but among others those of possession and authorship. In English, the preposition "by" once created a scandal in the American film industry when Otto Preminger had the temerity to advertise *The Man with the Golden Arm* as a film "by Otto Preminger." Novelist Nelson Algren and the Screenwriters Guild raised such an outcry that the offending preposition was deleted. Even the noun "author" (which I cunningly mask as "*auteur*") had a literary connotation in English. In general conversation, an "author" is invariably taken to be a writer. Since "by" is a preposition of authorship and not of ownership like the ambiguous *de*, the fact that Preminger both produced and directed *The Man with the Golden Arm* did not entitle him in America to the preposition "by." No one would have objected to the possessive form: "Otto Preminger's *The Man with the Golden Arm*." But even in this case, a novelist of sufficient reputation is usually honored with the possessive designation. Now this is hardly the case in France, where *The Red and The Black* is advertised as "*un film de Claude Autant-Lara*." In America, "directed by" is all the director can claim when he is not also a well-known producer like Alfred Hitchcock or Cecil B. De Mille.

Since most American film critics are oriented toward literature or journalism rather than toward future film-making, most American film criticism is directed toward the script instead of toward the screen. The writer-hero in *Sunset Boulevard* complains that people don't realize that someone "writes a picture; they think the actors make it up as they go along." It would never occur to this writer or to most of his colleagues that people are even less aware of the director's function.

Of course, the much abused man in the street has a good excuse not to be aware of the *auteur* theory even as a figure of speech. Even on the so-called classic level, he is not encouraged to ask, "Aimez-vous Griffith?" or "Aimez-vous Eisenstein?" As for less acclaimed directors, he is lucky to find their names in the fourth paragraph of the typical review. I doubt that most American film critics really believe that an indifferently directed film is comparable to an indifferently written book. However, there is little point in wailing at the philistines on this issue, particularly when some progress is being made in telling one director from another, at least when the film comes from abroad. The Fellini, Bergman, Kurosawa and Antonioni promotions have helped push more directors up to the first paragraphs of a review, even ahead of the plot synopsis. So we mustn't complain.

Where I wish to redirect the argument is toward the relative position of the American cinema as opposed to the foreign cinema. Some critics have advised me that the *auteur* theory applies only to a small number of artists who make personal films, not to the run-of-the-mill Hollywood director who takes whatever assignment is available. Like most Americans who take films seriously, I have always felt a cultural inferiority complex about Hollywood. Just a few years ago I would have thought it unthinkable to speak in the same breath of a "commercial" director like Hitchcock and a "pure" director like Bresson. Even today, *Sight and Sound* uses different type-sizes for Bresson and Hitchcock films. After years of tortured revaluation, I am now prepared to stake my critical reputation, such as it is, on the proposition that Alfred Hitchcock is artistically superior to Robert Bresson by every criterion of excellence and further that, film for film, director for director, the American cinema has been consistently superior to that of the rest of the world from 1915 through 1962. Consequently, I now regard the *auteur* theory primarily as a critical device for recording the history of the American cinema, the only cinema in the world worth exploring in depth beneath the frosting of a few great directors at the top.

These propositions remain to be proven and, I hope, debated. The proof will be difficult because direction in the cinema is a nebulous force in literary terms. In addition to its own jargon, the director's craft often pulls in the related jargon of music, painting, sculpture, dance, literature, theater, architecture, all in a generally futile attempt to describe the indescribable. What is it the old jazz man says of his art? If you gotta ask what it is, it ain't. Well, the cinema is like that. Criticism can only attempt an approximation, a reasonable preponderance of accuracy over inaccuracy. I know the exceptions to the *auteur* theory as well as anyone. I can feel the human attraction of an audience going one way when I am going the other. The temptations of cynicism, common sense and facile culture-mongering are always very strong, but somehow I feel that the *auteur* theory is the only hope for extending the appreciation of personal qualities in the cinema. By grouping and evaluating films according to directors, the critic can rescue individual achievements from an unjustifiable anonymity. If medieval architects and African sculptors are anonymous today, it is not because they deserve to be. When Ingmar Bergman bemoans the alienation of the modern artist from the collective spirit which rebuilt the cathedral at Chartres, he is only dramatizing his own individuality for an age which has rewarded him handsomely for the travail of his alienation. There is no justification for penalizing Hollywood directors for the sake of collective mythology. So invective aside, *aimez-vous* Cukor?

2. WHAT IS THE *AUTEUR* THEORY?

As far as I know, there is no definition of the *auteur* theory in the English language—that is, by any American or British critic. Truffaut has recently gone to great pains to emphasize that the *auteur* theory was merely a polemical weapon for a given time and a given place, and I am willing to take him at his word. But lest I be accused of misappropriating a theory no one wants anymore, I give *Cahiers* critics full credit for the original formulation of an idea which reshaped my thinking on the cinema. First of all, how does the *auteur* theory differ from a straightforward theory of directors? Ian Cameron's article "Films, Directors and Critics," in *Movie* of September 1962, makes an interesting comment on this issue: "The assumption which underlies all the writing in *Movie* is that the director is author of a film, the person who gives it any distinctive quality. There are quite large exceptions, with which I shall deal later." So far so good, at least for the *auteur* theory which even allows for exceptions. However, Cameron continues: "On the whole we accept the cinema of directors, although without going to the farthest-out extremes of the *la politique des auteurs* which makes it difficult to think of a bad director making a good film and almost impossible to think of a good director making a bad one." We are back to Bazin again, although Cameron naturally uses different examples. That three otherwise divergent critics like Bazin, Roud and Cameron make essentially the same point about the *auteur* theory suggests a common fear of its abuses. I believe there is a misunderstanding here about what the *auteur* theory actually claims, particularly since the theory itself is so vague at the present time.

First of all, the *auteur* theory, at least as I understand it and now intend to express it, claims neither the gift of prophecy nor the option of extracinematic perception. Directors, even *auteurs*, do not always run true to form, and the critic can never assume that a bad director will always make a bad film. No, not always, but almost always, and that is the point. What is a bad director but a director who has made many bad films? What is the problem then? Simply this: The badness of a director is not necessarily considered the badness of a film. If Joseph Pevney directed Garbo, Cherkassov, Olivier,

Belmondo and Harriet Andersson in *The Cherry Orchard*, the re-
sulting spectacle might not be entirely devoid of merit with so many
subsidiary *auteurs* to cover up for Joe. In fact, with this cast and this
literary property, a Lumet might be safer than a Welles. The realities of casting apply to directors as well as actors; but the *auteur*
theory would demand the gamble with Welles, if he were willing.

Marlon Brando has shown us that a film can be made without a
director. Indeed, *One-Eyed Jacks* is more entertaining than many
films with directors. A director-conscious critic would find it difficult
to say anything good or bad about direction that is nonexistent. One
can talk here about photography, editing, acting but not direction.
The film even has personality, but like *The Longest Day* and *Mu-
tiny on the Bounty*, it is a cipher directorially. Obviously, the *auteur*
theory cannot possibly cover every vagrant charm of the cinema.
Nevertheless, the first premise of the *auteur* theory is the technical
competence of a director as a criterion of value. A badly directed or
undirected film has no importance in a critical scale of values, but
one can make interesting conversation about the subject, the script,
the acting, the color, the photography, the editing, the music, the
costumes, the decor, etc. That is the nature of the medium. You
always get more for your money than mere art. Now by the *auteur*
theory, if a director has no technical competence, no elementary flair
for the cinema, he is automatically cast out from the pantheon of
directors. A great director has to be at least a good director. That is
true in any art. What constitutes directorial talent is more difficult
to define abstractly. There is less disagreement, however, on this first
level of the *auteur* theory than there will be later.

The second premise of the *auteur* theory is the distinguishable
personality of the director as a criterion of value. Over a group of
films a director must exhibit certain recurring characteristics of style
which serve as his signature. The way a film looks and moves should
have some relationship to the way a director thinks and feels. This is
an area where American directors are generally superior to foreign
directors. Because so much of the American cinema is commissioned, a director is forced to express his personality through the
visual treatment of material rather than through the literary content
of the material.

The third and ultimate premise of the *auteur* theory is concerned with interior meaning, the ultimate glory of the cinema as an art. Interior meaning is extrapolated from the tension between a director's personality and his material. This conception of interior meaning comes close to what Astruc defines as *mise-en-scène*, but not quite. It is not quite the vision of the world a director projects, nor quite his attitude toward life. It is ambiguous in any literary sense because part of it is imbedded in the stuff of the cinema and cannot be rendered in non-cinematic terms. Truffaut has called it the temperature of the director on the set, and that is a close approximation of its professional aspect. Dare I come out and say what I think it to be is an élan of the soul?

Lest I seem unduly mystical, let me hasten to add that all I mean by soul is that intangible difference between one personality and another, all other things being equal. Sometimes this difference is expressed by no more than a beat's hesitation in the rhythm of a film. In one sequence of *La Règle du Jeu* Renoir gallops up the stairs, stops in hoplike uncertainty when his name is called by a coquettish maid, and then, with marvelous post-reflex continuity, resumes his bearishly shambling journey to the heroine's boudoir. If I could describe the musical grace note of that momentary suspension, and I can't, I might be able to provide a more precise definition of the *auteur* theory. As it is, all I can do is point at the specific beauties of interior meaning on the screen and later catalogue the moments of recognition.

The three premises of the *auteur* theory may be visualized as three concentric circles, the outer circle as technique, the middle circle personal style and the inner circle interior meaning. The corresponding roles of the director may be designated as those of a technician, a stylist and an *auteur*. There is no prescribed course by which a director passes through the three circles. Godard once remarked that Visconti had evolved from a *metteur-en-scène* to an *auteur*, while Rossellini had evolved from an *auteur* to a *metteur-en-scène*. From opposite directions they emerged with comparable status. Minnelli began and remained in the second circle as a stylist; Bunuel was an *auteur* even before he had assembled the technique of the first circle. Technique is simply the ability to put a film together with some clarity and coherence. Nowadays it is possible to become a director without knowing too much about the technical side, even the crucial functions of photography and editing. An expert production crew could probably cover up for a chimpanzee in the director's chair. How do you tell the genuine director from the quasi-chimpanzee? After a given number of films, a pattern is established.

In fact, the *auteur* theory itself is a pattern theory in constant flux. I would never endorse a Ptolemaic constellation of directors in a fixed orbit. At the moment my list of *auteurs* runs something like this through the first twenty: Ophuls, Renoir, Mizoguchi, Hitchcock, Chaplin, Ford, Welles, Dreyer, Rossellini, Murnau, Griffith, Sternberg, Eisenstein, Stroheim, Bunuel, Bresson, Hawks, Lang, Flaherty, Vigo. This list is somewhat weighted toward seniority and established reputations. In time, some of these *auteurs* will rise, some will fall, and some will be displaced by either new directors or rediscovered ancients. Again, the exact order is less important than the specific definitions of these and as many as two hundred other potential *auteurs*. I would hardly expect any other critic in the world fully to endorse this list, especially on faith. Only after thousands of films have been re-evaluated will any personal pantheon have a reasonable objective validity. The task of validating the *auteur* theory is an enormous one, and the end will never be in sight. Meanwhile the *auteur* habit of collecting random films in directorial bundles will serve posterity with at least a tentative classification.

Although the *auteur* theory emphasizes the body of a director's work rather than isolated masterpieces, it is expected of great directors that they make great films every so often. The only possible exception to this rule I can think of is Abel Gance, whose greatness is largely a function of his aspiration. Even with Gance, *La Roue* is as close to being a great film as any single work of Flaherty's. Not that single works matter that much. As Renoir has observed, a director spends his life on variations of the same film.

Two recent omnibus films—*Boccaccio 70* and *The Seven Capital Sins*—unwittingly reinforced the *auteur* theory by confirming the relative standing of the many directors involved. If I had not seen either film I would have anticipated that the order of merit in *Boccaccio 70* would be Visconti, Fellini and De Sica and in *The Seven Capital Sins* Godard, Chabrol, Demy, Vadim, De Broca, Molinaro. (Dhomme, Ionesco's stage director and an unknown quantity in advance, turned out to be the worst of the lot.) There might be some argument about the relative badness of De Broca and Molinaro, but otherwise the directors ran true to form by almost any objective criterion of value. However, the main point here is that even in these frothy, ultra-commercial servings of entertainment, the contribution of each director had less in common stylistically with the work of other directors on the project than with his own previous work.

Sometimes a great deal of corn must be husked to yield a few kernels of interior meaning. I recently saw *Every Night at Eight*, one of the many maddeningly routine films Raoul Walsh has directed in his long career. This 1935 effort featured George Raft, Alice Faye, Frances Langford and Patsy Kelly in one of those familiar plots about radio shows of the period. The film keeps moving along in the pleasantly unpretentious manner one would expect of Walsh until one incongruously intense scene with George Raft thrashing about in his sleep, revealing his inner fears in mumbling dream talk. The girl he loves comes into the room in the midst of his unconscious avowals of feeling and listens sympathetically. This unusual scene was later amplified in *High Sierra* with Humphrey Bogart and Ida Lupino. The point is that one of the screen's most virile directors employed an essentially feminine narrative device to dramatize the emotional vulnerability of his heroes. If I had not been aware of Walsh in *Every Night at Eight* the crucial link to *High Sierra* would have passed unnoticed. Such are the joys of the *auteur* theory.

NOTES ON THE *AUTEUR* THEORY IN 1970

Now let's see where we were when we were so rudely interrupted by the shrill cackling of the unbelievers. We were talking about the late André Bazin and his attitude toward the *politique des auteurs* first promulgated by François Truffaut and about the paradoxically active and passive role of the director in the art and history of film. But that was back in 1962 ("Notes on the Auteur Theory in 1962"), and though the wench is not dead, that was another country. The critical landscape was still relatively barren, and it was possible to stake a claim on extensive deposits of intellectually untapped movie-making. Actually almost the entire American cinema had been consigned to oblivion before the *auteur* controversy compelled a reappraisal of panned and neglected movies like *Dinner at Eight, A Man's Castle, Secret Agent, She Married Her Boss, Angel, Holiday, Bringing Up Baby, The Magnificent Ambersons, They Were Expendable, Letter from an Unknown Woman, Fort Apache, Lady from Shanghai, Wagonmaster, The Golden Coach, Strangers, Kiss Me Deadly, Seven Men from Now, Baby Face Nelson, Vertigo, The Searchers, Touch of Evil, Bitter Victory, Johnny Guitar* and even *Psycho*, a movie it was culturally fashionable to despise back in 1960 when I began reviewing films in the *Village Voice*, my favorable review of *Psycho* having prompted a poison-pen barrage from *Voice* readers at that time. Hence, when Richard Corliss renders lofty judgments on the decline of Hitchcock from *Psycho* to *Topaz*, he neglects to mention that Hitchcock had been considered in grievous decline even at the time of *Psycho*. The battle of the Sixties was thus concerned largely with a re-evaluation of the Fifties, Forties and Thirties and, in the cases of Keaton, Sternberg and Griffith, even the Twenties. I never set out to guarantee the future but rather to consolidate the past, and this I feel I have done or at the very least helped get done. It is hard to believe today that there was ever a time when there were absolutely no books on the films of Alfred Hitchcock. Now in 1970 there are at least half a dozen book-length critical studies of Hitch, and the word *auteur* has entered the English language. (The New York *Times* Encyclopedic Almanac now defines an *auteur* as "a film-maker, especially a director, notable for his creativity and personal style.")

My erstwhile enemies may while away their ersts to their hearts' content. For my own part, I believe the time has come to move on to necessary modifications of a policy that has stood the test of time fairly well in the realm of film scholarship. As I said back in 1962, the *auteur* theory was proposed as a first step rather than a last stop in film aesthetics. Unfortunately, I was quoted out of context and even misquoted in publications with larger subscription lists than *Film Culture*, and, as a consequence, many fatuously self-serving testimonials about the function of film criticism were allowed to circulate in gaseous form. With so many puffed-up critical egos arrayed against me, it was only a matter of time before they started deflating each other. Indeed, one of the ironies of the *auteur* controversy is the loathing many of the anti-auteurists now openly express toward each other. This grotesque feuding tends to substantiate the warnings of the late André Bazin about the perils of purely impressionistic criticism.

Still, in the long run, as Disraeli once observed, we are all dead. And thus heartened as I am by my own gradual vindication and the falling out among my enemies, I am in no mood to forget and forgive. For the time being, however, I shall limit myself to some marginal observations on the lingering paradoxes of the *auteur* controversy. I shall present these observations in the form of notes to suggest the ellipses of that elaboration which is yet to come.

1. The original Sarris–Kael controversy was not so much over *auteurs* as over genres. Miss Kael, in her misapplied feminist zeal, is attuned more to kiss-kiss than bang-bang. It is her misfortune (though not ours) that the American cinema has always been stronger in bang-bang than kiss-kiss. Whereas Miss Kael believes that Barbra Streisand's cavortings in trashy musicals are worth thousands of words of gushingly Kaeleidoscopic prose, I believe that

movies like *Point Blank, Gunn, Madigan* and *Once Upon a Time in the West* are infinitely more interesting than any of Barbra's barbarities. And that is about all that can be said on the subject short of the Me Jane, you Tarzan fulminations Miss Kael originally invoked to add a new dimension to her *ad hominem* arguments. Unlike the great Garbo in *Ninotchka*, Miss K has always made too much of an issue of her womanhood. Even so, I have no special quarrel with Miss K's obsessive concern with Miss Streisand. Not that I have any desire to continue playing good old Charlie Brown to Miss K's Lucy, but I can't really discern any overriding moral issue involved in the conflicting tastes of two movie reviewers. Besides, even Miss K's most fervent admirers do not hold her to the humdrum standards of coherence and consistency to which the rest of us are accountable. Her critical apparatus has more in common with a wind machine than with a searchlight, and when all the papers and ticket stubs have stopped blowing around, it is difficult for the more orderly readers to find their bearings. Miss K is more an entertainer than an enlightener, and she is singularly ungenerous (at least in print) to her colleagues. She disdains the good manners (however teeth-clenched) of the scholarly community, and she scorns all the little film magazines that spawned her. For all her professed feminism, she has not been conspicuously kind to the increasing number of distaff reviewers in the field. Indeed, the increasingly perverse otherness of film criticism seems to cause her genuine distress despite all the success and recognition she has received. Her toleration of dissent is comparable in degree to Spiro Agnew's, and her capacity to communicate with any critic she hasn't spiritually castrated is virtually nil. Consequently, there is no point in arguing with Miss K; the most one can do is coexist in the same sphere of influence without succumbing to the Perils of Pauline, a tagline I invented seven years ago and still find timely.

2. Are some genres superior to others? Not necessarily and not by definition. Nonetheless there is a reflex action in high-brow circles to counterpose the tragedies of the noble Greeks, the earthy Elizabethans and the cerebrally seventeenth-century French against the relatively debased catch-all genre of bourgeois melodrama with which most movies of the twentieth century can be identified. To say you enjoy movies is thus comparable to saying you enjoy bour-

geois melodrama, and how can you possibly have such bad taste, you who have savored the great treasures of antiquity? Movies also lack the density and texture of the great novels of the past three centuries. Even the most dedicated film enthusiast would have to concede that on the whole the cinema has attracted not so much the super-renaissance artists is required aesthetically as the sub-renaissance artists it could accommodate professionally. Also, the cinema has shown a disconcerting affinity to relatively minor schools of literature and drama. More good movies have been made from W. S. Burnett's novels than from Fyodor Dostoevsky's. Ultimately, however, the metaphysics of melodrama in the movies is intimately bound up with their aesthetics. Jean-Luc Godard has observed that the cinema records the process of dying, with screen players inching ever closer to death with each second of screen time. However, the nature of the film industry has been such that actors and actresses have never been available for any given film for more than a few weeks or a few months, almost never as long as a year or two. Carl Dreyer has recalled in an interview with Michel Delahaye that the old actress who played the title role in *The Parson's Widow* knew she was dying when she was making the picture, but she assured Dreyer that she would last out her role, and she did, and her professional and existential tenacity was, by some sort of cruelly poetic logic, precisely the theme of *The Parson's Widow*. Robert Walker (*My Son John*), Spencer Tracy (*Guess Who's Coming to Dinner?*), Robert Donat (*The Inn of the Sixth Happiness*) and, above all, Carole Lombard (*To Be or Not To Be*) have similarly survived iconographically on the screen despite the immediacy of their earthly demise shortly after the end of shooting. The extent to which actors (documentary) not only interpret but augment characters (fiction) gives the screen a double aesthetic image. The inescapable realism of the documentary image restricts the scope and stature of the fictional image. But nowadays most professed admirers of classical tragedy are speaking of literary texts rather than staged spectacles, and no one suggests that the cultural tone of the screen was enhanced by Christopher Plummer's recent incarnation as Oedipus. As for the psychological and sociological amplitude of the novel, the cinema is locked into the musical time mechanism of montage and can only approximate the nuances of the novel with its fits and starts of complex compositions and encroaching camera movements. Such fountainhead films as *Birth of a Nation* and *Potemkin* actually chained montage to the most superficial form of scarifying melodrama, but film historians have been misled by the sociological veneer of the two works into locating the aesthetic essence of cinema art in its social concerns. Realism and social consciousness thus became the artistic alibis of socially conscious film historians, and genre films without sociological veneer were cast into the dustbins of commercial entertainments. The unstudied genres took their revenge by flourishing as fables of directorial feelings. Even today while everyone is obsessed with what Godard is up to, Sergio Leone, especially in *The Good, the Bad and the Ugly* and *Once Upon a Time in the West*, is expressing his deepest feelings in an allegedly depleted genre. But these are merely arbitrary facts in the history of the film industry. If movies had evolved in other ways, we would have had other facts to consider. The *auteur* theory was therefore never a theory at all, but rather a collection of facts, a reminder of movies to be resurrected, of genres to be redeemed, of directors to be rediscovered. To sum up, montage, the double imagery of documentary and fiction, the use of fables to express feelings, the sheltering cultural inferiority complex of the medium, the industrial organization of moviemaking and the contrasting demands of repetition and variation, combined to create a situation in which movies managed to break the most sacred rules of art, and the first became last, and the last became first.

3. Like Molière's *bourgeois gentilhomme*, who was astonished to discover that he had been speaking prose all his life, many sages of structuralism will soon be astonished to discover that the cinema, like Sigmund Freud, has been structuralist all along without knowing it. Does structuralism present a grave threat to the *politique des auteurs?* The current editors of *Cahiers du Cinéma* seem to think so as they scramble to divest themselves of their previously pluralistic commitments. I welcome structuralist analysis of the cinema as a means of confirming original intuitions about individual movies. But the structuralists will have to work a great deal harder with their basic material. I am afraid there are no short cuts to film scholarship. How can we say with any scholarly confidence that a screen metaphor is dead unless we open all the celluloid coffins in the vaults?

Can any mere *litterateur* fully analyze the motorcycle metaphors in *Easy Rider* without having seen *Orphée*, *The Wild One*, *Rebel Without a Cause*, *Scorpio Rising* and the entire Hell's Angels hagiography from American-International?

4. I once hailed *Casablanca* as a glorious exception to the *auteur* theory. I was wrong! There was more to the career of Michael Curtiz than met my unfriendly eye at the time. It should be remembered, however, that Bogart and Bergman were making jokes about the terrible lines they had to read in this turkey, and the New York critical establishment of 1943 was shocked when the stupid Academy passed up *Watch on the Rhine* to give its Oscar to *Casablanca*, a picture the public discovered despite the reviewers of the time. *Watch on the Rhine* looks terribly turgid by contrast, but New York critics of both stage and screen have always seemed to gorge themselves on Lillian Hellman's Marxist mayonnaise.

5. There is at least part of me that has always been studio slicker rather than moviemane, and I can sense click effects as well as anyone. I remember Ralph Blasi once asking me if *The Unseen* was worth seeing. Not particularly, I said, and then he advised me that he had enjoyed *The Uninvited* with the same genre (spooky horror), the same director (Lewis Allan) and the same ingenue lead (Gail Russell) and probably the same composer (Victor Young). I then made myself clearer by asserting in terms of geometric proportions that *The Unseen* was to *The Uninvited* as *Passage to Marseilles* was to *Casablanca*, a futile effort to cash in by reproducing the spell and mood of an unexpected hit. On the other hand, *The Bride of Frankenstein* and *The Son of Frankenstein* are more spellbinding than *Frankenstein* itself. Even the principle of sequels demands more scholarship than the facile phrasemakers in the field imagine.

6. When I originally wrote my first Howard Hawks career article, I went out on a limb to argue that the Hawksian fluidity of camera movement and invisibility of editing in *His Girl Friday* was actually faster than Lewis Milestone's classical montage in *The Front Page*. At the time, and it was many, many years ago, remember, I was bluffing a bit because I hadn't seen *The Front Page*. Lo and behold! When I finally did get to see *The Front Page* at the British Film Institute, my theory held up, but I still recall the incident in a spirit of contrition. There is no substitute for seeing a picture, and now-

adays film scholarship is infinitely more feasible than it was only a few years ago.

7. Many of the arguments that have been hurled against me over the years have had a curiously familiar ring, being many of the arguments I myself had raised in the first days of my film criticism. Indeed there was a time when a Stanley Kramer film made my ten-best list. You can look it up. All I want to do is forget.

8. The recent Jean Renoir retrospective at the New York Film Festival confirmed that Renoir's career was no less trend- and period-dominated than that of any of his Hollywood colleagues. He did the mandatory stage piece at the beginning of talkies (Feydeau's On purge bebe), a sub-Pagnol piece (Chotard & Cie.), a Simenon–Maigret policier (La Nuit du Carrefour), a great literary classic (Madame Bovary), etc. Renoir is no less an artist for reflecting his time as much as he transcends it. One must render unto Renoir what is Renoir's and unto the cinema what is the cinema's, but there is enough on the screen for everyone and everything, for the auteur and the Zeitgeist, for the director and the scenarist, for the actor and the character, for the art and the myth, for the fact and the fable.

9. We see Mizoguchi the way the French see Ford, more through mythic configurations than novelistic nuances, and we see Mizoguchi's style up to a point. I recently saw an obscure Mizoguchi film at New York's Museum of Modern Art without any English subtitles, which left me up the Sea of Japan without a paddle. The program notes alerted me to the plot outline, but I was generally puzzled by the personal relationships, and the picture dragged along. Mizoguchi's treatment of eroticism interested me momentarily because he seemed to have invented a characterization of a young servant as a crawling peeping Tom partly to keep the camera moving and partly to devise a human point of view for the spectacle of sexuality. And then at the end the beleaguered heroine walks to a restaurant on a hillside overlooking the sea, and she orders something from a waiter in white, and the camera is high overhead, and the morning mists are bubbling all around, and the camera follows the waiter as he walks across the terrace to the restaurant and then follows him back to the heroine's table now magically, mystically empty. It is as if death had intervened in the interval of two camera movements, to and fro, and the bubbling mists and the puzzled waiter provide the

Orphic overtones of the most magical *mise-en-scène* since the last deathly image of F. W. Murnau's *Tabu*.

10. Genres and *mise-en-scène*. Are these the clues to my deepest concerns? It would seem that my strongest instincts are Christian rather than Marxist and that I believe more in personal redemption than social revolution, and therefore I am more moved by the majestic camera movements of Mizoguchi and Ophuls than by the meteoric montage of Eisenstein and Resnais. The ascending and descending staircases of Hitchcock are more meaningful than all the Odessa Steps.

11. The recent stock-market crash confirmed the accuracy of that deliciously vicious scene in Antonioni's *L'Eclisse* where Alain Delon's boss rationalizes the crash in the Milan Stock Exchange by observing that "we now know the customers we can really count upon" (i.e., the customers that have not been wiped out by margin calls). During the recent Wall Street debacle, the same sort of comment from brokerage bigwigs was reported almost daily in the financial pages of the New York *Times*.

12. As the movies have declined in mass appeal, we are stuck more and more with vulgarity without sociology, but movies have achieved a practical permanence they never possessed before. And so more and more the long view prevails over the immediate impression. A 16-millimeter print of Sam Fuller's *Forty Guns* is now circulating with Fuller's original ending and not the studio compromise that was inflicted on him. As much as I sympathize with Fuller's intentions, I do believe that he and his admirers are rewriting film history in an unconscionable way. It reminds me of the time many years ago when Roger Tilton would end a showing of Murnau's *Last Laugh* prematurely so that the class would not be corrupted by the ironically happy ending. We must look at the past, especially the movie past, as it was and not as we would have liked it to be. This kind of sentimental revisionism is too typical of the muddled effort to redeem the past by denying it ever happened. Like the Hammett-Chandler private eyes of yesteryear, the *auteurist* must probe ruthlessly into the past and accept the consequences. Nothing can faze this *auteurist*, least of all the revelation that "Rosebud" in *Citizen Kane* was originally a bicycle that Herman J. Mankiewicz once lost in Wilkes-Barre, Pennsylvania.

AUTEURISM VS. AMNESIA

An acidulous critique of *Performance* printed in the New York Sunday *Times* some months ago took writer-director Donald Cammell to task for daring "to plagiarize and subvert one of the most brilliant themes from one of the profoundest films of all time: Ingmar Bergman's *Persona*: the faces of Fox and Jagger melt together and, thenceforth, the two perform toward, against, and into each other." If Cammell can reasonably be charged with plagiarizing Bergman's visual device of "melting together" two faces—i.e., super-imposing one face on another—then Bergman himself can as reasonably be charged with plagiarizing that same effect in his 1967 *Persona* from Alfred Hitchcock's 1957 *The Wrong Man*. And, even in 1957 facial superimposition was a tired old trick out of the German Expressionist bag.

Elsewhere in the critique, Roman Polanski's *Repulsion* is cited as the stylistic source for the switch from color-present to black-and-white-past in *Performance*. As it happens, all of *Repulsion* is photographed in black-and-white, and even if it weren't, Roman Polanski could hardly be credited with inventing chromatic chronology. Almost a decade before *Repulsion* Alain Resnais' harrowingly ironic documentary on the Nazi death camps, *Night and Fog*, counterposed color and black-and-white as the visually dialectical equivalents of the tensions between past and present, history and memory. William Wyler's *The Collector* employed the same device a few years later as an amplification of dramatic psychology. When I noted Wyler's stylistic debt to Resnais in *The Collector* (and to Godard for the jump cuts borrowed from the 1960 *Breathless* to serve the more explicit melodrama of the 1962 *The Children's Hour*), a reader reminded me that the stylistic split between black-and-white reality (Kansas and all that) and color fantasy (Oz and all that) occurred originally back in 1939 in *The Wizard of Oz*. And only this year, Joseph L. Mankiewicz reminded me that the freeze-frame, far from having been invented as a film ending by François Truffaut for *The 400 Blows*, closed out the farcical festivities of George Cukor's *The Philadelphia Story* back in 1940.

The preceding samples of film lore are intended not so much to advance the cause of antiquarianism as to pinpoint the perils of academic amnesia in much of what passes for serious film criticism these days. As the number of instant cinema scholars increases daily, the temptation to bypass the tortuous past of film history increases also. How convenient it would be if all movies made before 1955 could be derogated as "primitive" or "commercial" or "vulgar." No long hours of tedious screenings would then be required of the film scholar. Film history could begin with Bergman, Fellini and Antonioni and end, I suppose, with Godard, and it wouldn't even be necessary to see and resee even the films of Godard, Bergman, Fellini and Antonioni after a complete line of illustrated scripts had been made available in book form.

Ironically, the very academicians who bemoan the supposed lack of historical and cultural curiosity in their students encourage these same students to ignore the bulk of film history by subordinating movies to every other art form. Hence, Bergman is merely a pretext to quote Strindberg, Fellini merely a visual aid for Dante, and Antonioni merely a footnote to Pavese. Not that Strindberg, Dante and Pavese are to be despised. I am as much for ecumenical erudition as the next renaissance man. But the time has come to acknowledge film scholarship as an end in itself and not merely as a means to revitalize the lesson plans of other cultural disciplines. That is not to say that every scholar in literature and the fine arts is forbidden to mention any film without having covered the whole area. What I am saying is that those scholars who have chosen to specialize in film are more likely to treat film as a cultural continuum than are the mere slummers from other sectors of academe.

Not so long ago this argument would have been academic in every sense of the word. The few published dispensers of film lore fell into either the fan or pan category. The fan category concentrated on gushy incantations of the gods and goddesses of the silver screen minus the distractions of sacrilegious distinctions. By contrast, the

pan category provided a litany of despair and disillusion to explain
how and why glorious cinemah had been betrayed by inglorious
movies. The net effect of both approaches was to deter intelligent
people from any intense contemplation of the flickering shadows on
the screen. Films were acceptable as an eccentric hobby, even as part
of the sociological context of their time, but not as a subject of intellectual concentration and academic specialization.

Of course, there were exceptions to this smug attitude in the relatively enlightened writings of Otis Ferguson, James Agee and
Manny Farber. Unfortunately, Agee's reviews were published posthumously out of the context of his immediate concerns, Ferguson's
was published belatedly in 1971 nearly two decades after his death,
and the still living Farber has also achieved hard-cover commemoration in 1971. The point is that these relatively sensible observers
of films never attained the influence (or affluence) they deserved
mainly because they did not indulge in the more fashionable forms
of anti-movie derision. Their influence even on film academe is still
less than it should be because they chose to write on *individual*
movies rather than on cinemah as a whole. To those unfamiliar with
most of the trees in the film forest, Agee's reviews of the Forties
seem cryptic, mystifying and esoteric. Better to pass over Agee for
those self-proclaimed film histories in which old newspaper clippings
are bound together with sociological glue. Even when Agee was lionized by the literary reviews, it was not so much because of his ab-
sorption in movies as in spite of it.

Hence, we have W. H. Auden's fashionably double-edged praise
of Agee's film reviews in 1944: "I do not care for movies very much
and I rarely see them; . . . I am all the more surprised, therefore, to
find myself not only reading Mr. Agee before I read anyone else in
The Nation but also consciously looking forward all week to reading
him again." Otis Ferguson was admired with similar ambiguousness
by Alfred Kazin, and Manny Farber is not without champions
among the cinephobes. But that isn't the point. The brilliant insights that came out of these men, as out of Vachel Lindsay, Robert
Warshow and Erwin Panofsky, came from their regarding movies
not with an upturned nose but with an open mind and heart. There
has to be more to fruitful film scholarship than a moviegoing mania,
but there has to be that at least. And why should it be any stranger

for a film scholar to be a movie buff than for a literary scholar to be a print freak?

Curiously, the resistance to serious film scholarship can now be found on both sides of the generation gap. Some of the Now people have difficulty remembering as far back as Richard Lester's romp with the Beatles in A Hard Day's Night six long years ago. To go back to such ancient works as Citizen Kane and The Blue Angel is comparable to studying Stonehenge. On the other side of the gap are those part-time scholars of film who remember Chaucer as if it were yesterday but find Keaton dated and irrelevant. And in between are the general run of book reviewers who deride every serious firsthand contemplation of film history as too specialized for the general reader. Hence, the visually sophisticated studies of Robin Wood on Hitchcock and Bergman and of Raymond Durgnat on Bunuel and Franju are ignored for the sake of still more empty-headed picture books with a fun-and-games frivolity in the text. No matter. The tide is turning slowly but surely as more films become available for study and reappraisal in 16 and 8 millimeter prints, on cassettes, in museums, institutes, revival houses and on television. Academic amnesia would seem to be doomed by the new arithmetic of film distribution.

If I counterpose auteurism to amnesia it is not because I wish to force a choice between Hitchcock and Bergman, but rather because I believe that a fuller understanding of Hitchcock and Bergman is possible when they are seen in the total context of the cinema. It is certainly permissible to talk about The Magic Flute in connection with Bergman's Hour of the Wolf. Bergman himself encourages the analogy with a gratuitous lecture on musical mise-en-scène transcending exposition to become incantation. But as Mozart's music is relevant to Hour of the Wolf, so is Murnau's visual mise-en-scène in Nosferatu, and Dreyer's in Vampyr, and Browning's in Dracula. How else can we do justice to the themes of vampirism Bergman introduces so overtly not only in Hour of the Wolf, but also in Persona? Again I am not forcing a choice between Mozart and Murnau, but rather suggesting a sensibility that can embrace both. There have been such sensibilities around for a long time, and it is time we started appreciating them.

POP GO THE MOVIES!

> Now in reality, the world have paid too great a compliment to critics, and have imagined them men of much greater profundity than they really are. From this complaisance the critics have been emboldened to assume a dictatorial power, and have so far succeeded that they are now become the masters, and have the assurance to give laws to those authors from whose predecessors they originally received them.
>
> —HENRY FIELDING, Tom Jones
>
> In point of fact, what is needed is a criticism of movies as a pop art which can have a critical currency beyond that of footnotes and preposterous learning.
>
> —LAWRENCE ALLOWAY, "Critics in the Dark,"
> Encounter, February 1964

Abstract aesthetics, especially on cinema, is generally the unreadable in search of the indescribable. Consequently, it would never occur to me as it has to Mr. Lawrence Alloway to analyze the corpus of Anglo-American film criticism for sense and sensibility. My strongest inclination is to let sleeping dogmas lie when it is such a thankless task to resurrect dead prose. Mr. Alloway, for better or worse, is undaunted by mere tedium. He tells us once more what we have been told so often and have never seriously doubted, that most writing on film does not belong to the ages. But who is Lawrence Alloway to lecture us at this late date on our deficiencies? The author's squib in Encounter offers at least a rudimentary introduction: "Lawrence Alloway is at present curator of the Guggenheim Museum in New York City. He has been a well-known English art critic, lecturer at the Tate Gallery and programme director of the Institute of Contemporary Arts. He was born in London (1926).

From time to time he has written about the cinema (see 'Monster Films,' in *Encounter*, January 1960) . . ."

From this brief description it would seem that Mr. Alloway possesses all the essential attributes of the compleat film critic, at least in literary circles. He writes about films only intermittently and in the most general terms, much like his distinguished alternate on *Encounter*, Nicola Chiaromonte. Alloway's well-chosen words gain added luster from the fact of his gainful employment outside the cinema, if not actually above it. That Alloway writes persuasively and can quote Hazlitt and Baudelaire in appropriate contexts is not to be denied, but it is doubtful that his *Encounter* polemic would have attracted much attention if he had not augmented the mystique of Movie-movies with the currently fashionable jargon of pop art. Ironically, the essential core of Alloway's argument originally appeared in the February 1963 issue of *Movie* ("Lawrence Alloway on the Iconography of the Movies"), where it was generally ignored. At that time I suspected that the editors of *Movie* had printed Alloway to further dissociate themselves from the more extreme tendencies of the *politique des auteurs*. I was tempted to submit a rebuttal, but I couldn't work up much enthusiasm against a movie-lover when I was up to my ears in controversy with movie-haters.

I must confess at this point that I still regard Alloway with mixed emotions. Many of the idiotic positions he attacks or dismisses are still entrenched in American academies from coast to coast. For example, there are prominent people who still believe that the cinema ended with *Potemkin*. (What's black and white and Red all over?) Alloway performs a public service by deflating the "conservative humanists" and their Luddite banners emblazoned with slogans against sound, color and CinemaScope. His blast at the slovenly sincerity of realist pronouncements is beautifully to the point:

Perhaps only in film criticism would it be possible to assume that capacious O.K. words like "honesty" and "reality" provide a general critical standard. A unified theory of cinema (though badly needed) will not be made by acts of exclusion on the basis of a sloganized vocabulary which prescribes the conditions and forms that reality can take.

Where I differ with Alloway is in his oversimplification of the notion of personal authorship in the cinema. Like most opponents of director criticism, Alloway assumes that the *politique des auteurs* denies the existence of writers, actors, composers, technicians and producers except as figments of the director's imagination. I would be the first to concede that any critical theory carried to extremes is absurd. When you become too addicted to the *politique*, you wind up listening to visiting Frenchmen whispering into your ear that Edgar G. Ulmer has just directed a nudist film anonymously. When you peruse Eversonian encyclopedics to their last footnotes, you find nothing peculiar in compiling filmographies of Gloria Jean and Rin-Tin-Tin. If you follow the daily reviewers slavishly, you end up believing that Christian-Jaque makes better movies than Robert Bresson. In fact, the philistinism of American reviewers makes *Sight and Sound* look like the house organ of the MacMahonists. (I might take this opportunity to apologize to Miss Penelope Houston for what she termed my "repellent" abbreviation of *la politique des auteurs* to the *auteur* theory. I had originally considered the more fragrant essence of *eau d'auteur*, but I decided that my Anglo-American detractors would maliciously mistranslate the theory as "Ode to the Author.") The point is that in America we are always overcompensating for the extremisms, real and alleged, of others, thus becoming extremists ourselves. Within the past year, particularly, the polemical tone of American film magazines has become so shrill that only the most dog-eared listeners could possibly derive any stimulation.

Yet, granting all the shortcomings of the American critical scene, it is difficult to believe that Alloway is seriously proposing a remedy. The terms in which he defines the cinema, whether as "the index of a Baudelairean art of modern life" with "modernity" defined by Baudelaire as "that which is ephemeral, fugitive, contingent upon the occasion" or as "the art-synthesis proposed by Wagner, the total-work to which all arts contribute," are terms vague to the point of vacuity, hypocritical genuflections to the authority of a personal past in the name of an impersonal present. Alloway's derogatory references to Jean Renoir and Carl Dreyer in tandem with a respectful citation of Nicola Chiaromonte suggest an astute awareness of the editorial climate at *Encounter*. Baudelaire and Wagner have been exhumed to buttress two of Alloway's dubious premises, Baudelaire the expendability and forgettability of movies, Wagner the hopelessly muddled collectivity of movie-making. In his eagerness to di-vest the cinema of personal responsibility and durable value, Allo-way transforms what is too frequently a dismal fact into a visionary ideal. Badness and banality become sociological virtues; familiarity breeds contentment. This is not the attitude of the true movie ad-dict who is too experienced to like everything he sees, but more the rationale of condescending content awareness without any deep commitment to formal excellence.

By casually mentioning a few pop directors and pop movies, Allo-way may intimidate the literarily conditioned editors and readers of *Encounter*, but his implicit praise of Henry King's work in wide screen along with that of Fuller, Cukor, Ray and Sirk is simply ludi-crous. A stylistic disaster like *This Earth Is Mine* is virtually an ob-ject lesson in how not to use Scope, particularly in one definitively inept composition of an endlessly lateral California-Last-Supper banquet table reflected in a shimmeringly blue pool. What is most disconcerting about Alloway, however, is not his apparently superfi-cial judgments but his obliviousness to aesthetic values of any kind. The fallacy of an all-wise antiquity is replaced by the fallacy of an all-meaningful modernity. The nostalgic yearning for hand-woven linen handkerchiefs is ridiculed in order to worship the efficiency and ex-pendability of Kleenex. This is part of the mystique of pop art, and there is a great deal to be said for its frank recognition of technologi-cal change. You may not like Campbell's Soup cans, but it is futile to pretend you still pick herbs in Arcady where the new housing development is located.

One might note in passing the curious significance Alloway at-taches to the allegedly rural bias of the late James Agee and the alleged fanaticism of Manny Farber on behalf of small-screen as op-posed to large-screen films. In both instances, fantastically dissimilar as they are, Alloway manages to align himself with modernity against tradition, and in this way modernity in the movies is reduced to the expediency of the now as opposed to the standard-setting memory of the then.

In a sense, pop art represents the latest step in the depersonaliza-tion of art for the greater glory and autonomy of the detached aes-thetic object. Shirley Jackson recently delivered a lecture maternally entitled: "Biography of a Story." After years of the textual technology of the New Criticism, the story has subtly evolved from a lifelike puppet to an unruly child with a life of its own. Its creator has been reduced to a progenitor, and Plato's "pregnancy of the soul" has acquired a new urgency in its metaphoric parturition. The work escapes and finally engulfs the artist; the object consumes the subject. This is the trend, the shape of things to come, the thought of shapes to come. There is no need to read sci-fi any more to detect increasing reciprocity between men and machines. Mechanical neuroses are already being diagnosed before human neuroses have been fully understood. The gap is narrowing between what we are and what we use or perhaps what uses us. This was the comic point of the Alain Resnais–Raymond Queneau *Le Chant du styrène*, which reminds me that what I think of when I think of modernity is Resnais and Godard and not the conventional pop film with the traditional morality of an era long antedating the modernistic surfaces of the Doris Day kitchen.

On the whole, I prefer the classical cinema to the modern, but classicism and modernity are terms inseparable from the notion of personal authorship. Alloway would undoubtedly disagree, but I wonder if he could implement his disagreement in a regular critical berth where he would be on the firing line, daily, weekly, or even monthly. Would he then be so eager to subscribe to his own smug advice: "What the film critic, who sits blindly through films week after week, could be expected to do is to contribute to an aesthetic of the typical film. Almost no work has been done in charting film cycles, for example."

Alloway's audacious strategy here, like Marshal Foch's in a moment of supreme disarray, is not without a certain charm. What the conventional anti-Hollywood critic has always condemned as lack of originality Alloway blithely redefines as a cycle. Curiously, the only cycles Alloway mentions specifically in his *Encounter* article are encompassed in such violent genres as the western (modernity?) and the "dark, moody crime films." By a strange coincidence, these are the genres singled out by the late Robert Warshow in his famous socio-aesthetic pieces cast in the Platonic mold of liberal preconception. These two genres, along with the musical, are the genres most admired by the *Cahiers du Cinéma* critics. The three American sound films tied for first place in the most recent *Cahiers* poll were

The Searchers, Singin' in the Rain and Vertigo; and Scarface was not too far behind.

Apparently there are cycles and there are cycles. Alloway does not state his position on Betty Grable extravaganzas, Ma and Pa Kettle (too rural perhaps), the Carry On carrion (too British perhaps), the Arliss–Muni–Garson benefactors-of-mankind series, Charlie Chan, Mr. Moto, Mr. Wong, Blondie, the children's hours. Even the cycles he does mention seem dubiously contrived. "Ten years ago," he informs us, "there was the Weapon-western, which included Winchester 73, Colt 45, Springfield Rifle, Only the Valiant (Gatling gun), and The Battle at Apache Pass (cannon). These and other films were not only about the power new weapons gave their owners, but about the social impact and consequences of new weapons." First two obvious points: When does a critic chart the course of a cycle? The so-called Weapon-western cycle ran about two years from 1950 to 1952. The film critic, who sits blindly through films week after week, would have so many crisscrossing cycles to contend with that it would be a miracle if he could find the time and space to relate every Weapon-western to every other Weapon-western. Even in this prehistoric period in pre-Alloway criticism, audiences were struck by the relative profusion of weapon titles, but I wonder how much more any critic could add to what Mr. Alloway has said about the Weapon-western in the excerpt I quoted. Besides, there are all kinds of overlapping. The Gatling gun is employed significantly not only in Mark Twain's A Connecticut Yankee in King Arthur's Court but also in Cecil B. De Mille's 1940 Northwest Mounted Police. Colt 45 comes closest to the overriding technological interest Alloway suggests and is also by far the silliest movie in the group.

Admittedly, out of force of auteur habit, I look at Alloway's Weapon-westerns through directorial personalities or lack of same. Winchester 73 (Anthony Mann, reportedly begun by Fritz Lang), Springfield Rifle (Andre de Toth), Only the Valiant (Gordon Douglas), The Battle at Apache Pass (George Sherman), Colt 45 (Edwin L. Marin). Mann's style is violent, tenacious, perverse. De Toth's is nasty, unpleasant, unstable. Douglas is an efficient technician without much personality, Sherman an unpretentious artisan on the B or C level, and Marin strictly poverty row. Back in the early Fifties, Mann was not much better known than Marin, and no one except Manny Farber reviewed directors at that level anyway, at least not here in America. Yet audiences agreed that *Winchester 73* was a much better as well as bigger western than *Colt 45*. Looking at those two movies today, I see that *Winchester 73* has much more in common with *T-Men* and *The Tall Target* than with *Colt 45*. The grinding psychological sadism of *Springfield Rifle* is much more in tune with *Pitfall* than with the other Weapon-westerns. Actually, *Springfield Rifle* is almost a titular trap for Alloway. The Springfield in question doesn't appear until near the end of the film, and then virtually as an afterthought. The bulk of the film is a nervous counter-espionage intrigue in which the hero intentionally degrades himself, is abandoned and then unintentionally betrayed by his wife, finds his secret associates brutally murdered by a traitor so sympathetic that even the conventionally affirmative ending leaves a sour taste in the audience's mouth. A perfect project for De Toth, if not for Alloway.

I have never claimed that the *politique* explains everything. Like the Roman bidding in bridge, it is strongest with slam holdings, less precise with intermediate hands. I would love to abandon it if I could, but I am unable to find anything better. It is undoubtedly a handicap in sociological analysis, but I find most sociological analysis of films too primitive for serious consideration. The amount of information required is so prodigious in proportion to the scholarship actually performed that scholarly affectation ends up simpering over unintelligent conjecture. To the sociologist, movie audiences are (or were before television) inert blobs of habit plodding into movie theaters at unvarying intervals like undiscriminating zombies. Since all movies are equally significant, the sociologist can pick out movies at random and define society.

American society, according to Martha Wolfenstein and Nathan Leites, is represented by such films as *Love Affair*, *The Road to Morocco*, *Guest Wife*, *The Sailor Takes a Wife*, *Bells of St. Mary's*, *It Happened One Night*, *Two Guys from Milwaukee*, *The Well-Groomed Bride*, *Mildred Pierce*, *Pride of the Marines*, *Stolen Life*, *This Love of Ours*, *Night and Day*, *Till the End of Time*, *Adventure*, *My Reputation*, *Young Widow*, *Hold That Blonde*, *The Strange Love of Martha Ivers*, *Fallen Angel*, *Leave Her to Heaven*, *The Killers*, *Too Young to Know*, *Tomorrow Is Forever*, *To Each*

could not sustain the ꜰorest art theater for more than a week. ꜱ he point is that there ' ꜱ always been something absurd about wr' ꜰng for the low thouꜱ .ds about aesthetic experiences accessible t the high millions. ꜰ ꜱway cannot be singled out for this particu' ꜱr absurdity, but t' fact remains that even if movies have finall made the scene, t' ꜱr constituencies are still much too large to ꜱe adequately reꜱ ꜱsented in the rotten boroughs of pop art.

Anywꜱ , I still cling to the illusion of visual craftsmaꜱ nip transformeꜱ ꜱy the alchemy of projection and the mystique ꜱf mise-enscènꜱ .nto the highest form of personal creation. Such ꜱ Renaissance heꜱ ꜱy has little place in the pop philosophy of Lawrerꜱ e Alloway:

' ꜱetailed analysis of the work of pop directors who worꜱ within the commercial framework has certainly revealed some recurꜱ ꜱg factors which are, correctly, translatable into a personal style. Howꜱ ꜱer, such nuanced discrimination risks being more like the esoteric eꜱ ꜱertise of specialists than like the humanist's tribute to individuality. . . . The risk for film criticism is that the canon of individual authorsꜱ ꜱp, applied to an expendable art form, will simply lead to the insulaꜱ ꜱon of criticism within a kind of hobbies-corner specialism.

We are back to Baudelaire's expendability again. Yet, previously, Alloway has submitted a thumbnail review of *I Walk Alone*:

This film, produced by Hal Wallis, one of a cycle of dark, moody crime films, was a favourite of mine. The competition of upright, out-of-date, jailbird Burt Lancaster and treacherous, modern, adjusted Kirk Douglas, was rich in irony as well as violence. The night-club in movies of the time was a symbolic scene, like the Machiavellian Renaissance palace in Jacobean tragedy. It was an area of nocturnal leisure, where fashion and violence joined, where chance encounters were luxuriously framed, and it gave Lizbeth [sic] Scott a chance to sing. But Agee had no eye for this kind of urban imagery, a dream maybe, but a topical and knowing one.

Agee's offending review? Alloway thoughtfully reprints it:

Good performances by Wendell Corey and Kirk Douglas, a sharp scene about an old-fashioned gangster's helplessness against modern business methods. Some better than ordinary night-club atmosphere. Otherwise the picture deserves, like four out of five other movies, to walk alone, tinkle a little bell, and cry "Unclean, unclean."

Note that Agee seems to cover much the ground that Alloway later embellishes with Renaissance and Jacobean rosebushes, but then Agee was writing pop criticism for the moment whereas Alloway has had seventeen years to brood over the singing voice of Lizabeth Scott. What an expendable art form! If Miss Scott's incarnation in a 1947 movie is so memorable today, what hope is there for us Garbo-lovers to escape Her haunting presence this side of the grave? Still there is much that is sympathetic in Alloway's avowed tastes. I agree that Agee overestimated films by Laurence Olivier, John Huston and Georges Rouquier, but Agee did estimate. If Alloway declines to estimate, how can he explain the memorable qualities of a movie like *I Walk Alone?* In the apparently incomplete form in which he has couched his arguments, Alloway fails to explain why he cites the particular examples, usually violent and stylized, he does.

One should not be too finicky about aesthetic approximations, but it is possible that Alloway has fallen into a linguistic trap in his pursuit of movie iconography. I quote from his piece in *Movie* of February 1963:

In the movies, facing the silver screen, what does one see (and what do the critics of the movies write about)? Let me propose a schematic answer. There is, first of all, what Panofsky, writing about art, has called the "primary or natural subject," which in terms of movies, consists of the physical reality of the photographed world. Robert Warshow had described this dimension of the movies as follows: "What the camera reproduces has, almost always on the most literal level, the appearance of reality." Thus, an actor "need only be present, a passive object merely available to the camera's infinite appetite for the material. The actor as an object of perception is real and important irrespective of whether we believe in the character." Thus, the physical reality of the photographed objects relates naturally to the star system, which fans and sociologists, but not film critics, write about. The star whose personality and status are created as a product, is, when photographed, continually present in a more powerful form than the individual roles he or she may be playing. It is not Beau Geste as interpreted by Gary Cooper, but Gary Cooper himself that is the point. Who remembers Marilyn Monroe's name in *Niagara?* Thus, even the "primary or natural subject matter" is not without its iconographical potential.

One of Alloway's premises is demolished by his own examples. Critic Agee mentions two actors—Wendell Corey and Kirk Douglas —in a review of one movie. Sociologists Wolfenstein and Leites mention only three—Bob Hope, Humphrey Bogart and Lauren Bacall—in an analysis of no fewer than fifty-three movies. Thus it would seem, contrary to Alloway, that critics are far more star-struck than sociologists. At his best, Manny Farber can pin players to the wall of categories without a wasteful flutter:

Otherwise, the Hollywood talkie seems to have been invented to give an embarrassingly phony impression of the virile action man. The performance is always fattened either by coyness (early Robert Taylor), unction (Anthony Quinn), histrionic conceit (Gene Kelly), liberal knowingness (Brando), angelic stylishness (Mel Ferrer), oily hamming (José Ferrer), Mother's Boy passivity (Rock Hudson) or languor (Montgomery Clift).

Let's not be unnecessarily cruel, but no mere sociologist could come up with a passage like Farber's in a million years of foundation-backed moviegoing.

To return to the linguistic trap I mentioned previously, what does one see in the movies on the silver screen, if we may reinvoke Alloway's ironic fan-magazine imagery? One could insist with maddening pedantry that all we see are flickering impulses of light on a two-dimensional screen and that these impulses merely represent by some agreed conventions the physical reality of the photographed world. The dividing line between what is represented and what is actually seen is generally ignored in casual conversation. That is why Alloway's statements seem so reasonable at first glance. It is only when Alloway attempts to enthrone common sense as profound theory that he gets into trouble. As soon as we identify an entity called "Marilyn Monroe" as an iconographical element of *Niagara*, we incorrectly limit a variable element with an invariable name. The "Marilyn Monroe" of *Niagara* is hardly identical with the "Marilyn Monroe" of *Gentlemen Prefer Blondes, Some Like It Hot* or *The Misfits*. The "Marilyn Monroe" at the beginning of the shooting of *Niagara* is not the same "Marilyn Monroe" at the end of *Niagara*. The great fallacy of iconographical or sociological criticism is its excessive reliance on invariable terms for purposes of comparison. "Marilyn Monroe" becomes not one of many malleable materials in the art of film-making but a sociological archetype with a single level of meaning.

The cinema, as Jean-Luc Godard has observed, is the only art which records the process of mortality. The so-called fine arts are frozen in a moment of time. The live arts perish in their own time-space continuum. Music reverberates in an imaginary world of blind sublimity. Literature is locked in the symbolic structure of language. The cinema alone is consumed by the spectacle of life approaching death. Unfortunately, film criticism seldom considers the aesthetic implications involved in the distinction between real and filmic time. When Eisenstein demonstrated that anything goes as far as temporal distortion is concerned, the actor was completely forgotten as the intransigently counter-revolutionary agent operating against the smooth flow of dialectical montage. "Serious" Anglo-American film criticism is still suffering from the montage hangover, and this is where Alloway is on very strong ground. The star system has simply shattered analytical film aesthetics beyond repair. We have become too accustomed to human faces to settle for historical forces, and Eisenstein himself ended up with an integral frame, not so much for Stalin's sake, as Dwight Macdonald has suggested, as for Cherkassov's. How can you cut away from *that* face?

However, time is only one of the cinema's many dimensions. *What* we see on the screen is ultimately less important than *how* we see it. This is where the apostles of iconography part company with the mystics of *mise-en-scène*. Let me hasten to add that by the *how* I mean not merely visual style but also moral attitude and emotional temperature. By Alloway's standards or rather apparent lack of standards, the Coke machine in *The Stripper* is equal iconographically or possibly even superior to the Coke machine in *Dr. Strangelove*. After all, a Coke machine is a Coke machine is a Coke machine. At least linguistically. Similarly, Marilyn Monroe is always Marilyn Monroe on the printed page. If you begin making a distinction between one Coke machine and another or between one Marilyn Monroe and another, you enter the realm of the how, the gateway to human intention and *mise-en-scène*.

"Film criticism," according to Alloway with a vague echo of Marx for the subliminal edification of *Encounter*'s editors, "is haunted by the spectre of uniqueness." Well, pop audiences—that is, you and me and my Aunt Minnie—may not be haunted by any specter, but they are looking for something different. Popular taste oscillates between cycle and variation. If Alloway overestimates the cycle, Agee overestimated the variation. Both critics have underestimated the decisive role of directorial personality, but that is another thesis for another time.

I might note in conclusion that the Movie-movie of Alloway and Warshow, Agee and Farber, in whatever light they chose to see it, is apparently becoming extinct. The confidence Hollywood craftsmen felt just a few years ago is gone. No longer is there an audience out there waiting for something a little better than usual but willing to settle for something a little worse than usual. The kind of relaxed craftsmanship which went into a *Laura*, a *White Heat*, an *Awful Truth* and a *Casablanca* is no longer possible in today's hysterical atmosphere of hit or bust. It's all or nothing now, and uniqueness is no longer a specter but a fact of life. The package, the project, the pre-sell have replaced the studio assembly line. There is no point in mourning the good old days. In the first place, they were not really that good, and in the second, if we can preserve enough of the old films, so amazingly memorable for all their alleged expendability, we can build a classical foundation from which we can erect a spire to the more personal, more chaotic, more disorganized, more affected and possibly even more inspired future. I agree with Alloway that anti-Hollywood herald angels have a way of exaggerating the amount of talent lying around just waiting for the cinema to regain the purity and integrity it lost when the wicked businessmen took over in 1898.

Certainly there is no further need to be defensive about the cinema. Movies could have been a great deal better, and such eminent cinephobes as Edmund Wilson and Lionel Trilling would still despise them, and they could have been a great deal worse, and such eminent cinephiles as the late André Bazin and Alexandre Astruc would still have loved them. Warshow and Panofsky wasted too much energy on tortured rationalizations, indefensible to the cinephobes and self-evident to the cinephiles, of the proposition that a new art had been born in our lifetime. Writing mostly in hostile

publications, these two cultivated men were forced to explain why
they enjoyed Hollywood movies. Vox Populi! they cried. Now the
vox is fading, and our beloved art goes on devising its own definitions. The least we confirmed cinephiles can do for the cinema is
judge it seriously and sensibly. I like pop films as well as anyone.
Some of the best ones I know have been directed by Jean Renoir
and Carl Dreyer.

MISE-EN-SCÈNE

The subject of this piece was suggested by a letter from Dr. Irving Schneider of Chevy Chase, Maryland. Dr. Schneider writes in part:

I've been asked to write a review of psychiatric documentary films, teaching and research ones, primarily from a phenomenological point of view. With respect to some of the ideas I'm working up, I need a good working definition or explanation of the notion of mise-en-scène. Like camp and several other terms, I think I know what it means but I'm not sure. A search through theatrical dictionaries and film works yields no definition. Friends and I have used the term occasionally to refer to the sum of all the elements making up a film, and at other times to the placement of the actors within a setting, but none of us can agree on what the most common or accurate usage is.

I would appreciate it greatly if you could find the time and inclination to explain to me your understanding of the term, and perhaps tell me something of its origin in film criticism.

First of all, mise-en-scène (pronounced mise-en-Seine) is a French term endowed with a certain vague élan in these times. Its most restrictive definition is quite literally "the placing in the scene," a concept associated originally with the stage rather than the screen. It is simply what we call direction both on stage and on screen. The one who perpetrates mise-en-scène is at least theoretically the metteur-en-scène, but here we run into a paradox. Although mise-en-scène is always used with either a neutral or positive connotation, metteur-en-scène has acquired in the past decade a negative connotation. Back in 1954 Tony Richardson in *Sight and Sound* and François Truffaut in *Cahiers du Cinéma* discussed metteurs-en-scène as lesser mortals, for Richardson below creators and for Truffaut below *auteurs*.

In seeking to define the *metteur-en-scène*, Richardson went so far as to explore some of the issues of *mise-en-scène*.

The term as we shall see is exact. The essential characteristic of all of them is the disparity between what they are saying and how they are saying it. They are not content—or not able—like the true interpreter to submerge their personalities in the job of putting whatever they are tackling on to the screen. They must "do something with" their material, and the means become the ends. (In some ways it is similar to the traditional distinction between form and content. But form has a more specific meaning and it can be used, as can style, by the *metteur-en-scène* for his own purposes.) Inevitably with this goes a certain—to call it staginess has the wrong connotations—but a certain self-consciousness. The particular elements in which this manifests vary widely. It may be the decor, the staging, the editing, the photography; it may be in the basic attitudes and feelings the director has about his subject; it may be in his certainty of manipulating the responses of his audience; but in all of them is this consciousness of their own presentation.

Who are these directors Richardson has designated as mere *metteurs-en-scène*? Max Ophuls, Orson Welles, Jacques Becker, Carl Dreyer, F. W. Murnau, Josef von Sternberg, Luchino Visconti, Carol Reed, Elia Kazan, Georges Clouzot, René Clement, Fritz Lang, Marcel Carné and Yves Allegret. It is difficult to see how these particular people fall so neatly between "creators" like Eisenstein, Renoir, Vigo, De Sica, Bunuel and Donskoi at the top and Wyler, Stevens and Huston on the bottom. One might note a roughly ideological consistency in the policy of the alleged "creators," but we need not pursue the point any further. The fact of the matter is that the term "*metteur-en-scène*" has been invoked to separate the good guys from the bad guys. Significantly, however, Richardson never once used the term "*mise-en-scène*" to describe the work of the *metteurs-en-scène*. He preferred to go to the dance with "*entrechats*" and "*grande battements*" in order to describe the self-conscious stylists of the cinema. *Mise-en-scène* as style is a notion developed both semantically and philosophically in French film criticism.

What *mise-en-scène* means is perhaps less important than what it implies. We might start by considering what it is in terms of what it is not. I myself would never apply the term to the direction of documentaries, nor of cartoons, nor even of avant-garde abstractions. Not that there is any law against talking about Grierson's mise-en-scène in Drifters, or Disney's in Fantasia, or Stan Vanderbeek's in Mankinda. It's just that mise-en-scène is a tacky term in these contexts. Above all, mise-en-scène implies impurity, since the purer forms of cinema are generally too transparent of purpose to require the magical tricks of mise-en-scène. The touch of class in an ordinary detective mystery or a trashy woman's novel can be explained or explained away by the invocation of mise-en-scéne. Conversely, the big blobs of truth that often pass for humanistic cinema would be disgraced by any suspicion of stylistic embellishment. Then again, on a more serious level of cinematic discourse, we never talk about Eisenstein's mise-en-scène in Potemkin as we do about Murnau's in Sunrise or even later Eisenstein's in Ivan the Terrible. Here we must pause to chart the collision course of two oversimplified battle cries—namely, montage versus mise-en-scène.

The Marxist-montage theoreticians, who have dominated so-called "serious" Anglo-American film criticism for the past thirty years, have always argued that commercial movies, particularly those from Hollywood, had sold out their uniquely cinematic birthright of conceptual editing for a mess of theatrical pottage. Perhaps the most literate summation of this general attitude was provided by Dwight Macdonald in 1942 via a harsh critique of Eisenstein's Film Sense as a stylistic recantation on the stake of the Stalinist Inquisition.

Was it only a dozen years ago that, with pious excitement, we went to "little" movie houses—the very term has disappeared—to see the new films from Russia? Is it so short a time since many of us were writing on the cinema as the great modern art form, the machine art whose technique was most in harmony with the dynamism of the machine age, the art that most powerfully affected such peculiarly modern areas as Freud's subconscious and Pavlov's reflexes, the only art that could sometimes bridge the gap between serious creation and mass taste, so that Birth of a Nation, Chaplin's comedies, Potemkin, and a few other films might be said to have been the only works of our time that have seemed both popular and great? Our enthusiasm was not misplaced, our theories were not unfounded. And yet the wonderful possibilities that lay before the cinema 10 years ago have withered into the slick banality of Holly-

wood and the crude banality of the post 1930 Soviet cinema. The potentialities, which really existed, which, for that matter, still exist and in
even richer profusion, simply were not realized, and the cinema gave up
its own idiom and technique to become once more what it was before
Griffith: a mechanical device for recording stage plays. Like so much
else in the past decade, it crept back into the womb, into the uncon-
sciousness. It has been many years now since anywhere in the world, a
film has been made which, aesthetically speaking, is cinema at all.

The point or at least one point is that when Dwight Macdonald
started writing film criticism, people were babbling about montage
the way they babble about mise-en-scène today. Note how rigorously
Macdonald excluded most films from the aesthetic temple of "cinema." By contrast, the French criticism led by André Bazin in the
Thirties and Forties was more concerned with what films actually
were than what they should have been—that is, with cinema rather
than with metacinema. When sound came, the montage critics held
their hands over their ears. Not Bazin. He welcomed sound for its
naturalizing influence, and he was one of the first critics to perceive
that sound had taken over many of the expressive functions of montage. While the Macdonalds mourned Potemkin, the Bazins studied
Scarface. For the French, film history was a fait accompli rather than
a political fable about the subjugation of the masses through the
opiate of star worship.

The very fact that mise-en-scène comes to the cinema from the
theater implies a defiance of montage metaphysics. A film not cinema? Nonsense. You don't need montage for cinema. All you need
is a screen and a projector. "The curtain opens," writes Michel
Mourlet in a 1959 Cahiers du Cinéma. "Night falls in the auditorium. Presently a rectangle of light vibrates before us, and soon we
are soaking up sounds and gestures. Here we are absorbed by this
unreal space and time. More or less absorbed. The mysterious energy
which supports with various felicities the eddies of light and shadow
and their froth of sounds is called mise-en-scène." For Mourlet and
his admittedly extreme school of mise-en-scène specialists—too extreme in fact even for Cahiers to print without an introductory disclaimer—mise-en-scène is the stuff of which projection light beams
are made. Mourlet has his own list of good guys and bad guys, and
Mr. Macdonald might be interested in knowing that Alfred Hitch-

cock is one of Mourlet's bad guys. Why? Because Hitchcock, like his ancestor Eisenstein in Mourlet's genealogy, ignores the personalities of actors to concentrate on abstract forms. Mourlet believes that the essence of mise-en-scène is the direction of actors so that they may dominate their decor and communicate directly with the audience. Mourlet's theories lead to some bizarre judgments even by Cahiers standards, but nevertheless Mourlet does convey some of the antipathy engendered in movie lovers against the more solemn film aesthetes who labor so industriously to disinfect the cinema of our dreams and desires. Sure, we go to the movies for rousing dramatic entertainment, for beautiful women and virile men. So what?

Ultimately, however, mise-en-scène is not anti-montage, even though the emphasis is on the spectacle itself rather than on the dialectical relationships of separate shots and images. Perhaps Alexandre Astruc comes closest to expressing the mystique of mise-en-scène through an analysis of the art of the late Kenji Mizoguchi:

But Mizoguchi knows well that, after all, it is not very important for his film to turn out well; he is more concerned with knowing whether the strongest bonds between himself and his characters are those of tenderness or contempt. He is like the viewer who sees the reflection of pleasure on the features of the one he watches, even though he also knows quite well that it is not this reflection alone which he is seeking but perhaps quite simply the tedious confirmation of something he has always known but cannot refrain from verifying. So I consider mise-en-scène as a means of transforming the world into a spectacle given primarily to oneself—yet what artist does not know instinctively that what is seen is less important than the way of seeing, or a certain way of needing to see or be seen.

The cinema is an art less of origination than of magnification. It is the only art I know where more comes out than goes in, and the difference can be called mise-en-scène. We might say that mise-en-scène is the gap between what we see and feel on the screen and what we can express in words. It is the gap between intention and effect. Most of the great classical directors worked intuitively rather than intellectually, and yet their art is genuinely profound. This too is mise-en-scène, a delirious subjectivity at work in an objective art form, the recognition of human purpose through the operation of a machine.

An analysis of mise-en-scène depends to some extent on a cinema of formulas and genres. We can distinguish better between Renoir and Bunuel because they both worked on the material of Octave Mirabeau's *Diary of a Chambermaid*. If both Renoir and Bunuel had been as purely personal as some theoreticians demand, there would be no basis of comparison. The way Renoir directed Paulette Goddard and the way Luis Bunuel directed Jeanne Moreau tells us a great deal more about their attitudes toward women than any explicit confession would reveal. Mise-en-scène is a shaping of an objective core. Take away the objective core, and you have pure personality without mise-en-scène. In answer to Dr. Schneider's letter, I would suggest a definition of mise-en-scène which includes all the means available to a director to express his attitude toward his subject. This takes in cutting, camera movement, pacing, the direction of players and their placement in the decor, the angle and distance of the camera, and even the selection of the content of the shot. Mise-en-scène as an attitude tends to accept the cinema as it is and enjoy it for what it is—a sensuous conglomeration of all the other arts.

THE AESTHETICS OF ANDRÉ BAZIN

What Is Cinema? by André Bazin consists of ten essays selected and translated by Hugh Gray with remarkable fidelity to the letter and spirit of the original. The essays were originally written between 1945 and 1957 in a variety of periodicals, including *Cahiers du Cinéma,* that fountainhead of the *nouvelle vague.* Some of Bazin's most flavorsome pieces are not included in this collection. I miss particularly his extraordinary eulogy of Humphrey Bogart, his critique of the *politique des auteurs* and an analysis of the western more scholarly and comprehensive than that of the late Robert Warshow. Hugh Gray was probably guided in his selection by an instinct for the essential, the basic, the ontological, if you will, in Bazin's aesthetics. No matter. Few books on any subject manage to be at once so profound and so readable.

It is not a question of agreeing or disagreeing with this or that position in the book. Bazin is as central a figure in film aesthetics as Freud is in psychology, and if some of us feel we have gone beyond Bazin, we must acknowledge in all honesty that it was Bazin who literally opened our eyes to the cinema. If I consider Bazin a greater film critic than, say, Agee or Warshow, it is not because Bazin was necessarily more perceptive or more talented than his American contemporaries but rather because the cultural climate for cinema was friendlier in Paris than it was in New York. Unlike Agee and Warshow, Bazin could be something more than a film critic without being something else than a film critic.

Bazin's greatest contribution to modern aesthetics is the restoration of interest in the integrity of visual space. If Bazin did not actually demolish the montage theories of Eisenstein, Pudovkin and Kuleshov, he did succeed in reducing these theories from imperatives to options. The typical Anglo-American film historian of pre-

Bazin vintage would look at the Odessa Steps sequence in *Potemkin*
and then look at a Hollywood movie pityingly for its lack of montage, which Bazin defines quite simply as "the ordering of images in
time." Bazin made mincemeat of Eisenstein's *Film Sense* and *Film
Form* by redefining the uses of montage in such an orderly way that
the screen would never look the same again. Bazin observes:

As regards montage, derived initially as we all know from the masterpieces of Griffith, we have the statement of Malraux in his *Psychologie
du cinéma* that it was montage that gave birth to film as an art, setting
it apart from mere animated photography, in short, creating a language.

The use of montage can be "invisible" and this was generally the case
in the prewar classics of the American screen. Scenes were broken down
for just one purpose, namely, to analyze an episode according to the
material or dramatic logic of the scene. It is this logic which conceals
the fact of the analysis, the mind of the spectator quite naturally accepting the viewpoints of the director which are justified by the geography
of the action or the shifting emphasis of dramatic interest.

But the neutral quality of this "invisible" editing fails to make use
of the full potential of montage. On the other hand these potentialities
are clearly evident from the three processes generally known as parallel
montage, accelerated montage, montage by attraction. In creating parallel montage, Griffith succeeded in conveying a sense of the simultaneity
of two actions taking place at a geographical distance by means of alter-
nating shots from each. In *La Roue* Abel Gance created the illusion of
the steadily increasing speed of a locomotive without actually using any
images of speed (indeed the wheel could have been turning on one
spot) simply by a multiplicity of shots of ever-decreasing length.

Finally there is "montage by attraction," the creation of S. M. Eisenstein, and not so easily described as the others, but which may be
roughly defined as the reenforcing of the meaning of one image by
association with another image not necessarily part of the same episode
—for example the fireworks display in *The General Line* following the
image of the bull. In this extreme form, montage by attraction was
rarely used even by its creator but one may consider as very near to it
in principle the more commonly used ellipsis, comparison, or metaphor,
examples of which are the throwing of stockings onto a chair at the foot
of a bed, or the milk overflowing in H. G. Clouzot's *Jenny Lamour*.
There are of course a variety of possible combinations of these three
processes.

Whatever these may be, one can say that they share that trait in common which constitutes the very definition of montage, namely the creation of a sense or meaning not proper to the images themselves but derived exclusively from their juxtaposition. The well-known experiment of Kuleshov with the shot of Mozhukhin in which a smile was seen to change its significance according to the image that preceded it, sums up perfectly the properties of montage.

Montage as used by Kuleshov, Eisenstein, or Gance did not give us the event; it alluded to it. Undoubtedly they derived at least the greater part of the constituent elements from the reality they were describing but the final significance of the film was found to reside in the ordering of these elements much more than in their objective content.

Bazin went on to elaborate what he meant by "objective content" in the short time he had to live, and when he was through, film history had regained its evolutionary purpose. It was not for Bazin to dictate the course of this evolution, but merely to chart it. In the works of such disparate directors as Welles and Rossellini, Bazin detected a new dignity for the image itself in itself. Unfortunately, Bazin's ideas have to be seen in the historical perspective of their own time and not second-guessed with 20–20 hindsight. It is not Bazin's fault that an English translation has been so long in coming. The soundness of his reasoning and the eloquent thrust of his arguments should still delight most of his American readers, but he is no longer the romantic cause that he once was, at least to this devotee. We are living in a post-Bazinian age as far as the international cinema is concerned. The most gifted directors shun any style that suggests manipulation of the audience. Even Hollywood movies are becoming more like windows and less like mirrors. New realities are engulfing us from one end of the world to the other, and yet we are not as happy as we thought we would be.

I tend to agree with Dr. Gray when he agrees with Jean Mitry's challenge to Bazin's conception of the image "as being evaluated not according to what it adds to reality but what it reveals of it." Mitry contends that the camera reveals not reality itself but a new appearance correlated to the real, but restructured in a frame as arbitrary and artificial as the gilded frame of a painting. But if I agree with Gray and Mitry against Bazin, it is because too much of the modern cinema has abandoned its obligation to restructure reality into meaningful forms. Reality is too often flung at our faces like a dead mackerel to show that the artist is not interested in manipulating us. He merely wishes to punish us for presuming to think ourselves qualified to judge him. Bazin was too civilized to encourage such disorder, but such disorder is one of the fruits of the freedom and self-consciousness to which Bazin contributed. The loveliest things in *What Is Cinema?* are Bazin's recognitions of those moments when audience and film are in magical rapport. His aesthetics is a loving, rigorous, almost ruthless means of eliminating all obstacles between the spectacle and the spectator. Even the film director was expendable in Bazin's quest for the clarity of a total rendering of reality. The American reader can reassure himself that Bazin never reached his ultimate destination but that along the way he demonstrated once and for all that there can be a moral distinction between a cut and a camera movement.

THE NEED FOR FILM

The relationship of art museums to movies is one of condescension and necessity. That is to say, condescension on the part of art museums and necessity for old movies that have no place else to go. As far as anyone knows, there is little affinity between the art collector and the movie collector. This is an unfortunate situation when one reaches the level of a Rockefeller or a Hartford. It becomes a question of millions for paintings by Renoir père but not a penny for movies by Renoir fils, and it is more than possible that posterity may enthrone the movie-making Renoir above his painting pater. All this has little to do with the snobbish calculations of the so-called patrons of the so-called arts. Paintings are as negotiable as currency and represent a better long-term investment than jewelry. A collector with an authenticated original painting enjoys the plutocratic pleasure of exclusive possession; and an army of critics, curators and experts are available for the convenient computation of his tax losses. The intangibles of displaying the status symbols of official culture are, of course, incalculable, particularly for the socially insecure nouveau-riche collector.

The ulterior benefits of collecting old movies are difficult to discern. It is hard to determine what constitutes an "original" print of a movie unless one so considers the negative from which all prints are copied, and the only value of the negative is in providing prints to be projected. Faded old prints are actually of less value to the collector than newer, cleaner copies. There are also the frequently grubby and quasi-criminal circumstances surrounding the acquisition of old movies. A painting gains its value from the prestige of the artist even if the purchase is negotiated with an avaricious art dealer. Until recently most movies lacked any such prestigious authorship, and even with the modern tendency to group films according to director, the director himself seldom has anything to do with the rights to the print. The rights to movies usually belong to producers, studios or other corporate entities. Dwight Macdonald has often chortled in print about elegant museum tributes to such creative giants as Samuel Goldwyn and Joe Levine. Mr. Macdonald doesn't seem to know or care that these heart-felt tributes to the Messrs. Goldwyn and Levine were inspired less by the producers themselves than by the precious treasures they were donating to posterity. What's one papal tribute more or less when the Sistine Chapel is at stake?

For private collectors, however, the situation is more desperate. They are usually forbidden by law to possess prints of old movies, and consequently they must operate in a very secretive atmosphere with other collectors and enthusiasts. Ironically, it is these private collectors, these movie pirates, who may be the last hope for the survival of many old movies. It is not a matter entirely of individuals. There are also pirate nations like Czechoslovakia and China who may have saved many Hollywood masterpieces for their cinemathèques and the rest of the civilized world simply by illegally duping the rented Hollywood prints when they were originally circulated by the American companies. One of the stunning revelations of the 1966 Montreal Film Festival was the 1917 John Ford western *Straight Shooting*, resurrected from, of all places, the Prague archives!

Fortunately, most European countries take the cinema far more seriously than it is taken in America. Aside from the Museum of Modern Art and the Gallery of Modern Art in New York, it is difficult to think of any art museums in America that have even seriously considered doing anything constructive about the last lively art to date. The motto of the museums seems to be: Let MOMA do it! The film people at MOMA have always complained of insufficient backing and financing from the Art Proper People all the way upstairs to the Rockefellers. Granting that inadequate budgets disarm in advance any criticisms of MOMA, the Gallery of Modern Art, the extraordinary George Eastman Film Library in Rochester and the movie-wise moribund Library of Congress. Granting also that the Hollywood film companies are the biggest villains of the piece, and only television prevented them from letting all their old movies crumble into dust in their vaults. Granting every extenuating circumstance, it is

still possible to quarrel with the general tendencies of film curators
to behave as custodians of good taste.

A few examples may be in order here. I will not mention the
names of the people involved simply because I wish to emphasize
the principle rather than any personalities out of a past too easy to
second-guess. Some years ago the curator of one institution was
offered the entire collection of Buster Keaton silents. A financial
decision was involved here since there was a cost factor in transfer-
ring the films to fireproof stock. The curator in question selected
four of the Keaton features and returned the rest. In a similar situation in an institution abroad, the curator told his donor to send the
truck around and unload every can of film. The curator of the first
institution has denounced the curator of the second as "a mere enthusiast without critical standards." My sympathies are entirely with
the curator-enthusiast over the curator-critic. It is not for curators to
decide what films should be preserved and what films should not. As
for the shortage of funds, perhaps if more films were collected, more
money would become available. Old Hollywood movies are particularly precious in their total context because so many directorial, acting and technical careers keep overlapping from one film to another
in an integral universe with its own charms and conventions.

Unfortunately it is the Hollywood film that has suffered most
from curatorial snobbery in the past. The critical climate has
changed appreciably in the past decade, but no one will ever be able
to calculate the lost opportunities to amass old movies. Late as it is
to save old movies from oblivion, certain suggestions should at least
be considered:

Curators should collect as much as possible of old Hollywood
movies and not be too finicky about the new movies being offered.
Ultimately, it takes less imagination to preserve Jean Renoir's *Rules
of the Game* and Ingmar Bergman's *The Naked Night* than to save
Lola Albright's performance in *Cold Wind in August*. Curators
should not worry unduly about the aesthetic quality of what they
rescue from oblivion. Alain Robbe-Grillet's *L'Immortelle* may leave
something to be desired as a mimicry of *Marienbad*, but future gen-
erations will derive as much benefit from a bad Alain Robbe-Grillet
movie as from a bad play by Henry James, not to mention the sensual supplication of Françoise Brion in the title role. What would

we give today for some bad Greek tragedies as a basis of comparison with *Aeschylus, Sophocles* and *Euripides* and as an index of Athenian taste.

The time may have come for all FOOFS (Friends of Old Films) to unite behind a federal subsidy program for preservation of old movies. A rotation program for prints could solve the problem of determining which of many institutions from coast to coast would house the collection. The federal government is a dubious entity for production subsidy. One could imagine Senator Eastland's committee discussing a projected film on Black Power, but the issue of preserving old movies should not unduly challenge the provincial sensibilities of Congress and the White House.

Perhaps the time has come also for all companies to declare an amnesty on pirated prints so that private collectors and international archives can pool all their resources, thus enabling us to determine once and for all how much of our moviegoing past we will be able to pass on to our children. The amnesty and the subsidy should coincide in one massive national effort to preserve an art form and an archaeological treasure for future historians.

THE AMERICAN FILM INSTITUTE

The American Film Institute (with its attendant edifice complex) has not yet been formally established, but already the noise of factional firecrackers resounds from New York to Los Angeles. Certain individuals and groups are "in" and others are "out," and everybody wants a slice of the pie which may amount to more than $5 million. As a not so innocent bystander I would like to make a few impertinent observations.

1. Anti-Establishment people always seem shocked when the Establishment fails to finance anti-Establishment art. People who expect federal funds with no strings attached should remember that American politicians tend to sniff suspiciously even at privately financed art. The Hollywood Ten were blacklisted as a result of a Congressional investigation into the operations of a privately financed industry. Does anyone really believe that the House Un-American Activities Committee would ever pass up the opportunity to investigate the expenditure of federal monies? Cecile Starr, William Starr and Kirk Bond have questioned the credentials of such enlightened dignitaries as Roger Stevens, Gregory Peck and George Stevens, Jr. However, if the American Film Institute begins considering individual projects, Senator Eastland of Mississippi will be looming over the horizon. Civil rights, Vietnam and the love affairs of homosexuals will hardly qualify as acceptable subjects. Could Stanley Kubrick have obtained federal financing for *Dr. Strangelove?* I wouldn't bet on it. What about *Sons and Daughters of Vietnam*, the movie version of *MacBird!*, or the film biography of Malcolm X? Forget it. Even *How to Succeed in Business Without Really Trying* might strike some solons as pinko propaganda. Let's not even discuss Capitol Hill guidelines for the treatment of sex on

the screen. Antonioni, Fellini and Bergman would be considered de-
generates by a clear Congressional majority.

That a film renaissance can be subsidized into existence is a notion that dies hard. The film schools in Poland and Czechoslovakia
are cited as examples of what can be done with government support,
but the situation in America is entirely different. The film industry
here exists independently of the government, and no American Film
Institute, however lavishly endowed, can guarantee distribution and
exhibition. The Iron Curtain countries are more restricted in the
number of films available to audiences. In America, we are glutted
with products from all over the world. As a critic, I have a hard time
keeping up with all the screenings and openings each week. Aside
from the output of the film industry, the importations and the revivals, there is an ever-expanding underground. New talent is always
welcome, but it would be an exaggeration to suggest that the public
is panting for youth to express itself on film. Jean-Luc Godard's films
cannot find commercial release, Bergman's latest had a disappoint-
ing run, Fellini's latest was a flop, as was Polanski's. So much for the
so-called art-house audience that is starved for new art.

2. Besides, why this passion for subsidizing new, untried film-
makers? Jean Renoir, Josef von Sternberg and King Vidor are still
alive even if the production rosters don't indicate it. Elia Kazan has
had difficulty finding money for personal projects. Why not some
federal money for proven masters of the medium, if for anyone?
Hollywood's heartlessness toward its own is too familiar to be re-
prised here. What is not so familiar is the intolerance of certain
academic types toward anyone who has ever engaged in commercial
film-making. A whole generation of film pedants have been brought
up to believe that the only good directors were long ago and far away.
Students are taught to preserve their souls from Hollywood while
preparing for the production of TV commercials or, worse still, industrial documentaries. Still, an apprenticeship is an apprenticeship,
and rather than pour money on promising film students, the government might try opening up the various unions to new talent, by
special legislation if necessary.

3. The federal government could perform one useful service by
forcing all film companies to supply a print of every film for which a

copyright is claimed. The Library of Congress would then serve as the central clearinghouse for the storage and distribution of original prints to interested institutions. The Library of Congress should have started performing this service a half century ago. Time has run out for most of the silent cinema, and time is now beginning to run out for the talkies. Unfortunately, neither the film industry nor film academe have displayed much fervor for the cause of print preservation. I would like to nominate William Everson as the first curator of the National Film Archives. No one in America is more dedicated and fair-minded on this issue.

4. Many proposals for film education sound like giant lottery schemes to achieve a masterpiece in the shortest possible time. I can't conceive of any film scholar in America being qualified to decide that one student above all others should be launched on a full-scale production while all his classmates are turned away empty-handed. Film historians find it impossible to agree on the best directors of the past. By what occult process can anyone detect the best directors of the future?

It would seem wiser to subsidize the cost of film stock and equipment so that students in film courses could have more leeway for experimentation. Perhaps practical film courses could be started as early as high school on an elective basis. Some talents mature later than others, and film is a particularly nebulous realm for talent evaluation anyway. Film-making is a craft as well as an art, and who is to say which should come first? My own limited experience with the new camera generation suggests that the more film they shoot and process, the sooner they will begin to understand the difference between a craft and an art.

5. I don't believe the American Film Institute will do any harm no matter how it is finally constituted. I am basically on the side of all film institutions as part of the medium's struggle for respectability. I do fear that the excessively high expectations arising out of the extravagant rhetoric of promotion will lead to disillusion and demoralization when pint-sized Pudovkins turn out dud movies. I think we should learn to crawl before we take the great leap forward. Perhaps the government can first subsidize every teacher of film to make his or her own film just to prove that film-making can indeed be taught.

Then try selling it to Joe Levine. Defeat may be probable, but the experience will be edifying. For every teacher defecting to a director's chair on the Riviera there will be hundreds of wiser and humbler instructors of the most magical and most elusive of all the arts.

THE ILLUSION OF NATURALISM

Jean-Luc Godard, that paragon of paradox, takes time out in *La Chinoise* to rewrite film history by challenging traditional notions of what is real and what is not real. Lumière, Godard argues through a mouthpiece character, was no more a pioneering realist than Méliès was a mere magician. Lumière did photograph the reality of trains steaming into a station or of workers filing out of a factory, but these were painterly subjects fashionable with the Impressionists of the late nineteenth century. By contrast, Méliès may have staged the state visit of a Balkan monarch to France with actors and fake sets, but nonetheless he transformed the cinema into a kind of Brechtian newsreel. Hence, Méliès came closer to reality and modernity through artifice than Lumière did through literal reproduction.

Godard's critical position is of course perverse to an extreme. He is not so much reevaluating Lumière and Méliès as he is redefining the cinema in terms of his own temperament. Godard intrudes too conspicuously into his own films to be considered the faithful recorder of reality à la Lumière, and yet he is too involved politically with the present to allow himself to be dismissed as a fanciful stylist à la Méliès. By reversing the roles of Lumière and Méliès, Godard justifies the contradictions of his own aesthetics.

Godard's aesthetic paradox in *La Chinoise* is not entirely self-serving. He is concerned also with facile distinctions between reality and artifice in the writings of film historians. The Lumière–Méliès dichotomy is particularly pernicious in its oversimplifications of fact and fiction. Godard would argue that the history of the cinema is the story of a reconciliation of apparent opposites. That he himself embodies this reconciliation demonstrates his theory without necessarily disqualifying its objective validity for cinema as a whole. Consequently, Godard's films celebrate the marriage of Lumière and Méliès with such finality as to make an article on screen naturalism seem hopelessly archaic. Or, so it would seem if Godard were taken as the last word on the subject. As it is, Godard's films represent, consciously or unconsciously, only the most recent efforts of movies to seem more "real" than what has been screened before. This impulse to seem real can be designated as Naturalism, although the term has acquired a pejorative connotation in the past two decades. I employ it merely to relate cinema to the historical processes that alone justify the catch-all terminology of critics and theoreticians—there is no point in pursuing the semantics of Naturalism. Specific examples of its varied guises will easily prove the ultimate futility of Naturalism as an artistic movement.

Before the birth of the cinema, Naturalism was invoked to describe certain literary and theatrical tendencies of Chekhov, Ibsen, Strindberg, Zola, Hebbel, Hauptmann, Brieux and Belasco, among many others. A term that can encompass both the eloquent ellipses of Chekhov and the ponderous stage effects of Belasco is obviously inadequate for any nuanced discussion. Nowadays it is fashionable to treat Naturalism as a transitional stage between Romanticism and Realism, as if Naturalism were a naïve preoccupation with homely details. Some years ago Edouard de Laurot criticized the film version of Paddy Chayefsky's Marty for not transcending its "naturalism" with an ideologically focused realism. Similar criticisms are leveled every season at drab dramas that fail to soar above the kitchen sink on wings of poetic imagination. Interestingly enough, a critic may refer to "poetic realism" but never to "poetic naturalism." Naturalism cannot be diverted by adjectives from its lumpy literalism.

Naturalism in the cinema, however, has never meant exactly the same thing as Naturalism in the theater. Not only is there a question of historical lag, the cinema having been born a full generation after the drama had been domesticated in Ibsen's doll's house, but also a curiously persistent love-hate relationship between the theater and the cinema that transforms the dramatic naturalism of one medium into the stylized theatricality of the other. Indeed, most film aestheticians have defined screen naturalism in terms of the medium's divorcement from the theater; whether that theater is romantic, poetic, symbolic, classic, realistic or naturalistic makes no difference in the argument. The film versions of *A Doll's House*, Zola's *Thérèse Raquin* and Chekhov's *Uncle Vanya* do not constitute naturalistic cinema nearly so much as assorted affectations of greasepaint and contrivance. First, the patina of time reveals what these plays have lost of their journalistic contemporaneity—the most obvious of all naturalistic criteria. Second, too much of the action occurs indoors, and mere exteriority has long been a test of screen naturalism, as the following passage from Paul Rotha's *The Film Till Now* demonstrates:

In contrast with this movement in the studios, there has appeared a small group of directors who showed a preference for constructing their films around natural incidents and with real material; a tendency that had possibly grown out of the early Western picture. Robert Flaherty, Ernest Schoesdack, Merian Cooper, Karl Brown, and William Howard formed the nucleus of this group, to whom there should be added James Cruze, John Ford, and Victor Fleming, by reason of their isolated pictures which fall into this category. To Flaherty, however, must be given the full credit for the first film using natural resources, the inspiring *Nanook of the North* in 1922, followed later by the beautiful *Moana*, in 1926. Other remarkable pictures characteristic of the naturalistic movement to be noted were *Grass, Chang, Stark Love,* and *White Gold,* all films that stood out sharply from the common run of American movies.

Rotha's views have both influenced and reflected the general line of Anglo-American aestheticians in defining Naturalism in the cinema in terms of a reality unique to the medium. The western, for example, is naturalistic only because of the authentic look of its landscape. Otherwise, no genre is more stylized and romantic and symbolical than this mythic meeting place of centaurs and six-shooters. Rotha is of course not committed to the ethos of the western as such but rather to that aspect of the western which attains its ultimate development in the documentary. By taking his camera into an Eskimo's igloo in 1922, Robert Flaherty had presumably taken the cinema beyond the influence of the theater. Thus *Nanook of the North* marks the beginning of the documentary movement that dominated film aesthetics in the English-speaking world for a generation. Not that *Nanook* was the first cinematic recording of reality but rather that it combined the impulse toward Naturalism with the creation of an organic work of art. In short, Nanook represented the fusion of authentic content with meaningful form to the extent that a chunk of nature was converted into art.

Unfortunately Nanook, like Naturalism, turned out to be more ambiguous in its aesthetics than its champions realized at the time. Naturalism in the theater is a mannered application of the concrete to an abstract medium. Naturalism in the cinema is almost a reflex of the medium itself. The theater was born of ritual, the cinema of reportage. Consequently, the term "naturalistic cinema" is almost tautologous.

Nanook the Eskimo is real in the sense that he is not an actor playing a role. We see him in his natural habitat rather than on some studio set. Robert Flaherty spent many months learning Nanook's routines and rituals and then filmed a loose account of the Eskimo's day-by-day existence. Since Nanook comes from a relatively primitive society in which man still hunts for his food, he makes a relatively picturesque subject for the camera. Hence, Nanook is too exotic a subject to fully satisfy the naturalistic movement. John Grierson, one of the foremost theoreticians of the documentary movement, criticized Flaherty for a Rousseau-like romanticism which was irrelevant to the problems of modern industrial civilization. Grierson's documentaries such as Night Mail and Drifters countered Flaherty's exoticism by selecting more typical subjects for scrutiny. Whereas Flaherty was essentially an explorer with no particular ideological axes to grind, Grierson and his colleagues had been profoundly influenced by the montage theories of Eisenstein and the resultant romanticism of machinery. Flaherty's Eden was pastoral and primitive; Grierson's dynamic and progressive. Flaherty's camera tended to stay focused on the faces of his subjects as he trailed them across their natural landscapes. Grierson was more concerned with the rhythms and images of mechanical movements and industrial processes—hence his films came to life in the cutting room.

Neither Flaherty nor Grierson solved the problem of recording the inner reality of their characters with a scrupulously documentary camera. The problem was less serious for Flaherty because his exotic explorer's taste enabled him to select heroes with a life style primarily visual and physical. Grierson, like Eisenstein, attempted to heroicize the masses, and in the process sacrificed men for Man. Grierson could show us what workers looked like, but he could never express what they felt and dreamed as individual beings.

The documentary movement tended to be too genteel for most audiences and some critics. The "revolutionary" view of workers and peasants was respectful to the point of tedium. Sex, crime and violence were dismissed as commercial devices of the studios. The documentary movement, like much of the Thirties Left, was inordinately puritanical: Karl Marx sipped tea with Queen Victoria.

Since mass audiences almost invariably preferred films of fiction to films of fact, the search for naturalistic elements spread to the so-called commercial film. The western, as we have noted, was cited for its natural exteriors. The early gangster films were applauded for depicting lower-class urban life (however garishly). Hollywood screwball comedies were appreciated for the behavioral naturalism of their players. Frank Capra earned the mantle of Naturalism for the imaginative bits of business he devised for players in such Depression fables as It Happened One Night, Mr. Deeds Goes to Town and Mr. Smith Goes to Washington. Behavioral naturalism was a curious concept that covered every breach of decorum from the stylized pantomimes of Chaplin, Keaton and Lloyd to the noisy anarchy of the Marx Brothers.

The cinema was long obliged to conceal its debt to the theater in order to be considered cinematic. The standard ploy in play adaptations was the insertion of gratuitous outdoor scenes between the various dialogues. This extra-theatrical excursion was known in Hollywood as "taking the movie outdoors." The late André Bazin's great contribution to film criticism was his audacious assertion that the cinema could be most faithful to itself by being faithful to the theatricality of the plays it adapted to the screen.

Nonetheless film criticism is haunted by the ghost of Naturalism. Too much talk, however expressive, is still considered in some quarters as alien to the "visuals" of the medium. And natural landscapes, however inexpressive or irrelevant, are still considered eminently "cinematic."

The impulse toward Naturalism is also expressed in the anti-Aristotelian criterion of sociological probability. Graduate students in English used to worry about Willy Loman's status as a tragic hero. By contrast, the most influential film critics of the Thirties were more likely to place Sophocles on trial for ignoring the problems of the common man. In 1935 Meyer Levin of *Esquire* defended *The Informer* of John Ford, Dudley Nichols and Liam O'Flaherty against *The Scoundrel* of Noël Coward, Ben Hecht and Charles MacArthur on the grounds that the protagonist of the Ford film informed on his best friend out of solidly economic motives whereas Noël Coward's veddy fancy scoundrel was motivated solely by a satanic flair for the aesthetics of evil. One unfortunate consequence of the criterion of sociological probability is the banality of failure in such ill-advised ventures as *Umberto D, The Luck of Ginger Coffey* and *Raisin in the Sun*. Nonetheless a certain class prejudice persists in naturalistic aesthetics. If the upper classes are treated at all, they must be caricatured (De Sica), satirized (Fellini), pitied for their aimlessness (Antonioni).

The Hollywood happy ending was denounced for many years, and for a time the "poetic realism" of Carné and Prévert in *Le Jour se leve* and *Quai des brumes* was hailed for the relative naturalism of its pessimism. Subsequently, Carné and Prévert were denounced for their morbidity, which allegedly contributed to the fall of France or at least too faithfully reflected the mood in which France fell. Similarly, Siegfried Kracauer in *From Caligari to Hitler* implicated the entire pre-Nazi German cinema for being too decadent to rouse the masses against Fascism. In the Twenties and early Thirties, however, German films were hailed for their pessimism as an "adult" antidote to Hollywood's sunny optimism. The notion of pessimism as a naturalistic effect is tied partly to a notion of philosophical probability and partly to a preference for the conventions of tragedy over the conventions of comedy. Ironically, many politically oriented critics have denounced the criterion of pessimism for its failure to affirm the possibilities of the human condition.

The coming of *cinéma-vérité* in the Fifties and Sixties has given the documentary movement the means to penetrate to the inner life of its real-life subjects. Jean Renoir recently observed that television talk programs were more relevant to contemporary cinema than all the new camera tricks. However, there was an aesthetic clash between the montage of the old-style documentaries and the steady camera set-up required for *cinéma-vérité*. Consequently, sound was divorced from image to effect a marriage between visual naturalism and verbal spontaneity. In the end, as in the beginning, the fundamental motivation of Naturalism in the cinema is to escape the influence of theater; yet ironically there is a growing nostalgia among knowledgeable film aestheticians for direct sound and all it implies of the essential theatricality of the cinema.

CENSORSHIP IN THE PERSPECTIVE OF 1969

When New York police seized Andy Warhol's *Blue Movie*, it was announced that the initial complaint had been filed by a member of the Citizens for Decent Literature from Watertown, New York. According to *Variety*, "the citizen in question apparently travelled the 400-odd miles [between Watertown and New York City] for the purpose of lodging said complaint." Still, police action against even the most salacious movies has been more the exception than the rule in New York City in recent years. Once the most repressed large city in America, New York has become one of the most liberated, and much of the credit (or blame) goes to Mayor John Lindsay's relaxed cosmopolitanism. Also, the Earl Warren Supreme Court passed many anti-censorship rulings, one of which obliterated the New York State Board of Regents as an organ of movie censorship.

Whereas in 1961 I went to Paris (and even London) for cinematic pleasures forbidden to New York, the pendulum has swung so far in the opposite direction that in 1969 New Yorkers saw more of the Lesbian seduction scene from *The Killing of Sister George* than did Londoners and more of the sexual congress and exposed genitalia (male and female) from *I Am Curious—Yellow* than were permitted to Parisians.

However, the Puritan tradition is still lurking in legislatures, courthouses and police stations across the length and breadth of America. Even without judicial encouragement, theater managers, projectionists, ticket takers and ushers are being arrested and harassed by law-enforcement officers and vigilante groups. At this moment with President Nixon holding prayer meetings in the White

House, liberals Earl Warren and Abe Fortas gone from the Supreme Court and Mayor Lindsay very gravely threatened in this year's mayoralty election by two law-and-order candidates, no one knows how much longer the screen will remain relatively free to show the Truth about the Facts of Life. Hence, it would be premature to bemoan the New Frankness in cinema at a time when we may yet be cast back into the dark ages of the Hays Office when married couples had to sleep in twin beds and all sinners had to be punished.

Andy Warhol's *Blue Movie*, like most of his cultural enterprises, is a derisive mockery of the very genre he exploits, in this instance the quasi-pornographic movie of redeeming social value for the sake of its defense in court. Indeed, Paul Morrissey, Warhol's articulate producer, immediately challenged the authorities to show why *Blue Movie* was any more objectionable than *I Am Curious—Yellow*. But Warhol breaks the rules, however hypocritical, by plunging right into his hard-core pornography, after which his two participants (Viva and Louis Waldon) discourse on such social issues as Vietnam, Mayor Lindsay and the garbage strike. Vilgot Sjöman had the good grace to spend a whole hour in *I Am Curious—Yellow* punishing the audience with his social insights before satisfying its prurient curiosity. Apart from the rhetorical reflex of defending the artist against society on every possible occasion, it is difficult to become concerned, much less inspired, by the issues involved in *Blue Movie*, *I am Curious—Yellow* and all the other cheerlessly carnal exercises in film-making.

Nowadays, more than ever, criticism is becoming as fragmented as creation. We are talking about different things at different times. That is to say that the sexual revolution is indeed interesting in itself. The evolution of the sexploitation movie in America deserves a separate chapter heading, though mainly sociological and only marginally aesthetic. Whereas once the film critic waited apprehensively for the novelistic adaptation to spring an embarrassingly sexless subterfuge, today's adaptors are as likely to embellish novels with additional vices and perversions. Hence the screen versions of Carson McCullers' *Reflections in a Golden Eye* and Philip Roth's *Goodbye Columbus* are in some ways more clinically explicit than the originals. But what has this to do with Art or Truth or even Realism? Not very much thus far.

By any reasonably objective standard, the movie fare of 1939 is, in retrospect, more interesting and more exciting than that of 1969. This doesn't mean that we can or should go back to where we were. For one thing, we can see 1939 more clearly now than we could at the time, and what seemed decadent then seems classical now. Similarly, 1969 may emerge in retrospect, if not like 1939, perhaps like 1929, a year in awkward transition, not from silence to sound, but from the dramatic discretion of the public performance to the denuded documentation of the private experience. Already we have become familiar with body-dubbing as a sequel to voice-dubbing and stunt-doubling. We have been officially informed that Britt Eklund's bared bosom in *The Night They Raided Minsky's* and Mia Farrow's in *Rosemary's Baby* and the rear view of Elizabeth Taylor on the staircase in *Reflections in a Golden Eye* were those of doubles.

Eventually, it seems, performers lacking ideal proportions may find stardom as difficult to attain or maintain as did the vocal defectives of the late Twenties. But more important, the sexual revolution and the attendant obsession with nudity may be making the screen more bourgeois than its erstwhile Marxist critics ever imagined. We were told for years in the serious historical texts on the cinema that censors and studios conspired to keep the truth from the masses, the implication being that once the censors and the studios were routed, a genuinely revolutionary cinema would come into existence. What has happened instead is that one set of fantasies has been replaced by another. And the change is less political than commercial.

On the positive side, the Negro is beginning only now to come into his own as a dignified and even heroic figure on the screen, but the relative stability of the ghetto market has had more to do with the rise of Sidney Poitier and Jim Brown than can be attributed to a more meaningful reduction in white racism. Similarly, the youth market has replaced the woman's market, so that movies have now switched from soap opera to dope opera, replacing one form of self-pitying sentimentality with another. As wives were always neglected, mistreated or misunderstood by their husbands, so now are young people neglected, mistreated or misunderstood by their elders. All young people seem to have exactly the same problems and the same values, despite differences in class, income, race, sect and even sex.

Thus the pot-smoking hippies, like the adulterous victims of back streets and brief encounters before them, come predominantly from the ranks of the bored bourgeoisie.

In this context, the increasing frankness of the screen implies a social malaise it is under no obligation to explore. We are back again to Antonioni's commercially convenient diagnosis of eroticism as the disease of our age. Of course, we are all sick, and our society is sick, and our system is sick, and we can't wait to take off all our clothes and cross-copulate and wife-swap and engage in polymorphously perverse diversions. But contrary to the expectations of optimistic liberals that the public would soon tire of libidinous license, audiences continue to prefer Antonioni's explicit disease to his implicit cure. And it may be that even the resurgence of the Right in America will not be able to stem the hedonistic tide which seems to be the logical consequence of capitalism and materialistic individualism. The Puritans predicted that the bikini would never cross the Atlantic. Nor the mini-skirt. But they did, and America herself topped these outrages with the topless and the see-through. And now no one, least of all the Puritans, knows where it is all to end.

This longtime moviemane can only regret that we didn't have a little less freedom a little earlier. I recall back in the Forties how a dozen actresses turned down the lead in *Voice of the Turtle* because the whole point of John Van Druten's gentle comedy would be lost on the screen without the mandatory bedroom scene. Eleanor Parker finally accepted a part that lost all of its charm by being denied the slightest *soupçon* of sex. Today *Voice of the Turtle* would be more likely to lose its charm by an excessive transformation of vertical grace into horizontal gaucherie.

We have come from an era when no one went to bed with anyone else to an era when people spend more time in bed than Oblomov ever did and to even less purpose. The fantasy of superhuman restraint has been replaced by the fantasy of superhuman release, and the truth has been passed about halfway on the path of the pendulum. Even the most revolutionary among us probably misses some of the charming footwork of actors and actresses as they circumvented the truth of the libido. But it must be remembered that the censors allowed us nothing when we asked for so little, and so now it is only fitting that we allow the censors nothing no matter how base the screen becomes. There can be no compromise with censorship even when there is regret for some of the lost charm of repression and innocence.

CITIZEN KAEL VS. CITIZEN KANE

> Voice in the Wind, a heartfelt shoestring quickie shot in 13 days,
> is a pretty awful moving picture, I realize, but I was touched by its
> sincerity and by a number of things in it, and was sympathetically
> interested in a good deal more. It is being advertised as "a strange
> new kind of moving picture," and that makes me realize, as the
> excitement over the "originality" of Citizen Kane used to, that al-
> ready I belong to a grizzling generation.
> —JAMES AGEE, The Nation, March 18, 1944,
> reprinted in Agee on Film

Pauline Kael's two-part article on *Citizen Kane* ("Raising
Kane," *The New Yorker*, February 20 and 27, 1970) reportedly
began as a brief introduction to the published screenplay, but, like
Topsy, it just growed and growed into a 50,000-word digression from
Kane itself into the life and times and loves and hates and love-hates
of Pauline Kael. My disagreement with her position begins with her
very first sentence: "*Citizen Kane* is perhaps the one American
talking picture that seems as fresh now as the day it opened." I can
think of hundreds of "American talking pictures" that seem as fresh
now as the day they opened. Even fresher. *Citizen Kane* is certainly
worthy of revival and reconsideration, but it hardly stands alone even
among the directorial efforts of Orson Welles. To believe that
Citizen Kane is a great American film in a morass of mediocre Hollywood movies is to misunderstand the transparent movieness of *Kane*
itself from its Xanadu castle out of *Snow White and the Seven
Dwarfs* to its menagerie out of *King Kong* to its mirrored reflections
out of old German *doppelganger* spectacles. Not that Miss Kael
makes any extravagant claims about the supposed greatness of the

film on which she has devoted so much newsprint. "It is a shallow
work," she decides, "a *shallow* masterpiece."

One wonders what Miss Kael considers a *deep* masterpiece.
U-Boat 29 perhaps? Actually, the closest she comes to comparing
Kane with the higher depths of cinema is in a parenthetical aside of
dubious relevance: "Like most of the films of the sound era that are
called masterpieces, *Citizen Kane* has reached its audience gradually
over the years rather than at the time of release. Yet, unlike the
others, it is conceived and acted as entertainment in a popular style
(unlike, say, *Rules of the Game* or *Rashomon* or *Man of Aran*,
which one does not think of in crowd-pleasing terms)."

Man of Aran, with its excessive sea-pounding on the sound track
making it as falsely exotic in its own time as *Ramparts of Clay* is in
ours, was certainly never conceived in crowd-pleasing terms. But
Rules of the Game and *Rashomon* are something else again even in
French and Japanese respectively. If anything, both films are more
rousingly entertaining and more satisfyingly lucid than *Kane*. Their
emotions are stronger, their gestures broader, their climaxes more
violent, their narratives more vigorous, their visual styles less ostentatious, and, no small consideration, their women infinitely warmer
and more sensual. Besides, the comparison is even factually ques-
tionable. *Rules of the Game* has never been too popular anywhere,
but *Kane* and *Rashomon* were instant sensations when they reached
the right audiences. It is no derogation of *Kane* and *Rashomon* to
say that they are immediately impressive whereas *Rules of the Game*
takes longer to appreciate because of the apparent artlessness of its
ironies. Not that Miss Kael bothers to commit her own personal
prestige to the greatness of any film. Note, for example, the cau-
tiously impersonal construction of "films of the sound era that are
called masterpieces." Perhaps this tone of cold-fish objectivity is the
price a normally warm-blooded film critic must pay to climb Onward
and Upward with the Arts at *The New Yorker*.

The plot thickens considerably when Miss Kael drifts away from a
halfhearted analysis of *Kane* to the most lively gossip imaginable
about the alleged birth pangs and labor pains of the script. Bit by
bit, "Raising Kane" becomes an excuse to lower the boom on Orson
Welles so as to resurrect the reputation of the late Herman J. Mankiewicz. By interviewing only the sworn enemies of Orson Welles,

Miss Kael has made herself fair game for Mr. Welles and his more fervent admirers. At the very least, we may expect a reprise of the recriminations exchanged between Peter Bogdanovich and Charles Higham on the occasion of the publication of Mr. Higham's *The Films of Orson Welles*.

How much of the final script of *Citizen Kane* was written by Herman J. Mankiewicz and how much by Orson Welles? I don't know, and I don't think Miss Kael, Mr. Bogdanovich and Mr. Higham do either. Undoubtedly, there will be affidavits aplenty from all sides, but literary collaboration, like marriage, is a largely unwitnessed interpenetration of psyches. Miss Kael demonstrates conclusively that Mankiewicz *could* have written the entire script unaided, but she cannot possibly know where and when and how and from whom and from what he derived all his ideas. As it happens, RKO was successfully sued in 1950 for plagiarism on the officially credited Mankiewicz–Welles script of *Kane* by Ferdinand Lundberg, author of *Imperial Hearst*. Miss Kael tries to pooh-pooh Lundberg's lawsuit because of the shadow it casts on her own one-sided lawyer's brief for Mankiewicz. RKO might just as well have been sued, Miss Kael contends, by John Dos Passos for the passages on Hearst in *USA*. Precisely. Who among us can claim complete originality in anything? "Raising Kane" itself bears the byline of Pauline Kael and of Pauline Kael alone. Yet thousands of words are directly quoted from other writers, and thousands more are paraphrased without credit. Miss Kael deserves her byline because she has shaped her material, much of it unoriginal, into an article with a polemical thrust all her own. Her selection and arrangement of material constitutes a very significant portion of her personal style.

Similarly, Orson Welles is not significantly diminished as the *auteur* of *Citizen Kane* by Miss Kael's breathless revelations about Herman J. Mankiewicz any more than he is diminished as the *auteur* of *The Magnificent Ambersons* by the fact that all the best lines and scenes were written by Booth Tarkington. It is only by virtually ignoring what *Citizen Kane* became as a film that Miss Kael can construct her bizarre theory of film history—namely, that *Citizen Kane* along with all the best moments in movies of the Thirties must be credited to a consortium of *New Yorker* writers gathered together by Harold Ross at Chasen's, the West Coast auxiliary of the Algonquin. Indeed, Miss Kael writes of Harold Ross in "Raising Kane" with much the same awed tone employed by General Lew Wallace in writing of Christ in *Ben Hur*. Writing of a Ross visit to Hearst's San Simeon, Miss Kael lacks only a divinely capitalized "H" ("He" for "he") to achieve a completely Biblical tone: "Harold Ross must have wondered what drew his old friends there, for he came, too, escorted by Robert Benchley."

What is most startling about "Raising Kane" is how little it adds to old stories that have been circulating in film magazines with fewer readers than *The New Yorker*. For example, *Persistence of Vision*, edited by Joseph McBride and published by the Wisconsin Film Society Press in 1968, contains not only McBride's *Kane* analysis which Miss Kael snickers at in "Raising Kane" without bothering to identify the author, but also an extended quote from John Houseman to Penelope Houston out of the *Sight and Sound* of Autumn 1962:

. . . we had done some work together on *Heart of Darkness*, which was to have been his first picture at RKO, and on something called *The Smiler with the Knife*. After I'd gone back East, Orson continued trying to find a subject. We had a mutual and very brilliant friend, Herman Mankiewicz, a celebrated Hollywood figure, who had recently broken his leg under tragicomic circumstances that I haven't time to go into. Having goaded each studio in turn into dismissing him, he had sunk to working on some of our radio shows. Orson arrived one night in New York, and over dinner told me that Mankiewicz had come up with an idea for a movie: a multi-faceted story about William Randolph Hearst in which Welles would play the title-part and direct. He asked me whether I would work with Mankiewicz as editor and collaborator on the script. I agreed and returned to Hollywood. After several conferences, at which Mankiewicz continued to develop his ideas, we moved him—nurse, plaster cast and all—up to a place in the mountains called Victorville, about a hundred miles from Los Angeles. There we installed ourselves on a guest ranch. Mankiewicz wrote, I mostly edited and the nurse was bored. Orson drove out once for dinner. At the end of three months we returned to Los Angeles with the 220-page script of *Kane*, later called *Citizen Kane*.

This is a delicate subject: I think Welles has always sincerely felt that he, single-handed, wrote *Kane* and everything else that he has directed— except, possibly, the plays of Shakespeare. But the script of *Kane* was especially Mankiewicz's. The conception and the structure were his, all the dramatic Hearstian mythology and the journalistic and political wisdom which he had been carrying around with him for years which he now poured into the only serious job he ever did in a lifetime of film writing. But Orson turned *Kane* into a film: the dynamics and the tensions are his and the brilliant cinematic effects—all those visual and aural inventions that add up to make *Citizen Kane* one of the world's great movies—those were pure Orson Welles.

The Houseman–Houston interview reads like a digest of "Raising Kane," and Joseph McBride was obviously aware of this interview when he analyzed *Kane* as "a tragedy in fugal form; thus . . . also the denial of tragedy." Aside from cackling at still another film scholar for the benefit of the philistines, Miss Kael creates the impression that McBride and his ilk never had the foggiest notion that Herman J. Mankiewicz had written the screenplay. McBride's greatest sin in apparently his willingness to consider *Citizen Kane* as a work of art rather than in Miss Kael's terms as "kitsch redeemed," a culturally defensive attitude for readers and editors who would be shocked to have any movie taken too seriously. Indeed, by the time Miss Kael is through taking *Kane* apart, it seems considerably more flawed than *The Owl and the Pussycat*. More important, *Kane* is viewed by Miss Kael almost exclusively as a product of the newspaper yarns that preceded it and not at all as an influence on the inner-space excursions of Fellini and Kubrick that followed it. McBride explicitly compares *Kane* to 8½ and is not that comparison more apt than Miss Kael's likening of *Kane* to *The Front Page*, for Pete's sake. And what is the black slab in *2001*, but the burnt sled "Rosebud" of *Kane*, the black slab representing the memento of an old civilization and "Rosebud" the memory of an old man.

"*Citizen Kane*, The American Baroque" is the pretentious title of a solemn, pedantic, humorless re-evaluation of *Kane* on the occasion of its revival in 1956. The piece first appeared in the ninth issue of *Film Culture* (1956) and did not cause too much stir one way or another. The reviewer (or rather rereviewer) was a twenty-eight-year-old New York free-lancer (more free than lance) with a severely limited education in film history. He had just started reviewing movies in the mid-Fifties, first under the name of Andrew George

Sarris and then merely Andrew Sarris, and by 1956 he had decided that the three greatest films of all times were Odd Man Out, Citizen Kane and Sullivan's Travels. Then from 1961 through 1969 he held that the three greatest films of all time were Lola Montès, Ugetsu and La Regle du jeu, and now in 1970 he has replaced Lola Montès at the top with Madame de . . . He still likes Citizen Kane, Odd Man Out, and Sullivan's Travels, but not as much these days as The Magnificent Ambersons, The Third Man and The Miracle of Morgan's Creek, Hail the Conquering Hero and The Palm Beach Story, not to mention Sunrise, Liebelei, La Ronde, Day of Wrath, Ordet, Flowers of St. Francis, French Can-Can, The Golden Coach, Psycho, Vertigo, The Searchers, Diary of a Country Priest, Au Hasard Balthazar, Brink of Life, Oharu, Seven Chances, Sherlock, Jr., Steamboat Bill Jr., and Shop Around the Corner. Also, the Russians deserved a look-in at least for auld lang syne since there were more personal styles in heaven and earth than were dreamt of even in Orson Welles's eclectic philosophy. No matter. Citizen Kane seemed infinitely less original and revolutionary in 1971 than it had in 1941 or even 1956, and not only because time had passed but also because the past had become more timely. If Kane once seemed like a tree in a clearing, it now seemed like a tree in a very large forest, and not even the topmost tree at that.

Nonetheless, despite the current reservations of its author, "Citizen Kane, The American Baroque" has been well received by academicians in recent years and repeatedly anthologized, most recently in a fascinating compendium entitled Focus on Kane (edited by Ronald Gottesman) with contributions by Gottesman, Juan Cobos, Miguel Rubio, J. A. Pruneda, William Johnson, John O'Hara, Bosley Crowther, Otis Ferguson, Cedric Belfrage, Tangye Lean, Orson Welles, Bernard Herrmann, Gregg Toland, Roy A. Fowler, Peter Cowie, Arthur Knight, Jorge Luis Borges, André Bazin, François Truffaut, Michael Stephanick and Charles Higham. Some of these pieces constitute the kind of "incense-burning" against which Pauline Kael's wise-guy criticism seems to be directed in her wild-swinging, mayhem-causing "Raising Kane," but most of the pieces raise formal and philosophical questions far beyond the dimensions of gossip culled from old newspapers.

Borges (in 1945) interprets Kane, perhaps predictably, as that "centreless labyrinth" mentioned in Chesterton's *The Head of Cae-sar*. But Borges is curiously dubious about the place of *Kane* in film history: "I dare predict, however, that *Citizen Kane* will endure in the same way certain films of Griffith or of Pudovkin 'endure': no one denies their historic value but no one sees them again. It suffers from grossness, pedantry, dullness. It is not intelligent, it is genial in the sombrest and most germanic sense of the word."

Truffaut makes a curious reference to *The New Yorker* (no person's name is given) description of Welles as "a genius without talent." One might just as aptly describe *The New Yorker* as talent without genius, and Miss Kael's approach to *Kane* and Welles as more intelligent than insightful. She spends infinitely more time on preliminary (and subsequently discarded) drafts of the script than on the final form of the movie as it materialized on the screen. Her bias is thus, as always, inescapably literary rather than visual. And it follows that she would be impatient with the visual, aural and emotional coup represented by "Rosebud." "The mystery in *Kane* is largely fake," Miss Kael contends, "and the Gothic-thriller atmosphere and the Rosebud gimmickry (though fun) are such obvious penny-dreadful popular theatrics that they're not so very different from the fake mysteries that Hearst's *American Weekly* used to whip up—the haunted castles and the curses fulfilled."

The operative words in the preceding passage are "though fun," a familiarly quaint Kaelian reconciliation of what she can enjoy viscerally with what she can endorse cerebrally. As it happens, Miss Kael is not alone in being ashamed of "Rosebud." Orson Welles has long since repudiated "Rosebud," or at least since a 1963 interview with Miss Dilys Powell of the Sunday *Times* (London) excerpted by Peter Cowie in his *The Study of a Colossus*: "It's a gimmick, really," said Welles, "and rather dollar-book Freud."

I disagree with both Miss Kael and Mr. Welles on "Rosebud," with Miss Kael for the anti-genre prejudice her repudiation of "Rosebud" confirms and with Welles for—who knows—his canny instinct for self-preservation in repudiating "Rosebud" before it came out of Herman J. Mankiewicz's ghostly past to haunt him.

When I interviewed Joseph L. Mankiewicz in 1970 for *Show* magazine, I had no idea that he would reveal to me the origin of "Rosebud" as a bike that Herman J. Mankiewicz once lost as a child in Wilkes-Barre, Pennsylvania. Nor did I have any idea that there then was and always had been a bitter feud between the Herman J. and Joseph L. sides of the Mankiewicz family. All I knew was that I had forged a crucial link with the scenarist of a strangely compelling movie called *Ladies' Man* and *Citizen Kane*. But my feeling of discovery was based first of all on my abiding attachment to "Rosebud" as not only the key to but also the beating heart of *Citizen Kane* as a movie. It is "Rosebud" that structures *Kane* as a private-eye investigation of a citizen in the public eye, and thus brings us much closer to *The Maltese Falcon* and *The Big Sleep* and the burning R's on the pillowcases of *Rebecca*.

The problem with defending "Rosebud" as a narrative device is that its very vividness makes it a running gag in our satirically oriented culture. How can we possibly take "Rosebud" seriously, Miss Kael complains, after Snoopy has called Lucy's sled "Rosebud"? The same way, I suppose, we can take *Potemkin* seriously after Woody Allen has sent a baby carriage rolling down the steps of a Latin American palace in *Bananas*. Both Snoopy and Allen are paying homage to bits of film language transformed by the magical contexts of their medium into poetic metaphors. But whereas Eisenstein's baby carriage moves from prop to agitprop as it becomes an archetypal conveyance of revolutionary fervor, "Rosebud" reverberates with psychological overtones as it passes through the snows of childhood (*les neiges d'antan*) into the fire, ashes and smoke of death. Indeed, the burning of "Rosebud" in Xanadu's furnace represents the only instance in which the character of Kane can be seen subjectively by the audience. It is as if his mind and memory were being cremated before our eyes and we were too helpless to intervene and too incompetent to judge. It is an act of symbolic summation and transfiguration worthy of Truffaut's passionately paradoxical tribute to the film itself: "It is a demonstration of the force of power and an attack on the force of power, it is a hymn to youth and a meditation on old age, an essay on the vanity of all material ambition and at the same time a poem on old age and the solitude of exceptional beings, genius or monster or monstrous genius."

The redeeming value of "Rosebud" is its suggestion that men of a certain size and scope and stature are not fully accountable even to history. This implied absence of accountability tends to slow the flow of moralistic molasses dumped over Kane on the most dubious pretexts. Through the years I have seen *Kane* about thirty times, but until very recently I never bothered to wonder what Kane's side of the story might have been if there had been somewhat more of his story on the screen. What, for example, is Jed Leland so outraged about in his rambling reminiscences of a rich friend with feet of clay? That Kane's two marriages failed? Leland's apparently sexless existence hardly makes him more "human" on that score than Kane. Besides, Kane's two wives never remotely suggest the stuff of which Rosebuds are made. Ruth Warwick's Emily is frigid, prissy, conservative and, from her quietly hysterical aversion to the idea of Bernstein in her son's nursery, at least incipiently anti-Semitic. Dorothy Comingore's Susan is harsh, raucous, vulgar and almost maniacally mediocre. Ray Collins's embattled Tammany tiger seems every inch the thief and scoundrel Kane claimed him to be, and Leland himself seems to have no greater ambition in life than to be a drunken dilettante full of moral superiority. If Miss Kael had analyzed the Kane–Leland relationship more fully on its own terms, she might have traced a parallel between Kane and Leland on one track and Hearst and Mankiewicz on the other. There is probably a great deal of Mankiewicz in Leland, and especially in that moment of alcoholic self-righteousness when Leland attacks Kane for not knowing how to get drunk. *In vino veritas* and all that. Hearst might even stand for all the Hollywood moguls in Mankiewicz's moralistic rhetoric. But the Leland–Kane relationship doesn't play so one-sidedly in the delicately pitched intimacy provided by Joseph Cotten and Orson Welles. Cotten is an actor who can swim under the surface of a characterization with less splash than Welles, and so when Cotten–Leland talks about drinking with Welles–Kane, he could be talking also about acting. Welles can't really lose himself in a part the way Cotten can, perhaps because Welles has so much more to lose. Even so, Welles and Cotten climb piggy-back on each other's lines with such zestful expertness that there is less conflict than complicity in their big renunciation scene. Leland becomes Kane's alter ego in the peculiarly Wellesian pattern which later couples Othello and Iago, Arkadin and Van Stratten, Falstaff and Hal, and Quinlan and Vargas, not to mention Welles and Cotten in repeat interperformances in *Journey into Fear* and Carol Reed's *The Third Man*. Indeed, when you add up everything Welles did after *Kane* and compare it with everything Mankiewicz did before and after *Kane*, the sour humor and intransigent ambiguity of *Citizen Kane* would seem to arise more from the personality of Welles than from that of Mankiewicz. What Mankiewicz has provided is an apparently big subject with faint hints of scandal from one side and large helpings of social consciousness from the other. And "Rosebud," a symbol that turned out to be more personal than social.

Back in 1941, Bosley Crowther qualified his enthusiastic review of *Kane* with a complaint about "Rosebud" and the unsolved mystery of Kane: "And the final, poignant identification of "Rosebud" sheds little more than a vague, sentimental light upon his character. At the end Kubla Kane is still an enigma—a very confusing one." Two days after his initial review, Crowther developed his reservations in a Sunday follow-up:

And when the significance of "Rosebud" is made apparent in the final sequence of the film, it provides little more than a dramatic and poignant shock. It does not clarify, except by sentimental suggestion, the reason for Kane's complexity. And so we are bound to conclude that this picture is not truly great, for its theme is basically vague and its significance depends upon circumstances. Unquestionably, Mr. Welles is the most dynamic newcomer in films and his talents are infinite. But the showman will have to acquire a good bit more discipline before he is thoroughly dependable.

Crowther's rejection of "Rosebud" as an explanation of Kane is consistent with his later pans of *Wild Strawberries* and *L'Avventura* for their apparent self-indulgence and obfuscation. Crowther's most influential period in film criticism was the Forties when his social approach to films coincided with the world-saving concerns of his readers. "Rosebud" is much closer to the arched fishing pole and line of the protagonist's father in *Wild Strawberries* than to the outstretched soldier's hand crumpling up near a butterfly in *All Quiet on the Western Front*.

Few American films up to *Citizen Kane* had been grown up enough to suggest that we never really grow up, and a boy torn away from his mother at an early age, like Kane, like Welles, least of all. The grandeur of "Rosebud" as a memory is that it is meaningless and trivial to anyone but Kane. Its horror is its confirmation that we

are isolated from each other by so much more than our politics and
morals, by nothing less, in fact, than our very selves. The only way
critics and audiences of the period could stomach the profound pessimism of Citizen Kane was to misconstrue it as a detailed denunciation of a certain kind of American plutocrat. In this respect, the
scenario is curiously sluggish and undeveloped next to a political hal-
lucination like the Capra–Riskin Meet John Doe which opened
shortly before Citizen Kane and had about a million times more
polemical Americana. Miss Kael never mentions Meet John Doe or
Mr. Smith Goes to Washington or The Grapes of Wrath or The
Great Dictator. Why Hearst should have been a more daring target
in 1940 than Hitler I have no idea, and, even today, the California
lettuce growers seem to have lost few of their fangs from The
Grapes of Wrath. By any standard, the few minutes of political talk
sprinkled in Citizen Kane would seem fairly superficial in a high-
school civics textbook. But the mystical process by which the Mercury Players parade across a haunted screen never seems to lose its
power to fascinate us.

Millions of viewers (including this reviewer) who watched the
Academy of Motion Picture Arts and Science presentations of April
15, 1971, were given to understand that Orson Welles had accepted
in advance an honorary award from John Huston via a piece of film
from Spain where Welles was presumably working on some assignment or other. The scenario for this bit of remote-control contrivance
had become familiar in recent years: Appreciative Artist Too Busy
Abroad to Come to Hollywood but Honored Just the Same. Huston concluded the charade by announcing that he would stop off in
Spain (on his way to Ireland) to deliver the Oscar to Orson. But if
Hollywood scuttlebutt is to be believed, not only was Welles in
town all the time; he shot the "Spanish" footage in his own Los
Angeles apartment the week before, and then capped the jest by
receiving the statuette from Huston at a local restaurant immediately after the Oscar ceremony. Thus while George C. Scott was
attracting all the attention with his public defiance of convention,
Welles and Huston, two merry pranksters of an earlier era, were
slipping in their own private joke without ever letting their tongues
out of their cheeks.

In their time Welles and Huston had been subjected to the same
brand of Faustian rhetoric masquerading as criticism. Both directorial careers started out with a bang in 1941, Welles with *Kane*,
Huston with *The Maltese Falcon*. Both found themselves a continent away when an ambitious project was being butchered in the
cutting room, Welles in South America during the martyrdom of
The Magnificent Ambersons, and Huston in Africa during the reduction of *The Red Badge of Courage*. Both men had bummed
around Europe in their youth, and never really lost their wanderlust
sufficiently to settle down in Hollywood for the more tedious tasks
of movie-making. Both men supplemented their directorial careers
with acting, and both men ended up disillusioning their earliest admirers. But there is really no need to shed crocodile tears over their
alleged decline.

Cinema, like politics, is the art of the possible. There are too
many conflicting temperaments and forces at work at every stage of
production to achieve purity of creation. And not only in Hollywood, as Pauline Kael seems to suggest in "Raising Kane." It is only
because she is so blissfully unaware of French and Japanese philistinism that she can treat Renoir and Kurosawa as miraculously unfet-
tered creatures of inspiration in comparison with their Hollywood
counterparts. Besides, most of her *New Yorker* readers salivate sympathetically to the mere mention of Renoir because the name reminds them of the kind of paintings they would like to possess.
After a disastrous screening of *The Rules of the Game* at the Harvard Club in New York, I can assure Miss Kael that most of her
readers would despise all but one or two of the master's movies,
painter father or no painter father. As for Kurosawa, his samurai epics
are more or less imaginative imitations of the Hollywood westerns
Miss Kael professes to despise on principle.

And what of the many screenwriters associated with Renoir, Kurosawa, Antonioni, Fellini and, on occasion, even Bergman? When
shall we read *their* stories with any portion of the extended detail
Miss Kael has devoted to the late Herman J. Mankiewicz. Indeed, if
foreign directors had to satisfy the Screenwriters Guild requirement
of writing at least 55 percent of the dialogue to qualify for a writing
credit, very few of the art-house deities would qualify. It is therefore
maliciously misleading of Miss Kael and her cohorts to argue that

directors like Hitchcock, Ford and Hawks had nothing to do with the preparation of their scripts when the astonishing stylistic continuity of their careers demonstrates the contrary. Only recently John Gielgud (no *auteurist* he) casually remarked on a talk show that Hitchcock had "written in" big parts for Peter Lorre and Robert Young to rival Gielgud's original lead role in *Secret Agent*. Hollis Alpert has taken up the cudgels for Miss Kael in the *Saturday Review* as part of his long crusade for greater recognition of the screenwriter. (Ironically, Alpert once won an award for criticism from the Directors Guild, and I never.)

As much as I respect Alpert's point of view, I must point out that *auteurism* was never intended to enthrone all directors above all writers but rather to identify the source of a style in movies worthy of memory. Often there is more than one source, and it is up to the critic to track down every contribution whenever possible. What I find peculiar, however, is the malignant anti-auteurism in the writings of Kael and Alpert as if *auteurism* were an established religion that had carried the day. As it happens, Sarris, Kael, Alpert, Kauffmann and even noted "mass critics" King Weed and Gene Shallow are jammed in a phone booth far from the madding crowd. (I don't even consider such voluntary exiles from the public pulse as John Simon, the greatest film critic of the nineteenth century, and Gene Youngblood, the greatest film critic of the twenty-first.) The point is that we are all splitting hairs over questions only vaguely understood and appreciated by the majority of our readers. Still, I must make every effort to keep the record as balanced as possible, and it is in this spirit of scholarly rectification that I am raising some *Kane* of my own.

As Miss Kael makes clear in her own article, it is not entirely the fault of Orson Welles that Herman J. Mankiewicz has tended to be the forgotten man of *Citizen Kane*. Indeed, nothing Miss Kael writes about Mankiewicz is inconsistent with F. Scott Fitzgerald's cruel but candid write-off in a letter to Maxwell Perkins dated April 23, 1938 (from *The Letters of F. Scott Fitzgerald*, edited and with an introduction by Andrew Turnbull): "Hard times weed out many of the incompetents, but they swarm back—Herman Mankiewicz, a ruined man who hasn't written ten feet of continuity in two years, was finally dropped by Metro, but immediately picked up by Columbia! He is a nice fellow that everybody likes and has been brilliant, but he is being hired because everyone is sorry for his wife—which I think would make him rather an obstacle in the way of making good pictures. Utter toughness toward the helpless, combined with super-sentimentality—Jesus, what a combination!"

Miss Kael digs into the dry rot that had set in almost thirteen years before Fitzgerald's letter: "It was a lucky thing for Mankiewicz that he got the movie job when he did, because he would never have risen at the *Times*, and though he wrote regularly for *The New Yorker* (and remarked of those of the Algonquin group who didn't, 'The part-time help of wits is no better than the full-time of half-wits'), *The New Yorker*, despite his pleas for cash, was paying him partly in stock, which wasn't worth much at the time. Mankiewicz drank heavily, and the drinking newspaperman was in the style of the *World*, but not in the style of the *Times*."

Miss Kael does manage to score a coup for Mankiewicz's authorship of *Kane* with an elaborate description of his misadventure in October 1925 with a review of Gladys Wallis (the wife of Samuel Insull) in *The School for Scandal*. Mankiewicz reportedly collapsed on his typewriter in a drunken stupor à la Jed Leland with his unspeakable (and unprintable) notice still in the carriage. By contrast, Miss Kael hastily downgrades the significance of the fact that the name Bernstein meant something in the early life of Welles. We must turn to Peter Cowie's *The Study of a Colossus* for the information "that Welles' own mentor in youth was a certain Doctor Bernstein who presented him, among other things, with a puppet theatre when he was in his infancy." Could this puppet theater have been the atrocity about which the first Mrs. Kane complains at the breakfast table? Fortunately Miss Kael's is not likely to be the last word on such speculations.

Not that Miss Kael can be charged with excessive charity toward Mankiewicz's weaknesses and afflictions. Especially memorable in a horrible way is her zestful retelling of an Ezra Goodman anecdote from *The 50 Year Decline and Fall of Hollywood* about an alleged gaffe perpetrated by Mankiewicz all over the dinner table of a fastidious Hollywood producer named Arthur Hornblow, Jr. According to members of the Mankiewicz family, the Goodman anecdote was heavily embroidered, and it does seem strange that a supposed champion of Mankiewicz should repeat such an unflattering account verbatim.

Even Mankiewicz's looks at the time of *Kane* undergo a harsh surveillance by Miss Kael: "It would be hard to explain his sudden, early aging and the thickening of his features and the transparently cynical look on his face in later photographs." Miss Kael's moralizing extends to Mankiewicz's *modus operandi*: "Mankiewicz had been hacking out popular comedies and melodramas for too long to write drama; one does not *dictate* tragedy to a stenotypist." No, one presumably writes tragedy in a garret with a goose quill. Suddenly we perceive that "Raising Kane," like Miss Kael's previous production story on *The Group*, is a saga with no heroes or heroines apart from Miss Kael herself. Orson and Herman, the two protagonists and antagonists of "Raising Kane," are reduced to the dimensions respectively of an exhibitionistic egomaniac and a self-destructive hack. Meanwhile, Miss Kael's gyroscopic ego preserves her moral superiority over all semblances of otherness. She heaps her scorn promiscuously over radicals and reactionaries, swimming-pool Stalinists and movie-industry moguls, young right-on students and old silent-movie buffs, Bazinians and Kracauerites. And in the process of putting everyone else down, she replaces the scholarly oversimplifications of the past with her own idiosyncratic oversimplifications. Hence, every movie made before 1929 is eradicated from the stream of film history through this curious tribute to the hitherto despised early talkies: "And the public responded, because it was eager for modern American subjects. Even those who were children at the time loved the fast-moving modern-city stories. The commonplaceness—even tawdriness—of the imagery was such a relief from all that silent 'poetry.' The talkies were a great step down. It's hard to make clear to people who didn't live through the transition how sickly and unpleasant many of those 'artistic' silent pictures were— how you wanted to scrape off all that mist and sentiment."

By her own calculation, Miss Kael was about eight years old when talking pictures came in, and it is not surprising that an eight-year-old should prefer speech to titles. Even today children tend to reject foreign films with subtitles. Television, if nothing else, has conditioned young people to listen to language rather than read it. But a generation of immigrants, among whom were my father and mother, actually learned English by reading the intertitles of silent movies. The point of view of this generation would differ from Miss Kael's, which is why a film historian cannot rely merely on childhood memories. I was born in 1928 just about when sound was coming in, and I can't depend on childhood memories at all for an appraisal of the silent era, but what little burrowing I have done has revealed a much greater diversity of style and content than Miss Kael's sweeping generalization would suggest. Twenties movies featured even more fun and knockabout humor than the Thirties, and not merely through their classic clowns—Chaplin, Keaton, Lloyd, Langdon, Laurel and Hardy, et al., but also through all sorts of relatively straight comedy players, including Marion Davies, the hapless obsession of William Randolph Hearst and the subject of Dorothy Comingore's shrill caricature as Susan Alexander.

Miss Kael is on even weaker ground when she credits all *The New Yorker* writers her stable of researchers could check out with effecting nothing less than a revolution in Hollywood tastes: "They changed movies by raking the old moralistic muck with derision. Those sickly Graustarkian romances with beautiful, pure high-born girls and pathetic lame girls and dashing princes in love with commoners, and all the Dumas and Sabatini and Blasco-Ibanez, now had to compete with the freedom and wildness of American comedy." Aside from taking a poke at Stroheim and Ingram, this passage is notable only for the fatuous falseness of its generalization. *Docks of New York, Sunrise, The Crowd, The River, Lonesome, A Girl in Every Port, Beggars of Life, That Certain Thing, Show People, The Jack Knife Man,* to name but a small sampling of the silents, were far closer to a kind of grubby grandeur than to Graustark.

A false record of film history is relevant here only to the extent that it contributes to a spectacular misinterpretation of *Citizen Kane* itself. After thousands of words of interesting gossip, "Raising Kane" brings us up short with the terse bulletin: "Which takes us right up to *Citizen Kane*, the biggest newspaper picture of them all—the picture that ends with the introduction of the cast and a reprise of the line 'I think it would be fun to run a newspaper.' " Here at least Miss Kael can be credited with a certain degree of originality, however bizarre, in treating *Citizen Kane* as the last of the Stop-the-Presses movies instead of the first of the Stop-the-World-I-Want-To-Get-Off films. What most other critics take to be a coffin, the irrepressible Miss Kael takes to be a barrel of laughs. A man dies, his best friends spits on his memory, his second wife becomes an alcoholic, a sled is burned, and everyone gets old in the process. Next Week, East Lynne.

But to support her oddly jocular reaction to Kane, Miss Kael is compelled to discount what Herman J. Mankiewicz actually did as a screenwriter for close to thirty years and try to place him as a person in the midst of the Algonquin Circle. Names are dropped with gay abandon, a Dorothy Parker here, a Nathanael West there. No need then to mention such relatively heroic Hollywood work horses as Robert Riskin and Dudley Nichols. They never dined with Harold Ross, and hence they don't count even though they wrote a hundred times as many funny lines as Parker and West put together. Besides, once you start mentioning genuine professionals like Riskin and Nichols, you have to start mentioning directors like Capra and Ford and McCarey, and they too had nothing to do with the Algonquin Circle. As for Herman J. Mankiewicz—that is, the real Herman J. Mankiewicz—his forte was never comedy at all but what Miss Kael would describe derisively as romantic melodrama. His most memorable movies before Kane are two interesting William Powell vehicles entitled Man of the World and Ladies' Man, and after Kane, two oddly convoluted movies for, respectively, Robert Siodmak (Christmas Holiday) and Nicholas Ray (A Woman's Secret), the latter movie strikingly anticipatory of brother Joe's All About Eve.

A man's life, as Kane suggests, is more than a jigsaw puzzle. Even when we have fitted all the pieces together, we may have difficulty understanding the completed portrait. It may be that Herman J. Mankiewicz's troubles started long before he came to Hollywood, but once there he encountered a crisis in film history which should at least be considered as part of his malaise. Back in 1931, the plot of Man of the World did not cause too much excitement. According to the Harrison's Reports of March 28, 1931:

The hero was a publisher of a scandal sheet. His system was to appear at the home of a wealthy person with an advance proof of some item that was to be printed about him. He would claim to be desirous of having this blackmailer prosecuted, but the person involved would never

consent to do this as it would be embarrassing. Instead he would pay
him hush money, which he thought would be turned over to the blackmailer, but which the hero would keep. At the home of one of his victims he meets the heroine. They eventually fall in love with each other.
He tells her about his past, but she is willing to marry him. The hero
later realizes the impossibility of this when his former sweetheart who
was his blackmailing assistant, tells him that he can never escape from
the past. He prints an item about the heroine and himself and presents
it to her uncle. In her presence he accepts a check for $10,000 as hush
money, and she is completely disillusioned. The police force him to leave
Paris and he goes to South Africa with his former sweetheart. The
heroine leaves for America, glad to be rid of him.

The story was written by Herman Mankiewicz. It was directed by
Richard Wallace. In the cast are William Powell, Carole Lombard,
Wynne Gibson, Guy Kibbee and others. The talk is very indistinct and
at times even difficult to understand. Not suitable for children, or even
for adults. Not a Sunday show. Not a substitution. Note: Two con-
cealed advertisements are used in this picture; mention is made of both
Duns and Bradstreets.

The exhaustively censorious coverage of *Harrison's Reports* neglects one slight plot detail. The hero tears up the check from his
beloved's uncle and lets the pieces flutter out to sea. This check-
tearing gesture is repeated more obliquely in *Kane* by Jed Leland via
a letter to Kane with the torn pieces of a check inside.

Ladies' Man, the next month, reflected more sordidness and self-
hatred than even *Man of the World*. Powell plays a self-mocking
gigolo, almost redeemed from his shameful profession by the true
love of Kay Francis, but finally destroyed by the unbridled passions
of a mother (Olive Tell) and daughter (Carole Lombard) team in
wicked high society. Powell's actual Nemesis is an implacable banker-
father-husband (Gilbert Emery) who intervenes for the sake of his
daughter after tolerating the indiscretions of his wife. It is the night
of the masquerade ball. Powell is dressed in the grotesque costume
of Potemkin to his elderly mistress's Catherine. The dignified husband comes to Powell's room and ends up hurling him from the
balcony. He then goes downstairs and takes his place alongside his
wife for the Grand March. She knows intuitively what has happened
and walks beside him fearfully but proudly. The police are waiting.
But the march continues round and round. William Everson has

compared this extraordinary figure of style to the climactic moments of Jacques Prevert in *Lumière d'Eté* (directed by Jean Grémillon) and *The Lovers of Verona* (directed by Henri Cayatte). They are, like the climactic moments in *Ladies' Man*, more the moments of a writer than of a director. If Sternberg had directed *Ladies' Man*, it might have been one of the great movies of the Thirties. Unfortunately, the director was Lothar Mendes, and the movie was consigned to oblivion except for the assiduous research of old-movie buffs. Still, I could see at last on the screen some prior evidence of the feeling that went into *Kane* and suddenly *Kane* itself took on a new coloration in the frightful tension between an old writer loaded down with fables of shame and guilt and a young director loaded down with fantasies of power and glory. For Mankiewicz, *Kane* may have been the last stop on this earth, and for Welles the first step on the moon.

The one expression critics invariably used to describe Herman Mankiewicz's dialogue was "grown-up," not witty or *New Yorkerish* or hilarious, but simply grown-up. And the dialogue in *Citizen Kane* is nothing if not grown-up. The trouble is that after 1933, serious grown-up screenwriters were increasingly plagued by a childish censorship, and only grown-up critics like Otis Ferguson and Meyer Levin even noticed the havoc that was being wrought. I suspect that Mankiewicz became more despondent and frustrated in this period, partly because his bitterness and cynicism could no longer find permissible plots in which to function and partly because Paramount itself was on the downgrade with its arty, adult projects. In all the space she has devoted in "Raising Kane" to an analysis of the script, Pauline Kael never mentions the brothel scene with Kane and Leland, a scene that the censors knocked out of Mankiewicz's original script, one of many elisions that tended to tip the viewpoint of the film from the more sensual Mankiewicz to the more theatrical Welles. Curiously, the rigid censorship that was in force in 1941 worked to the advantage of Welles *vis-à-vis* other directors with fewer hang ups about women.

Why then has Welles virtually obliterated Mankiewicz from view over the years? For one thing, Welles has continued living and, by living, incarnating *Kane*. Pauline Kael, Hollis Alpert and even the usually perspicacious Richard Corliss are in error when they blame the auteurists and other director-cultists for glorifying the director. Welles happened to be everything on *Kane*, producer, director, star and unit publicist. It is as if Marlon Brando, Stanley Kubrick and Darryl F. Zanuck were the same person. And yet it is Welles, more than any director up to his time, who made directing fashionably conspicuous. As Frank S. Nugent noted in the New York Sunday *Times* of June 12, 1938:

Speaking of Frank Borzage and George Stevens, as we expect to, brings up the matter of the unsung motion picture director. We remember a poll conducted by one of the theatre circuits not so long ago in which the patrons were invited to name their favorite stars, pictures, stories and directors. John Public and his wife sprinted through the first three categories and bluffed or quit cold on the fourth. Adolph Zukor, of all people, was voted the favorite director by some; Sam Goldwyn was another contender. As we recall it, Ernst Lubitsch won in a walk. His name seemed to be easy to remember. Actually, it was no contest.

Since this is a day of quizzes, spelling bees and all kinds of brain-teasers, we wonder how many persons could identify the following in terms of their recent, or their most outstanding pictures: Gregory La Cava, Leo McCarey, Wesley Ruggles, Clarence Brown, Fritz Lang, Alfred Hitchcock, Robert Stevenson, Michael Curtiz, Norman Taurog and Victor Fleming. Or would you score better if the professor asked you to name the director of *The Informer*, of *Mr. Deeds Goes to Town*, of *Wells Fargo*, or *A Slight Case of Murder* and *The Good Earth*? (Don't be upset if you wind up with a dunce cap: you could catch us just as easily.)

The point, if any, is not merely that we are apt to forget the director after the fact—which would be at most a pardonable lapse of memory—but that we frequently ignore him during it. In clearer words, most of us take a film's direction for granted, whether it is good or bad, and toss the laurel wreath or the poison ivy sprig at the players. Quite possibly the oversight works as often to the forgotten man's advantage as it does to his disadvantage. Still, we feel it's high time to make the director come out from behind those false whiskers and take his place in the hot glare of the cinema spotlight.

Actually the auteurists are still fighting an uphill battle to make movie audiences conscious of style, despite all the apparent published evidence to the contrary. The player is still the thing, be he

John Wayne or Dustin Hoffman or, to the immediate point, Orson Welles. Admittedly, Welles often shows a tendency to swallow up subordinate credits and thinner egos. For years he has been hinting broadly that he had everything to do with the carousel scene in Carol Reed's *The Third Man* and he has never gotten over the bad habit of directing other directors for whom he is ostensibly only acting, and sometimes barely that. This is the monstrous side of his personality, but since *Kane* he has displayed a great many more interesting and compassionate sides to this same personality, especially in movies like *The Magnificent Ambersons*, *Lady from Shanghai*, *Touch of Evil*, and *Falstaff*. Still, the plot line of *Mr. Arkadin* could be interpreted as a parable of an artist setting out to eliminate all his collaborators.

However, nothing is to be gained in the attempted resurrection of Herman J. Mankiewicz by painting him as something he is not, specifically the comic muse of the Marx Brothers in *Duck Soup* and *A Night at the Opera*, movies from which Mankiewicz was fired very early in the proceedings. By crediting Mankiewicz with these movies on the flimsiest evidence, Miss Kael defrauds writers Bert Kalmar and Harry Ruby, director Leo McCarey (*Duck Soup*), writers George S. Kaufman and Morrie Ryskind and director Sam Wood (*A Night at the Opera*) in much the same way that she claims Welles and the Wellesians have defrauded Herman J. Mankiewicz. Besides, the two funniest episodes in *Duck Soup*—the lemonade war between Harpo and Edgar Kennedy, the mirror sequence—are derived from old Charlie Chase and Laurel and Hardy farces, and McCarey directed both Chase and Laurel and Hardy in the silent era. So much for the Algonquin Circle as the sole dispenser of Thirties movie comedy. Miss Kael probably felt that a relationship, however tenuous, with the Marx Brothers would strengthen her argument that Mankiewicz was a man of mirth. She seems unaware that *Duck Soup* was a flop at the time of its release, and the Marx Brothers were let go at Paramount, as was W. C. Fields a few years later. A great many of today's comedy classics like *Bringing Up Baby* and *Holiday* were box-office failures in the Thirties. Paramount and RKO were two of the better studios of the Thirties and they paid the price by not harvesting the corn as assiduously as Metro did. When I look over the list of great films, here and abroad, that have failed to attract audiences in their own time, I find it difficult to endorse Miss Kael's neat conspiracy theory to explain why *Kane* did not do better than it did. It was no fault of Hearst's that *Kane* was a complete commercial flop in England, where Hearst had as little influence as Lord Beaverbrook had here. Also, the New York run began tapering off well before its tenth week, as if the word-of-mouth were getting around that *Kane* was a cold, gloomy movie at a time when cold, gloomy movies were not nearly as fashionable as they are today, and, even so, have you peeked at the grosses for *Persona* lately?

Nor do I agree that the Academy Awards might have turned the tide commercially. Miss Kael neglects to mention what actually did win the Oscar that year: *How Green Was My Valley*, a movie that, though it would not have gotten my vote over *Kane* at the time, is nonetheless the best movie, apart from *Sunrise*, ever to win an Oscar. (I think it is much more disgraceful that *Mrs. Miniver* won the 1942 Academy Award over *The Magnificent Ambersons*.) And even Welles could not quarrel with the choice of John Ford as best director in 1941 by both the New York Film Critics and the Academy. After all, Welles did study for *Kane* under Ford, Frank Capra, King Vidor and Fritz Lang, and if Miss Kael would take another look at *Stagecoach* and *The Informer*, she would find more expressionism than she suspects.

Despite her blatant bias against Welles, Miss Kael is to be commended for providing as much information as she has on the life and background of Herman J. Mankiewicz. Since his death in 1953 he has indeed been a forgotten man, eclipsed not only by Welles but by his younger brother, Joe. Richard Griffith credits the script *Kane* to Joseph Mankiewicz in the once authoritative film history coauthored with Paul Rotha and entitled *The Film Till Now*. To this day the *Film Daily Year Book* records the name of the Oscar winner for best original screenplay in 1941 (along with Orson Welles) as "John Mankiewicz." The late great French film critic Jean-Georges Auriol assumed that the Mankiewicz who had coauthored *Kane* (Herman) had also directed *Dragonwyck* (Joseph). Part of the problem is the anomalous position of the screenwriter in terms of autonomous creation, a position accurately described for all countries and all times by Alberto Moravia in *Ghost at Noon:*

I want to say a few words about the job of a script-writer, if only to give a better understanding of my feelings at that time. As everyone knows, the script-writer is the one who—generally in collaboration with another script-writer and with the director—writes the script or scenario, that is, the canvas from which the film will later to taken. In this script, and according to the development of the action, the gestures and words of the actors and the various movements of the camera are minutely indicated, one by one. The script is, therefore, drama, mime, cinematographic technique, mise-en-scène, and direction, all at the same time. Now, although the script-writer's part in the film is of the first importance and comes immediately below that of the director, it remains always, for reasons inherent in the fashion in which the art of the cinema has hitherto developed, hopelessly subordinate and obscure. If, in fact, the arts are to be judged from the point of view of direct expression— and one does not really see how else they can be judged—the script-writer is an artist who, although he gives his best to the film, never has the comfort of knowing that he has expressed himself. And so, with all his creative work, he can be nothing more than a provider of suggestions and inventions, of technical, psychological and literary ideas; it is then the director's task to make use of this material according to his own genius and, in fact, to express himself.

The proof that Moravia's maxims still pertain even after Miss Kael has reconsidered the roles of Welles and Mankiewicz lies in the fact that no one has proposed publishing the original first draft of the Kane script. What will appear in print (with "Raising Kane" as an added dividend prologue) is the final shooting script of the film now in the can. The published script of Kane will therefore not be an independent literary entity like a published play, but rather a printed reference to a can of film stored somewhere. If Citizen Kane had appeared as a Mercury Theatre production on stage before reaching the screen, there would be nothing to stop an enterprising producer from redoing it as a play or even making it as a film with, say, Mike Nichols directing Dustin Hoffman as Kane, Jon Voight as Leland, Alan Arkin as Bernstein, Ali MacGraw as the first Mrs. Kane and Barbra Streisand as Susan Alexander. That is why Don Mankiewicz's plaintive letter to the Voice associating his late father with Shakespeare and Orson Welles with Franco Zeffirelli doesn't really apply to the admittedly arbitrary situation of cinema. There is no ontological reason why screenplays cannot enjoy an independent literary existence and be remade at will every season. It is just the way things are that Herman J. Mankiewicz must play second fiddle to Orson Welles all through eternity.

But if Welles has never been singularly generous to Herman J. Mankiewicz, he was always more than generous to Gregg Toland, and I would support the majority view on Kane (against Kael) that the movie looks more extraordinary than it sounds. Indeed, it is bewildering how Miss Kael can evade the responsibility of systematic visual analysis in the case of a cinematographic landmark like Citizen Kane. She refers to Otis Ferguson's critique of Kane as the best review of the film without coming to grips with his denunciation of the film's talky, showy theatricality. She never shows the slightest comprehension of the aesthetic issues raised by the film, issues that are unresolved to this day. Nor does she acknowledge the possibility that critics of good mind and good will may thoroughly dislike Kane. Instead, she employs Kane as a club to batter many of her pet targets all the more vulnerable for being so vague. One would never read Pauline Kael to find out why the camera moves mystically toward and into the mirror after Kane and his myriad reflections have filed past. This would take Miss Kael into those dangerously stylistic speculations that are the great glory of film. But if we are to believe Miss Kael's protestations on the subject, she deplores any trace of mysticism or even mystery in the medium. The lights must be on at all times, and the mind clear, and the intellect engaged.

Still, one must wonder why Miss Kael's commercially successful collections of movie reviews have all exploited a conspicuously carnal relationship with her subject at least in their titles—I Lost It at the Movies, Kiss Kiss Bang Bang, and Going Steady. Methinks the lady doth protest too much. The great appeal of movies is emotional rather than intellectual. To believe otherwise is to lie to yourself and to your readers. Worse still, you spend your whole life scolding your most charming seducers because they do not go out to seek honest work. I think it is a mistake for critics to scold artists, or even to bemoan their bad luck. Whereas Miss Kael tends to be Faustian in these matters, I tend to be Adlerian. It is better to accept and appreciate the supposed "disappointments" of our time—Welles, Mailer, Salinger—for what they have done rather than for what they might

A LESSON PLAN FOR A COURSE IN FILM HISTORY

First my credentials. I have been teaching a variety of film-related courses for close to eight years, and I have been lecturing on film to lonely crowds for close to fifteen. My classes have ranged in size from a seminar six to a semaphore six hundred in such institutions as The School of Visual Arts (1965–1967) New York University (1967–1969), Columbia University (1969–1972), and Yale (1970–1972). I have spoken with films and without them, before films and after them and even during them (the last a practice guaranteed to foster lingering resentments). In the course of my academic career I have received many inquiries from other educators about my method and my message, and I have never known exactly how to respond. I happen to depend too much on improvisation, Socratic stimulation and contemporaneous involvement ever to freeze my curriculum into the mold of preconception. Hence, this brief rumination is not intended so much to supply permanent answers as to define some of the problems that arise in the teaching of film history.

One of the problems that does not concern me is the feeling shared by many non-film academics and many non-academic filmites that film should not be taught at all. Since film courses are here to stay, some one or other will have to teach them. If not I, then thou and who is to say that thou is any more qualified than I, or I that thou? Not I certainly.

Having disposed of the ontological problems of teaching film history, let us now proceed to the pedagogical options available in a relatively uncharted field. Among these options are the purely chronological (Edison, Lumière, Méliès, Porter, Griffith and all that), the technological (Kinetoscope, Panoptikon, Vitascope, Vistavision, Cinématographe, CinemaScope, Cinerama, wide-angle lens, deep focus, jump cut, fade, dissolve, iris, wipe, traveling shot, parallel editing, tilt, pan, zoom and all that), the stylistic (montage versus mise-en-scène, documentary versus fantasy, medium versus art form, movie versus film, objectivity versus subjectivity, realism versus expressionism, analysis versus acceptance and all that), the thematic (capitalism, socialism, anarchism, militarism, pacifism, religiosity, anti-clericalism, puritanism, liberalism, libertarianism, libertinism, etc.), plus all the attendant subdivisions by nations, genres, directors, writers, cinematographers, players, studios, production units et al.

The purely chronological approach is not entirely without merit even though it tends to obscure the density of film history by implying that a mere twenty or thirty films can serve as the expressive emblems of twenty or thirty thousand more. The earliest courses in film history tended to synthesize the chronological with the technological into what I once designated as the pyramid theory with *Potemkin* at its apex. By this theory it was stipulated that film history progressed until *Potemkin*, and then declined precipitously thereafter. It is extraordinarily difficult today to convince students in the Seventies that there was a time in the very late Fifties when most serious-minded film scholars firmly believed that the artistic development of the medium had ended in 1930. The pendulum has now swung so far in the opposite direction that Richard Schickel was forced (in a 1971 article in The New York Sunday *Times Magazine*) to adopt a defensive tone in upholding the artistic worth of the silent screen. Griffith, Murnau, Lang, Pabst, Sternberg, Stroheim, Flaherty, Eisenstein, Pudovkin, Dovjenko, Sjostrom, Stiller, Dreyer? Who are they? For that matter, even Chaplin, Keaton, Lloyd, Laurel and Hardy have to be reintroduced to a skeptical generation weaned on *Mad* magazine, Mick Jagger and Hermann Hesse.

Thus I find myself compelled to bridge the generation gap between my aged self and my students by resurrecting the traditional Anglo-Russian montage-documentary aesthetics against which I have been rebelling for the past fifteen years. I suppose it is like a Trotskyist being forced to explain who Stalin was in order to achieve self-definition. Similarly, I must assign readings in Eisenstein and Pudovkin and Rotha and Griffith and Kracauer and Spottiswoode and Reisz and Lindgren and Balázs and Manvell and Sadoul and Grierson and Bardèche and Brasillach and Wright and Arnheim and many others before I can make my students appreciate the shattering impact on my sensibility of the anti-montage formulations of the late André Bazin. Unfortunately, Bazin has been translated piecemeal into English at least twenty years too late for any polemical confrontation with the Old Guard of Film Scholarship. Neorealism and the New Wave have come and gone, Godard and Antonioni have risen and fallen, and all now seems confusingly eclectic. Even when I screen *Citizen Kane* and *Open City* for my students on successive weeks, it is difficult for them to perceive the aesthetic resemblance Bazin saw between these two meditations on *mise-en-scène*.

Gradually I have given up trying to reconstruct the aesthetic controversies of the past. I have found that the assigned readings are too strung out on the time machine and that only bits and pieces seem relevant at any given moment. Besides, students (and especially film students) don't seem to read nearly as much as they should anymore. There's nothing to be done for it except strip down the readings to the bare essentials—Pudovkin's *Film Technique and Film Acting* (Eisenstein's *Film Form* and *Film Sense* are invaluable to advanced students, but somewhat unwieldy and abstruse for beginners), André Bazin's *What Is Cinema?* woefully incomplete but wondrous withal and *The Cinema as Art* by Ralph Stephenson and J. R. Debrix, a routine though useful work with the advantage of its authors having modified Anglo-Russian orthodoxies with modern French heresies. These three books—the Pudovkin, the Bazin, the Stephenson and Debrix—serve somewhat shakily as thesis, antithesis and synthesis. It remains for the films and the lectures to take up the rest of the slack by making the abstract concrete.

A word then about the choice of films. Each teacher must consider his or her own temperament. When I started teaching I tended to impose a "line" and let the students take it or leave it. I knew they didn't like Griffith, and so I made it a point of honor always to start with a Griffith, preferably and outrageously with *Birth of a Nation*. Lately I have decided that *Birth of a Nation* is too distracting sociologically for any sustained formal analysis. The obvious second choice is *Intolerance*, a movie even Pudovkin and Eisenstein acknowledged as a decisive influence on their careers. Nonetheless, if I had to make a choice between *Birth of a Nation* and *Intolerance*, I would choose *Birth of a Nation*. It is a better movie, less sanctimonious and infinitely more important than its repentant successor. As it happens, however, both *Birth of a Nation* and *Intolerance* are so overbooked at the beginning of each school year that many film instructors may find themselves without either of these official landmarks. I have experimented from time to time with less familiar and less spectacular Griffiths such as the eminently Victorian *Broken Blossoms* (curiously effective with young audiences despite its racism and contorted sentimentality), *True-Heart Susie* (my favorite Griffith despite the corny cruelty of its titles, and certain passages with a cow that make the film seem more bucolic than pastoral), *Way Down East* (except for Lillian Gish's exquisite performance, entertaining but superficial melodrama on the Belasco level) and *Orphans of the Storm* (the Gish sisters both sublime and ridiculous in the context of Griffith's French Revolution).

Is Griffith worth all the trouble he causes with right-on students? I would say he is if only because of the dialectical tension he creates at the outset of the course, a tension without which I cannot span the generation gap. A more cynical rationale would be that after Griffith you can only go up in classroom rapport. No one, but no one, seems as far removed from the present day. Actually, the traditional courses of yesteryear made the appreciation of Griffith easier by preceding him with relative primitives like Lumière, Méliès, Porter and the Brighton School. Griffith thus fitted into the pyramid theory by virtue of his technological advances, but Griffith's personal vision was more or less lost in the shuffle. I choose to put Griffith to a sterner test by presenting him as the first of the great masters rather than as the last and the most advanced of the primitives. What preceded Griffith I'd rather describe in my lectures than book for my screen. Besides, I would argue that Griffith's most important stylistic contribution is not his editing at all but his creation of a subjective sanctuary for his players, a softly focused, closed-in, close-up sanctuary wherein players could express their innermost feelings without disrupting the objective serenity of the external world with diva displays. It is in this balance between the subjective and the objective that Griffith achieved the first authentic movies on this planet. I try to bring Griffith alive as an artist of another age and not merely as a contributor to the accumulated techniques of editing.

For editing we can wait for the Russians to give us the impression it is coming out of their ears. Eisenstein and Pudovkin are mandatory; Dovjenko, though deliriously lyrical, is optional. Curiously, the 1905 films of Eisenstein and Pudovkin—*Potemkin* and *Mother*—are emotionally more effective and technically less ambitious than their 1918 films—*October* and *The End of St. Petersburg*. If I had enough time and money I would show all four films and let the students puzzle out what Moussinac meant when he remarked that Eisenstein was a cry and Pudovkin a song. Lacking time and/or money, I would group the 1905 films together or the 1918 films and not mix the two periods. Dovjenko may be represented by either *Earth* or *Arsenal*, the latter wild, fantastic, ultimately baffling. I have tried for years to get Dovjenko's *Aerograd* and Pudovkin's *The Deserter* and have given up. Pudovkin's *Storm Over Asia* is probably his best but is not as paradigmatic as his more conventional montage classics. For a Women's Lib angle there is Room's extraordinarily sensitive analysis of an un-Russian ménage-à-trois, *Bed and Sofa*, a film that even Jay Leyda in his monumental study of Soviet cinema —*Kino*—has not been able to absorb into his socio-aesthetic. On the whole, the Russians are treated respectfully, even admiringly, in my class, but without the sparkling insights only a genuine enthusiast can provide.

The Germans are something else again: Murnau (*Nosferatu, The Last Laugh, Faust, Sunrise, Tabu*), Lang (*Dr. Mabuse, Die Niebelungen, Metropolis, Spione*), Pabst (*The Joyless Street, The Love of Jeanne Ney, Pandora's Box, The Diary of a Lost Girl*) provide any number of combinations to serve as a contrast to the Russian programs. Murnau stands as the precursor of such later masters of spiritually resonant mise-en-scène as Max Ophuls and Kenji Mizoguchi. I am still experimenting with Murnau since I do not presume to understand him fully, and yet his films never cease to amaze me. Lang and Pabst, however, display contrasting styles especially where they intersect at the genre juncture of Lang's *Spione* and Pabst's *Love of Jeanne Ney*. Whereas Lang moves fluidly from

shot to shot like the graceful storyteller he is, Pabst packs each shot
with enough expressive detail to fill a Freudian catalogue. Whereas
Lang is more romantic, Pabst is more erotic. Whereas Lang is more
fatalistic, Pabst is more clinical. The main thing is that students can
see these distinctions on the screen with directors as vivid as Lang
and Pabst. *The Cabinet of Dr. Caligari?* I really don't respect it
enough to overcome my boredom, and I seldom book it.

After Griffith, the Russians and the Germans (sometimes I book
the Germans ahead of the Russians) the class is ready to climb up
the wall, and so I wind up the term with Chaplin, Keaton, Lloyd,
Laurel and Hardy and, optionally, Langdon (whom I don't enjoy
that much). Here I take what I can get and send my classes out to
Chaplin and Keaton retrospectives around town to fill in the gaps.
One full term is about all I care to devote to the silent cinema. The
second term covers the period from 1930 to 1970, and I usually wing
it, starting with *The Blue Angel* and/or *Morocco* to demonstrate
how Sternberg broke through the sound barrier, and then trotting out
the best films of the best directors I can locate. Renoir and Clair and
Vigo cover the Thirties in France. Hitchcock, Hawks, Lubitsch,
Capra, McCarey, Ford and, of course, Welles represent the American cinema. Rossellini, Bunuel, Dreyer, Mizoguchi, Ophuls, Bresson, Antonioni, Fellini, Bergman, Kurosawa, Visconti, Godard,
Chabrol, Truffaut, Resnais represent the outside world. But there
are never enough slots to fit everyone in. How do I choose? Partly
out of my own ever-altering aesthetic, partly out of my instinct for
what can be made clear and what cannot. Hitchcock, for example, is
more teachable than Ford though I admire both equally. More and
more, however, my choices are determined by my budget and the
availability of films. Hence, I stay loose even to the point of doing
without *Citizen Kane*, the keystone of any course in film history, if
its price should go too high. Not that I worry unduly about the
availability of films for my classroom. Even if the supply of prints
dried up completely, I would simply adjourn my classes and have
them reassemble at movie houses around town. Film history can be
taught from any vantage point, and each year I assemble more memories to communicate to my students. I tell them again and again
that we are all caught in the flux of a continuing film history and
that there are no permanent landmarks to show us the way. Still,

without the anchors cast by Griffith, the Russians, the Germans and the great Hollywood comedians, my course would be floating too freely for comfort. I might add in conclusion that my approach to film aesthetics is descriptive rather than prescriptive, and that is why my lesson plan can never be much more detailed than this. The rest is improvisation and, hopefully, inspiration.

II.

PERSONAL STYLES

THE MAN WHO SHOT LIBERTY VALANCE

The Man Who Shot Liberty Valance is a political western, a psychological murder mystery and John Ford's confrontation
of the past—personal, professional and historical. The title itself
suggests a multiplicity of functions. "The man who" marks the traditional peroration of American nominating conventions and has
been used in the titles of more than fifty American films. In addition
to evoking past time, "shot" may imply a duel, a murder or an assassination. "Liberty Valance" suggests an element of symbolic ambiguity. This is all *a priori*. After the film has unfolded, the title is
reconstituted as bitter irony. The man who apparently shot Liberty
Valance is not the man who really shot Liberty Valance. Appearance
and reality? Legend and fact? There is that and more although it
takes at least two viewings of the film to confirm Ford's intentions
and at least a minimal awareness of a career ranging over 122 films in
nearly half a century to detect the reverberations of his personality.

The opening sequences are edited with the familiar incisiveness of
a director who cuts in the camera and hence in the mind. James
Stewart and Vera Miles descend from a train which has barely
puffed its way into the twentieth century. Their powdered make-up
suggests that all the meaningful action of their lives is past. The town
is too placid, the flow of movement too stately and the sunlight
bleaches the screen with an intimation of impending nostalgia. An
incredibly aged Andy Devine is framed against a slightly tilted building which is too high and too fully constructed to accommodate
the violent expectations of the genre. The remarkable austerity of the
production is immediately evident. The absence of extras and the
lack of a persuasive atmosphere forces the spectator to concentrate
on the archetypes of the characters. Ford is well past the stage of the

reconstructed documentaries (*My Darling Clementine*) and the visually expressive epics (*She Wore a Yellow Ribbon*). His poetry has been stripped of the poetic touches which once fluttered across the meanings and feelings of his art. Discarding all the artifices of surface realism, Ford has attained the abstract purity of a Renoir. James Stewart and Vera Miles are more than a Western Senator and his lady returning to the West. Ford's brush strokes of characterization seem broader than ever. Stewart's garrulous pomposity as the successful politician intensifies his wife's moody silence. She greets Andy Devine with a mournful intensity which introduces the psychological mystery of the film. Devine, Ford's broad-beamed Falstaff, must stand extra guard duty for the late Ward Bond and Victor McLaglen. Ford, the strategist of retreats and last stands, has outlived the regulars of his grand army.

Stewart seizes the opportunity to be interviewed by the local editor and his staff and entrusts his wife to Devine, who takes her in a buckboard to the ruins of a house in the desert. They sit in quiet, mysterious rapport until Devine descends to pick a wild cactus rose. Stewart is concluding his interview in the newspaper office when, through the window, the buckboard enters the frame of the film. We have returned to the the classic economy of Stroheim's silent cinema where the action invaded the rigid frame and detail montage took it from there. However, Ford reverses the lateral direction of the film up to this point to lead his characters into an undertaker's shop, where they are reunited with Woody Strode, also artificially aged.

A man is lying in a coffin. We never see him, but we learn that his boots have been removed, that he is being buried without his gun belt and that, in fact, he has not worn his gun belt in years. Although we never see the corpse, we feel the presence of the man. The mood of irrevocable loss and stilled life becomes so oppressive that the editor (and the audience) demand an explanation. At a nod from his wife, Stewart walks into the next room away from the mourners, away from the present into the past. Just as Vera Miles begins to open her hat box, there is a cut to Stewart introducing the flashback by placing his hand on a historical prop, a dismantled, dustridden stagecoach. From the cut from the hat box to that climactic moment nearly two hours later when we see a cactus rose on the coffin, the cinema of John Ford intersects the cinema of Orson

Welles. As Hitchcock and Hawks are directors of space, Ford and Welles are directors of time, the here and there, as it were, opposed to the then and now.

It is hardly surprising that the plot essence of the flashback is less important than the evocations of its characters. Whatever one thinks of the *auteur* theory, the individual films of John Ford are inextricably linked in an awesome network of meanings and associations. When we realize that the man in the coffin is John Wayne, the John Wayne of *Stagecoach, The Long Voyage Home, They Were Expendable, Fort Apache, She Wore a Yellow Ribbon, Rio Grande, Three Godfathers, The Quiet Man, The Searchers* and *Wings of Eagles,* the one-film-at-a-time reviewer's contention that Wayne is a bit old for an action plot becomes absurdly superficial. *The Man Who Shot Liberty Valance* can never be fully appreciated except as a memory film, the last of its kind, perhaps, from one of the screen's old masters.

The first sequence of the flashback is photographed against a studio-enclosed skyscape far from the scenic temptations of the great outdoors. A stagecoach is held up almost entirely in close-up. Again this is not *a* stagecoach but *the* stagecoach. James Stewart, an idealistic dude lawyer from the East, gallantly defends Anna Lee, a Fordian lady since *How Green Was My Valley,* and is brutally flogged for his trouble by Liberty Valance, a hireling of the cattle interests. Indeed, Lee Marvin and his equally psychotic henchmen convey an image of evil so intense that the unwary spectator may feel that the film is drifting into the Manichean conventions of horse opera. Unlike Welles and Hitchcock, Ford has never exploited Murnau's expressive camera movements which are capable of reversing moral relationships. Liberty Valance will be as much of a mad dog at the end as he is at the beginning. Every entrance he will make will be outrageous, but whip, gun and all, he represents something more than the pure villainy of the whining killers in *Wagonmaster.* As a political instrument of reactionary interests, Liberty Valance represents the intransigent individualism which Stewart is dedicated to destroy. However, Marvin and Wayne are opposite sides of the same coin, and when Wayne kills Marvin to save Stewart for Vera Miles, he destroys himself. Burning down the house in the desert he had built for his bride, he is washed away by the stream of history. Wayne is

seen for the last time walking away from a tumultuous convention
about to nominate Stewart as the man who shot Liberty Valance.

Ford's geography is etched in as abstractly as his politics. We are
told that the cattle interests operate north of the picket line, but we
never see the picket line, and we never have a clear concept of the
points of the compass. We are treated to a territorial convention
without any explicit designation of the territory seeking statehood.
(One may deduce one of the territories in the Southwest, Arizona or
New Mexico, from the sympathetic presence of a Spanish-American
contingent.) The alignment of farmers, merchants and townspeople
against the ranchers is represented by scattered Ford types—Edmond O'Brien with the drunken eloquence of a newspaper editor
sent west by Horace Greeley, John Qualen with the dogged tenacity
of a Swedish immigrant, Ken Murray with the harsh fatalism of a
frontier doctor. Even lower on the credit roster one sees the familiar
Ford gallery of scrambling humanity. There is still the same proportion of low humor, still disconcerting to some, derived from glut-
tony, drunkenness, cowardice and vainglory. Through the entire flashback Andy Devine fulfills his duties as town marshal by cowering
behind doorways to avoid Liberty Valance. Yet, Devine's mere par-
ticipation in the fierce nobility of the past magnifies his character in
retrospect. For Ford, there is some glory in just growing old and
remembering through the thick haze of illusion.

Godard's neo-classical political collage in *Le Petit Soldat* is
matched by Ford in a schoolroom scene where Stewart is framed
against a picture of Washington and Woody Strode against a picture of Lincoln. Ford's obviousness transcends the obvious in the
context of his career. For a director who began his career the year
after Arizona and New Mexico were admitted to the Union, the
parallel ambiguities of personal and social history project meanings
and feelings beyond the immediate association of images. No American director has ranged so far across the landscape of the American
past, the worlds of Lincoln, Lee, Twain, O'Neill, the three great
wars, the western and transatlantic migrations, the horseless Indians
of the Mohawk Valley and the Sioux and Comanche cavalries of
the West, the Irish and Spanish incursions and the delicately balanced politics of polyglot cities and border states.

In accepting the inevitability of the present while mourning the past, Ford is a conservative rather than a reactionary. What he wishes to conserve are the memories of old values even if they have to be magnified into legends. The legends with which Ford is most deeply involved, however, are the legends of honorable failure, of otherwise forgotten men and women who rode away from glory toward self-sacrifice. In what is perhaps the last political assemblage Ford will record, John Carradine, the vintage ham of the Ford gallery, matches his elocutionary talents on behalf of the cattle interests against Edmond O'Brien's more perceptive expression of a new civilization. When Carradine has concluded, a cowboy rides up the aisle and onto the speaker's rostum to lasso the rancher's candidate. This inspired bit of literal horseplay suggests a twinge of regret in the director's last hurrah for a lost cause. Shortly thereafter, Wayne strides out of the film past a forlorn campaign poster opposing statehood.

The shooting of Liberty Valance is shown twice from two different points of view. Even Kurosawa can be superficially clever with this sort of subjective maneuver. Ford's juxtaposition of an action and its consequences from two different points of view is far more profound when the psychological chronology is properly assembled in the spectator's mind. The heroic postures of Wayne, Stewart and Marvin form a triangle in time. The conflicting angles, the contrasting plays of light and shadow, the unified rituals of gestures and movements and, above all, Ford's gift of sustained contemplation produce intellectual repercussions backward and forward in filmic time until, on a second viewing, the entire film, the entire world of John Ford, in fact, is concentrated into the first anguished expression of Vera Miles as she steps off the train at the beginning of the film, and everything that Ford has ever thought or felt is compressed into one shot of a cactus rose on a coffin photographed, needless to say, from the only possible angle.

Although The Man Who Shot Liberty Valance achieves greatness as a unified work of art with the emotional and intellectual resonance of a personal testament, there are enough shoulder-nudging "beauties" in the direction to impress the most fastidious seekers of "mere" technique. There is one sequence, for example, in which Edmond O'Brien addresses his own shadow, repeating Horace Greeley's injunction to go west, which might serve as a model of how the cinema can be imaginatively expressive without lapsing into impersonal expressionism. The vital thrust of Ford's actors within the classic frames of his functional montage suggests that life need not be devoid of form and that form need not be gained at the expense of spontaneity. *The Man Who Shot Liberty Valance* must be ranked along with *Lola Montès* and *Citizen Kane* as one of the enduring masterpieces of that cinema which has chosen to focus on the mystical processes of time.

LOLA MONTÈS

"*Lola Montès* is, in my unhumble opinion, the greatest film of all time, and I am willing to stake my critical reputation, such as it is, on this one proposition above all others."

Thus spake Sarris in the *Village Voice* in 1963, just before the first New York Film Festival, at which the late Max Ophuls' ill-starred masterpiece was seen for the first time in America in more or less its original version. Almost eight years after its disastrous Paris premiere on December 22, 1955, *Lola* was screened at the Museum of Modern Art auditorium on September 19, 1963. The American reaction at that time was mixed, but generally respectful, and I did not press the point further. I waited for the film to secure a distributor and waited and waited and waited.

After fifteen viewings, *Lola* has yielded up to me not only its deepest beauties but also its most distracting faults. I fully understand why most other viewers can never love *Lola* as devotedly as I do. To be moved by *Lola Montès* is to feel the emotion in motion itself as an expression of a director's delirium, and this is not an easy task for the conceptualized vision of the average viewer, conditioned for years to frame-by-frame pictorialism by which every shot is milked for all it's worth. What makes *Lola* even more difficult to appreciate is its refusal to conform to the standard look of what most people tend to demand of a great film. *Lola* sins first and foremost by being photographed in garish color rather than in virtuous black-and-white and across a screen more wide than square. It is romantic rather than realistic, sensuous rather than severe. It glories less in the simplification of its style than in its elaboration as it glides and strides and turns and tracks across a fluid screen in the most dazzling display of baroque camera movement in the history of the cinema.

* * *

But it would be a mistake to assume from surface appearances that the film is all style without substance. Indeed, Lola Montès emerges today as one of the most profoundly personal statements on art and life ever projected on a screen. Back in 1955, however, it suffered the misfortune of opening in Paris under what amounted to false pretenses. Parisians had been conditioned by the advance publicity to anticipate a salacious superspectacle on the "sins" of Lola Montès. Martine Carol in the title role promised new sensations of sensual self-revelation in her established capacity as superstar of the boudoir. (Before Lola, and at a time when nudity was not nearly as commonplace as it is today, Martine Carol's bared bosom in Lucrezia Borgia had raised temperatures even in such relatively uninhibited realms as Sweden and Japan.) Lola had cost close to 700 million old francs (about one and a half million dollars), a figure that made it the most expensive film produced in France up to that time, and in France, as in America, no one ever expects a superproduction to turn out to be art for the ages. Furthermore, the film was based on a novel (La Vie Extraordinaire de Lola Montès) by Cecil St. Laurent, a hack historical novelist noted for the concupiscence of the Caroline Chérie series. It remained only for a fifty-four-year-old "commercial" director named Max Ophuls to confound all and sundry by treating reactionary material with a revolutionary style built around an expressionistic circus from which Lola's past cascaded in all directions in the form of fragmented flashbacks. It was as if an American audience had gone to see Betty Grable in Forever Amber and was treated instead to the Wellesian pyrotechnics of Citizen Kane.

Ophuls himself had never dramatized himself (like Welles, Vigo, Stroheim, Kubrick, et al.) as a daring innovator or avant-garde adventurer. Back in 1935, already in flight from Hitler, he declared in an interview: "I don't pretend to be an avant-garde director. The term horrifies me. It suggests contempt for the mass audience. I only feel that even in a commercial film one should try to do something a little different."

Nonetheless, Lola turned out to be his swan song. After more than a year of wrangling with the film's panicky producers, Ophuls went in 1957 to direct a theatrical production of Beaumarchais' The

Marriage of Figaro in Hamburg. Long afflicted with heart trouble, he died in a Hamburg clinic on March 26, 1957, one month before his fifty-fifth birthday. In death he became one of the most revered culture heroes for a new generation of French directors. Jacques Démy dedicated his first film, called simply Lola (1960), to Ophuls, and that same year François Truffaut wrote in a bit of business (for one of the gangsters in Shoot the Piano Player) involving a music box that plays the Georges Auric melody from Lola Montès.

Even today, however, the inescapable mediocrity of Martine Carol as an actress poses a problem for the average audience. Lacking the hypnotic magnetism of Dietrich's Lola in The Blue Angel, Arletty's Garance in Children of Paradise, Vivien Leigh's Scarlett O'Hara, or even the charisma of Ava Gardner's Barefoot Contessa, Martine Carol's Lola Montès becomes blankly unfocused next to the gleaming romantic sensibilities of Anton Walbrook's King Ludwig of Bavaria, Oskar Werner's idealistic German student, and finally and ultimately Peter Ustinov's ringmaster, who begins by manipulating Lola's legend for the masses and ends by worshiping Lola's presence in his otherwise emotionally empty existence. With the crisp crackle of his whip, Ustinov's ringmaster dominates the arena as if he were a director arriving on the set for the first day's shooting with a preconceived plan. It is his fate to be humbled by his helpless love for Lola as any artist is humbled by his attachment to his creation.

Hence, the emphasis of the film shifts from the object of love (Lola) to the cultural mechanism of love (the Romantic sensibility), and the film thereby succeeds thematically where it fails dramatically. There is no doubt that Ophuls' own feelings about Martine Carol's mediocrity, one of the commercial conditions of his craft, are affectionate rather than contemptuous. By recording with his gravest and most sympathetic style her pathetic straining for a sublimity she only dimly understood, Ophuls suggested that the banality of a life, any life, hers, his, ours, Lola's, could be given meaning and majesty by the beauty of art.

For some of us the name of Max Ophuls will always evoke a vertiginous whirl of elegance and splendor around a world seen and felt in terms of memory and mortality. This is the ultimate meaning of Ophulsian camera movement throughout his career (twenty-one films in twenty-five years of wandering, like Lola, through many countries); time has no stop. Montage tends to suspend time in the limbo of abstract images, but the moving camera records inexorably the passage of time, moment by moment, past the perishable splendor of settings that reflect in their cinematic impermanence all the absurdities of human vanity. It will all end in a New Orleans circus with Lola Montès selling for one dollar her presence to the multitudes, redeeming all men both as a woman and as an artistic reflection of their sensibilities, expressing in one long receding shot the cumulative explosion of the Romantic ego for the past two centuries. Although my reservations about the film's coldness at the core now make me drop it down a notch or two from the very summit of greatness, I suppose I love Lola Montès because it transforms cinematic expression into a religious experience for this age of increasing faithlessness and fragmentation.

AU HASARD BALTHAZAR

"My first impression was a very strong one," the Prince repeated. "On my way from Russia, passing through many German towns, I just looked about me in silence and, I remember, I never asked any questions. That was after a long series of violent and painful attacks of my illness, and I always relapsed into a state of complete stupor when my illness became worse and I had several attacks on the same day. I lost my memory and, though I was fully conscious, the logical sequence of my thoughts seemed to be broken. I could not follow the course of events consecutively for more than two or three days. That's how it seems to me. But when my attacks abated, I became well and strong again just as I am now. I remember I felt terribly sad. I even felt like crying; I was in a state of constant wonder and anxiety. The thing that affected me most was the thought that everything around me was foreign. I realized that. The fact that it was foreign depressed me terribly. I completely recovered from this depression, I remember, one evening at Basel, on reaching Switzerland, and the thing that roused me was the braying of a donkey in the market place. I was quite extraordinarily struck with the donkey, and for some reason very pleased with it, and at once everything in my head seemed to clear up."

"A donkey?" Mrs. Yepanchin observed. "That's strange. Still," she went on, looking angrily at her laughing daughters, "there's nothing strange about it. I shouldn't be surprised if one of us fell in love with a donkey. It happened in mythology. Go on, Prince."

"Ever since I've been awfully fond of donkeys. I feel a sort of affection for them. I began making inquiries about them, for I'd never seen them before, and came almost at once to the conclusion that it was a most useful animal—hardworking, strong, patient, cheap, and long-suffering. And because of that donkey I suddenly acquired a liking for the whole of Switzerland, so that my former feeling of sadness was gone completely. . . ."

—FYODOR DOSTOEVSKI, The Idiot

Robert Bresson's *Au Hasard Balthazar* was inspired at least partly by the donkey anecdote told by Dostoevski's Prince Myshkin. Robert Bresson's Balthazar is a donkey born, like all beings, to suffer and die needlessly and mysteriously. Hence, the Russian roulettish *au hasard* in both the title and the arbitrary fragmentation of the framing. It is not that we see everything from Balthazar's point of view as if from some blessed vision of a doomsday donkey but rather that we see past the meager milestones of Balthazar's existence to the fitful spasms of human vanity and presumption, the pathetic charades of good and evil, choice and necessity, tenderness and cruelty, order and chaos, joy and sorrow. To the spectacle Bresson has built around his beast of burden, Balthazar does not so much bear witness as breathe (and bray) from one dimension of time (the physical) to another (the spiritual). Balthazar is born among children and dies among a flock of sheep, partaking in the beginning of the illusion of innocence and in the end of the symbolism of innocence. And if we weep at the fate of Balthazar, it is not through a misplaced sentimentality for the fate of a creature unmindful of its ultimate destiny but through a displaced response to the heightened awareness Balthazar has inspired in us.

Au Hasard Balthazar is the seventh of nine films Robert Bresson has directed in twenty-seven years of a cultishly maximal and commercially marginal career. In their total context, Bresson's works are obsessively, often oppressively religious and not merely in their subjects, but also in their style, which is another way of saying that Bresson practices what he preaches. The recently concluded Bresson retrospective at the Museum of Modern Art traced the evolution of his style from the dramatic dialectics of Jean Giraudoux (*Angels of Sin*) and Jean Cocteau (*Les Dames du Bois de Boulogne*) into the voluptuous passivity and impassivity of his more controlled works. Indeed, Bresson virtually abandons histrionic expression after his first two films, relying instead on one-shot non-professionals with meaningfully blank faces. But even in *Angels* and *Dames* there are curious intimations of a tension between theatrical gestures and the Bressonian inevitability and implacability that engulf them. Thus, Jany Holt's penitent murderess leaves the young novice (Renée Faure) who has died in the struggle for the murderess' soul. We know long before the camera completes its long tracking movement that the penitent will surrender to the police voluntarily and proudly. Long before I finally saw the movie I had heard about Jany Holt's affirmative fist-clenched extension of her downturned wrists to be manacled. My mind's eye had assumed a baroque treatment of this gesture with the director's virtually thrusting the hands into the camera. Not so. Bresson causes the hands to flow laterally on the screen as the culmination of a reverse tracking shot from right to left, after a long walk from left to right. The effect was more fluid and less abrupt than I had anticipated in advance. At the very outset of his career. Bresson was thereby dedicated to dedramatizing his material for the sake of a spiritual certitude. Similarly, Maria Casares in *Les Dames du Bois de Boulogne* had a line ("*Je me vengerai*") that I had read in an illustrated text long before I heard it on the screen. I imagined all sorts of histrionic readings for that most ultimate of all vows from a woman scorned, but I never imagined that Maria Casares would read the line as quietly as she actually did under Bresson's direction (if not repression).

By the time of *Balthazar*, Bresson has abandoned dramatic spectacles altogether. A passion for precision now so dominates his work that the extraordinary unity of his method and his meaning becomes almost boring. A recurring Bressonian mannerism is the shot of a place held long after the people have departed. The world, Bresson implies, indeed demonstrates, will be here long after we have gone. We must learn to accept the visual depopulation of this world as a token of our own imminent departure. A gang of curiously contemporary hooligans, wholly evil and malicious, spread an oil slick on the road and wait for a car to skid off the embankment. We wait with the mischief-makers, share their boredom and impatience, and then hear the sound of a crash without being visually released by the spectacle of destruction. We remain chained to the agents of evil on their terms, not ours, and Bresson will not deliver us to our own evil fantasies. This then is the key to his austerity, the rationale of his anti-drama. He never bandages a moral wound if he can let it fester instead and if in letting it fester he can cause a spiritual delirium in his characters.

But let us not overlook the fact that *Au Hasard Balthazar* is an extraordinarily sensual film. As a donkey conveyed Mary to her Divine Destiny, so did it also figure in mythology as the symbolic evocation of sensuality. For Bresson it is sufficient for Balthazar to oppose his ancient significations to the cruel modernity of machinery, and thus be tortured with the same vile eroticism employed to seduce his mistress. The carnal humiliation of the character played by Anne Wiazemsky unfolds with the same rhythm of metaphysicial anticlimax characteristic of all the other episodes of the film. It is only Balthazar's sublime self-absorption that can provide any lasting perspective on Bresson's fragmented human dramas.

There is one extraordinary episode in which Balthazar meets the animals of a circus in an eyeball to eyeball confrontation that is as expressive cinematically as it is evocative philosophically. Balthazar even goes through the futile motions of rationality by performing feats of arithmetic with his hoof at the behest of a trainer for an audience yearning to believe, as always, that animals truly have souls. But it is not to be. Balthazar must keep his rendezvous on a hillside with a very private destiny.

Au Hasard Balthazar plucks out the roots of existence and presents us with a very morbidly beautiful flower of cinematic art. Bresson's vision of life and his cinematic style may seem too bleak, too restrictive, too pessimistic for some, perhaps for many. Indeed, I cannot in all candor consider myself the most devoted Bressonian, and I have long ago renounced any ambition to do a definitive analysis of anything to which my entire sensibility does not respond, and there are large gaps in my psyche Bresson leaves untouched. And yet, all in all, no film I have ever seen has come so close to convulsing my entire being as has Au Hasard Balthazar. I'm not sure what kind of movie it is, and indeed it may be more pleasingly vulgar than I suggest, but it stands by itself on one of the loftiest pinnacles of artistically realized emotional experiences.

JAMES STEWART

I have been commissioned to write a piece about James Stewart on the basis of a cryptic remark which appears in a book of mine entitled *The American Cinema:* "The eight films [Anthony] Mann made with James Stewart are especially interesting today for their insights into the uneasy relationships between men and women in a world of violence and action. Stewart, the most complete actor-personality in the American cinema, is particularly gifted in expressing the emotional ambivalence of the action hero."

"The most complete actor-personality in the American cinema"? Now what could I have possibly meant by that? Perhaps simply that Stewart has incarnated and articulated a uniquely American presence on the screen throughout his long career, and a presence moreover that is more complex than it seems at first glance. I would add that Stewart is primarily a screen actor and a Hollywood screen actor at that. His few forays on the stage have not been of such a quality as to challenge the Gielguds, the Oliviers, the Richardsons, the Redgraves and the Scofields. Still, he is their better on the screen where behavioral consistency in a world of objects and vistas is more important than the vocal realization of a character from a printed page. This judgment would probably cause more gnashing of teeth in New York with its long tradition of mindless Anglophilia in the theater than in London with its perverse appreciation of American vitality and physicality.

Indeed, I recently had a quarrel with the British editors of a reference work I was preparing, they arguing that Burt Lancaster and Kirk Douglas were more crucial entries than Laurence Olivier and Ralph Richardson and I arguing the opposite. Actually, my first intimations of Stewart's having been grossly underrated came in Paris in 1961 at screenings of Alfred Hitchcock's *The Man Who Knew Too*

Much and John Ford's *Two Rode Together*. Two sequences stand
out in my mind, and in both there is an unforgettable image of
Stewart's long legs awkwardly stretched out as a metaphorical confirmation of his quizzical countenance. The excessively cerebral
French, of course, know a good physical thing when they see it, and
François Truffaut has acknowledged the influence of the riverbank
sequence in *Two Rode Together* in which Stewart sits and talks
with Richard Widmark on a similar Truffaut sequence in *Jules and
Jim*.

However, Stewart's lanky physicality was not so much a key as a
clue to the deeper meanings of his acting personality. To get to these
deeper meanings requires an examination of the artistic contexts in
which he has functioned most effectively. After all, feelings on the
screen are expressed not so much by actors as *through* them. Hence,
we can't really trace Stewart's contribution without dragging in such
directors as George Stevens (*Vivacious Lady*), Frank Capra (*You
Can't Take It with You, Mr. Smith Goes to Washington* and *It's a
Wonderful Life*), Ernst Lubitsch (*The Shop Around the Corner*),
Frank Borzage (*The Mortal Storm*), George Cukor (*The Philadelphia Story*), Alfred Hitchcock (*Rope, Rear Window, The Man
Who Knew Too Much* and *Vertigo*), Otto Preminger (*Anatomy of
a Murder*), John Ford (*Two Rode Together* and *The Man Who
Shot Liberty Valance*), Robert Aldrich (*Flight of the Phoenix*) and
the aforementioned Anthony Mann. But Stewart has never really let
down even in bad movies, and this unrelenting professionalism and
tenacity are qualities often lacking in even the greatest stage actors
when they venture into the relatively fragmented screen.

All in all, Stewart has appeared in over seventy movies since his
screen debut in 1935 in some forgotten Metro trifle tagged *Murder
Man*. He was twenty-seven then—lean, gangling, idealistic to the
point of being neurotic, thoughtful to the point of being tongue-
tied. The powers-that-be at Metro were slow to recognize his star
potential. Through the 1930s Stewart made his biggest impact on
loan-out to other studios, to Columbia for the Capras with Jean Arthur, to RKO for the Stevens with Ginger Rogers, to United Artists
for *Made for Each Other* with Carole Lombard, to Universal for
Destry Rides Again with Marlene Dietrich.

By the time Metro realized they had a prodigy on their hands,

Stewart was off to the war for five years during World War II, and when he came back he had had enough of Leo the Lion and began free-lancing. He already had an Oscar on his mantelpiece for *The Philadelphia Story* and an award from the New York Film Critics for *Mr. Smith Goes to Washington*. But somehow he never regained his stride with critics and audiences. His extraordinarily emotional performance in *It's a Wonderful Life* was overlooked in a year galvanized by the classical grandeur of Laurence Olivier in *Henry V* and the sociological scope of the wildly overrated *The Best Years of Our Lives*. *Magic Town* was an out-and-out flop, *Call Northside 777* a stolid semi-documentary, *On Our Merry Way* the occasion of a reunion with old buddy Henry Fonda in a John O'Hara sketch. Stewart later played a cameo in clown make-up for Cecil B. De Mille in *The Greatest Show on Earth*, but he was drifting more and more to action pictures and wacky farce comedies. In *Rope*, he was miscast somewhat as an irresponsible intellectual and submerged both by the lurid subject and Hitchcock's single-take technique sans visible cuts.

But in *Rear Window, The Man Who Knew Too Much* and *Vertigo*, Stewart supplied Hitchcock with three of the most morbidly passionate performances in the history of the cinema, and again he was overlooked by critics hypnotized by the dreary Philco Playhouse realism of Paddy Chayefsky's *Marty* and Terence Rattigan's *Separate Tables*. This was an era in which feeble talents like Ernest Borgnine and David Niven were winning Oscars for characterizations that proclaimed their own drabness. Stewart never changed type. As he became older, he tried to look younger. Unfortunately, the best way to win awards in Hollywood is to plaster a young face with old-age make-up. Artificial aging, however grotesque it may seem to the bored camera, is an infallible sign of "character" for those who confuse the art of acting with the art of disguise.

Stewart, alas, was always Stewart, and he gradually slipped out of the cultural mainstream. In his personal life he fell afoul of the redoubtable Margaret Chase Smith when he was mentioned for a general's commission in the Air Force Reserve. In England, actors are knighted for their services. In America, they are suspected of lurid frivolity. *Strategic Air Command* expressed his devotion to the Air Force at a time when hawkdom was beginning to be viewed in many quarters as a potentially dangerous outlet for patriotism. *The FBI Story* was sickeningly reverent toward J. Edgar Hoover, and *The Spirit of St. Louis* somewhat pointlessly proud of Charles Lindbergh. Besides, Stewart was embarrassingly old for a part the unlamented John Kerr had turned down out of political scruples.

Through the 1950s and 1960s, Stewart had his share of clinkers. He was no happier doing the Rex Harrison stage role in *Bell, Book and Candle* than he had been a generation earlier doing the Laurence Olivier role in *No Time for Comedy*. His performance in *Harvey* was less effective than Frank Fay's on the stage, and Fay operated on a fey vaudeville level over which Stewart's screen persona usually towered. But put Stewart in the middle of good English players in *No Highway in the Sky* and *Flight of the Phoenix* and *The Man Who Knew Too Much*, and he dominated the proceedings as only the greatest star personalities were capable of doing. And put him in a western, and he gave it a gritty grandeur worthy of the Waynes and the Fondas and the Scotts and the Coopers.

Indeed, it was when Stewart became too old to be fashionable that he became too good to be appreciated. Suddenly his whole career came into focus as one steady stream of moral anguish. Hitchcock brought out the overt madness in him, the voyeurism (*Rear Window*), the vengefulness (*The Man Who Knew Too Much*), the obsessive romanticism (*Vertigo*). Ford brought out the cynic and opportunist in him. Mann brought out the vulnerable pilgrim in quest of the unknown. Otto Preminger's glazed gaze in *Anatomy of a Murder* reminded us once again of Stewart's dogged tenacity.

That Stewart even had the opportunity to enrich and expand his mythical persona into his sixties and our seventies is a fortunate accident of film history. But enriched and expanded he has become through the steady pull of his personality which has evolved over four decades from American gangly to American Gothic. If we take care of the small matter of preserving his seventy-odd films for posterity, he shall truly belong to the ages, perhaps as a relic of the moral fervor that once shaped even the more intelligent among us. In any event, the cumulative effect of all his performances is to transcend acting with being, the noblest and subtlest form of screen acting.

BUSTER KEATON

Only a day before the Nobel Prize in Literature was awarded to Samuel Beckett, I confided to my class in film history that Buster Keaton's vision of the world was in some ways more profoundly absurdist than Samuel Beckett's. The following week I joked with jovial paranoia about the action of the Nobel Committee as merely the latest proof of a conspiracy of the Literary Establishment against the fledgling scholars of film. I then reaffirmed my cultural heresy and waited for cries of outrage from the linear louts. Unfortunately, there were no challenging ripples of disbelief, no intimations of interdisciplinary impudence. Not only do we live in an age when shock statements are taken as a matter of course; we accept also the most arrant sensationalism as a calculating stratagem: tentative, probing, even psychodramatic.

Perhaps all along I was really addressing all the eminently cinephobic professors from my Columbia College and Graduate English days. Not so much addressing them really as exorcising them, and not even them so much as the smug cinephobia of their cultural environment. Perhaps I have never gotten over the guilt I felt back then when I used to sneak away from classes down to the Nemo (now defunct), the Olympia (now an ethnic house) and the Thalia (still the dumpiest art house in the Western world). Indeed, the shadows of literary snobbery still loom menacingly over all my endeavors to the point where I often feel that I am shamefully subverting my students by showing them movies on class time. Not that I have any hard feelings against the literary world for protecting its cherished privileges. Nor do I wish to convert cinephobes to a medium they profess to despise. All that I ask is that they reserve judgment on films and film-makers (Keaton included) until they have had an opportunity to study said films and film-makers (Keaton in-

cluded) first hand on the screen. To put it more bluntly: I have read
Beckett. Have the cinephobes seen Keaton? Recently? If not, their
film scholarship is sadly deficient and their liberal-arts education
woefully incomplete. That's all. A word to the wordily wise should
be sufficient.

But why compare Keaton to Beckett at all? What has a professional vaudevillian turned filmic acrobat to do with a reclusive writer
cast in the modern mold of chic alienation and despair? Rudi
Blesch, Keaton's biographer, suggests that Keaton anticipated Beckett
in the absurdity of his (Keaton's) vision. It is possible that Beckett's
pessimism may have been influenced by Keaton's pratfalls. Possible
but not especially logical. Although Beckett (1906–   ) was born
only eleven years after Keaton (1895–1966), he might as well have
been born in another century. Beckett was a late starter at least in
the theater. He was in his fifties when *En Attendant Godot* was
produced (in Paris in 1953). But Keaton was a relatively early
starter, appearing in his first two-reelers with Fatty Arbuckle in 1917,
directing his own two-reelers by 1920 and his own feature-length
films by 1923. Granting that film-making at its most individualistic is
a relatively collective form of creation compared to writing, it is safe
to say that Keaton was a more prolific artist than Beckett and that
having started much earlier he burned out much sooner. That Keaton's burning out may have been caused largely by Hollywood's
wasteful industrial processes does not concern us at the moment.
Limiting ourselves to Keaton's most productive years, we find a veri-
table symphony of movements, gestures and imperturbable expressions in perfect harmony with almost every conceivable catastrophe
known to man, machine and nature.

Keaton's relatively brief burst of creativity barely spanned the decade of the Twenties between the first of his nineteen shorts (*The
High Sign*) in 1920 and the last of his dozen silent features (*Spite
Marriage*) in 1929. Until very recently, most of the works from this
period were unavailable to the general public. Even the most avid
American scholar was fortunate if he could get to see more than four
or five of the thirty-one Keaton films. Hence, the late James Agee's
classic essay, "The Golden Age of Comedy," did more for Agee's
reputation as a critic than for Keaton's reputation as a clown. Without the opportunity to check out Keaton's credentials first hand,

most readers of Agee's article tended to subordinate Kea
vague troika of a tradition, with Charles Chaplin and Har(
on either side of a comic noted inordinately for his great st

Now, fortunately, almost all of Keaton's works are available in 16
millimeter, and Raymond Rohauer has been circulating a Keaton
Retrospective. Keaton's lost years have finally been resurrected,
and the results are staggering. On the level of satire, Keaton has
taken on the Mafia (*The High Sign*), do-it-yourself doltishness
(*One Week*), grotesque gallows humor (*Convict 13*), household
ecology (*The Scarecrow*), slum sentimentality (*Neighbors*), an up-
roariously Freudian image of sticky paper currency as the equivalent
of excrement in man's obsessional existence (*The Haunted House*),
the megalomania of show biz (*The Playhouse*), law and disorder
(*Cops, The Goat*), misapplied technology (*The Electric House*),
family feuds (*Our Hospitality*), assembly-line absurdity (*The Navi-
gator*), the American matriarchy (*Seven Chances*) and the ridicu-
lousness of war (*The General*).

It is not, however, as a satirist that Keaton is pre-eminent but
rather as a pessimist in perpetual motion. Keaton's images do not
necessarily have to mean anything. They often exist solely for their
beauty and grace. When Keaton flows into his machinery as if to
provide a demonstration of entropy at work, he is not so much satir-
izing man's relationship with the machine as celebrating it. A
French critic-animator has noted Keaton's similarity as a film-maker
to later animators by virtue of his elaborate solutions to mathemati-
cal and geometrical puzzles on the screen. No other film-maker in
history has concerned himself so conscientiously with plastic potentialities. There is a fantastic sequence in *The Goat* in which Keaton
flees his pursuers by mounting a clay model of an equestrian statue
just before the model is to be unveiled by its sculptor. Chaplin uses a
similar gag in the opening of *City Lights*, but once the satiric potentialities of the shot have been exhausted, Chaplin scampers away
from the statue. By contrast, Keaton remains mounted on the clay
horse until it begins to sag and crumple under his weight, and the
sculptor, a bearded nincompoop in a beret, proceeds to break down
and weep. Keaton's expression here is mercilessly pragmatic. What
good is a clay horse (art?) if you can't mount it to your own advantage. There is ultimately something unabashedly ruthless about Kea-

ton's comedy, which chills his humor. (His recurring "darky" jokes are but one symptom of the most uninhibitedly American film art since D. W. Griffith's.) If anything, Keaton's American unconscious is one of the richest treasure chests of social myth ever extracted from any artist in any medium.

Beckett, after Hitler and Buchenwald, found it philosophically appropriate that the theater be stripped down to its barest essentials and starkest configurations, but Keaton expanded and elaborated his comic spectacles to the point of bursting his stylized genre with an excess of physical and topographical documentation. Still, I cannot help feeling that the melancholy emanating from Keaton's oeuvre, out of an age of official optimism, is artistically more fascinating than the more studied pessimism that pours from Beckett's punctuated pauses and silences. If I prefer Keaton to Beckett, it is because I feel that Keaton was swimming against a current, and Beckett is swimming with it. Actually, it is not so much Keaton versus Beckett as Keaton-film versus Beckett-theater, which brings us imperceptibly and inevitably to the one palpable contact between Beckett and Keaton: The Samuel Beckett *Film* directed by Alan Schneider in 1965, with Buster Keaton.

Schneider's direction of Keaton in *Film* is nothing short of catastrophic, but only if we retain any memory of the classic Keaton. Buster's presence in the film is certainly no more crucial to its conception than the late Bert Lahr's was to the conception of *Waiting for Godot*. But whereas Lahr's casting was an inspiration, Keaton's was an imposition. The fact that the film is silent not only takes away Beckett's greatest strength as an artist—his sublimely succinct dialogue; it adds also to the pretentiousness of the project. Keaton would never have participated in such an overtly symbolic enterprise if he hadn't needed the money. Curiously, certain morbid characteristics of Beckett's personality emerge more clearly in the film precisely because of the lack of morbidity (and mortality) in Keaton's persona. Beckett's paranoia about prying eyes (of dogs, cats, parrots, goldfish and even self-reflecting mirrors) is rendered unconvincingly by Keaton in curiously menacing flourishes with overcoats and other drape-drab garments and fabrics. Keaton's metaphorical eyepatch and fuzzy vision, his ostentatious awkwardness is a travesty of the alertness and agility that characterized Keaton in his mobile period;

ID: 2296000015067

e, even though a
   Overdue charges
aterials and pay

ID:0296002006017
er ; foreword by Rennard

and it is doubtful that the real Keaton would keep feeling his own pulse even if he had lived to be a hundred in the process. Beckett's instinctive addiction to stasis in film as in theater is clearly consistent with his frightful memories of the camps and ovens, but Keaton's life force was motion, and to have denied him this even in his old age was to consign him, albeit unconsciously, to the scrap heap of film history.

Buster Keaton did not therefore belong in Samuel Beckett's film. Rumor has it that Keaton was not even originally the first choice for the role, and so no blame attaches to anyone for the misalliance. But what does that do to the alleged connection between Beckett and Keaton? Not much, really. Yet the comparison is still apt. What Keaton arrived at intuitively out of a combination of a relatively rootless childhood, a fantastic physical adaptability and a suitably uninhibited medium still in the midst of its birth pangs, Beckett formulated intellectually out of his confrontation with the nightmare of modern history. Whereas Keaton's cinema may have once seemed somewhat innocent in its improvisations and feats of derring-do, it now seems extraordinarily prophetic and profound in its mythic configurations of all the catastrophes that have befallen us since 1929. Still, Keaton gives us hope, as Beckett does not, that man somehow possesses the beauty, grace and energy to overcome all obstacles to his continuing survival. And most magically of all, Keaton's films compel us to accept survival even at the risk of sadness. How much more voluptuously self-satisfying is the self-pity we can wallow in while we wait for Godot!

BARBARA LODEN'S *WANDA*

That Barbara Loden, a woman, happens to be the director of *Wanda* invites the contemporary reviewer to all sorts of speculations about a distinctly female point of view on film. The trouble is that there have been relatively few women directors in the history of the medium, and of these even fewer have been more than marginally prominent. Hence, when a Barnard student film society approached me recently with a request for suggestions for a program of woman-directed films, I hemmed and hawed and harumphed. Woman-written films are something else again. Anita Loos alone could keep (and has kept) MOMA hopping for months on end, and Betty Comden, Frances Goodrich, Ruth Gordon, Sonya Levien, Frances Marion, Jane Murfin and Bella Spewack were no slouches either, not to mention Mae West and Ayn (*Love Letters*) Rand.

And these are but the Hollywood contingent. If we add up all the European and American credits, the woman's role in screenwriting is seen to be a massive one. For that matter, *Five Easy Pieces* was written by a woman (Adrien Joyce), and I leave it to the more esoteric experts to determine whether the woman's hand shows up in the characterizations. But women directors are something else again. Lillian Gish stated the Victorian attitude toward the hurly-burly of Hollywood directing after her first and only directorial assignment (*Remodeling Her Husband*—1921) by remarking more in sorrow than in anger that directing was no job for a lady. And so it isn't, but it is becoming increasingly apparent that directing can be a job for a woman.

Up to the present time, however, the most distinguished woman director in film history has been Leni Riefenstahl, and Miss Riefenstahl may present ideological problems to the present leadership of Women's Lib. Alexander Dovjenko's widow was a possible runner-up for the films she completed from her illustrious husband's notes. Dorothy Arzner, Jacqueline Audrey and Ida Lupino were to be credited with some respectable movies, while lost in the mists of history were Mrs. Sidney Drew, Lillian Ducey, Julia Crawford Ivers, Frances Marion, Vera McCord, Frances Nordstrom, Mrs. Wallace Reid, Lois Weber and Margery Wilson. (The unwary researcher is hereby advised that Monta Bell and Marion Gering qualify as certified males.) Very recently, however, the field has widened to include Vera Chytilova, Shirley Clarke, Juleen Compton, Joan Littlewood, Elaine May, Susan Sontag, Nadine Trintignant, Agnes Varda and Mai Zetterling, and this is only in the realm of relatively commercial cinema. The talented Canadian Joyce Weiland leads the contingent of women film-makers in the experimental, abstract, poetic, avant-garde, underground categories.

But what does one say about a woman qua woman director that is not condescendingly sexist? One can take the Jane Austen—Emily Brontë approach and say that whereas Miss Brontë wallowed in her own womanhood, Miss Austen rose above hers and was therefore more universal, which has always struck me as a roundabout way of expressing a straightforward literary preference for Miss Austen over Miss Brontë. I cannot think of any pejoratively "feminine" quality which is not found in a vast number of male artists. Indeed, the fluttery, excessively lyrical, unduly intuitive characteristics which are commonly labeled feminine are often precisely the qualities superior women tend to discard in order to be taken seriously by the male establishment. And it is certainly not in these obvious ways that I take Wanda to be a movie by a woman. Quite the contrary. Barbara Loden comes on stylistically hard rather than soft, analytical rather than rhapsodic, harsh and awkward rather than smooth and graceful. Nonetheless, she gives herself away in a manner that is all the more touching for being so instinctual.

Up to the time bonnie Wanda encounters her unromantically criminal Clyde (Michael Higgins), the film is constructed as a series of alienating friezes of man (and woman) submerged in the mineral kingdom of coal, rock, steel, glass, asphalt. Miss Loden's style alternates between Antonioni on the hillsides (two-dimensional pointillism) and Fellini on the horizon lines (de Chirico in Disneyland). But once Miss Loden stops sketching her environment and begins inhabiting it, her characterization comes to life. The museum shots of the milieu are superseded by intensive cross-cutting between two loners groping for each other across the infinite distances in the front seat of a moving car. None of Godard's lyrical windshield two-shots shot from outside the car alongside Coutard. Barbara Loden is inside the car, body and soul, and she keeps looking at the man to whom she has entrusted her life, and sometimes he is in profile looking ahead at the road and sometimes he is in full shot looking sidewise from the road at her.

And always he is gruff in his groping way. He gives her money to buy a hat so as to discard the haircurlers that make her a caricature of lower-middle-class America. He wants her to have class. He buys her a dress and throws her slacks out on the turnpike. An unconscious touch of American affluence is in that gesture when compared to a similar situation in François Truffaut's The Soft Skin in which Jean Dessailly induces Françoise Dorleac to change from slacks to a dress so that he can look lecherously at her legs while he is driving. But there is no question of throwing away the slacks in the land of De Maupassant. And more important, Truffaut cannot resist showing the audience the lecherous spectacle of Miss Dorleac's legs. Barbara Loden, by contrast, withholds the sensual spectacle of her own legs until they are about to be used and abused by the man in her life. No anticipatory glances at the legs. Only eyeball-to-eyeball confrontations via head shots.

And when her man has been killed, and she allows herself to be picked up by a soldier in a brown uniform and he tries to impose his chromatic bulk over her body on the front seat of his car, she breaks away and runs into the forest and breaks down into tears that inform her tired flesh that she had been emotionally alive for so short a time and we don't really need the spider web to round out the sequence but somehow I didn't mind it and the movie seems at an end but keeps starting up again and again until it is mercifully extinguished in a freeze frame and all in all it is the extraordinary good fortune of Barbara Loden the director to have had Barbara Loden the actress to manipulate with such impulsive immediacy.

III.
GENRES

THE MUSICAL: THE FRED AND GINGER SHOW

A medley of eight Fred Astaire–Ginger Rogers musicals of the 1930s has winged its way into town. The medley consists of *Top Hat, Follow the Fleet, The Gay Divorcee, The Story of Vernon and Irene Castle, Shall We Dance?, A Damsel in Distress, Swing Time* and *Carefree.* Actually, Joan Fontaine pinch-hits for Ginger in *A Damsel in Distress,* and just for the record two missing Astaire–Rogers caprices of that epoch—*Flying Down to Rio* and *Roberta* —are litigiously unavailable. (I must confess that I have always wanted to see *Roberta* not so much for Astaire and Rogers as for Irene Dunne singing "Smoke Gets in Your Eyes.") The movies represented are not all of a piece. Of the ones I have seen—and I have seen all but *A Damsel in Distress*—I much prefer *Swing Time.* Why? Who can say for sure? On stage or screen, the musical is the hardest genre to evaluate sensibly and coherently.

Just so I don't seem to be abandoning the franchise on heavy-think to the belatedly giddy spring sunshine, it might be noted that Fred Astaire often pops up in weighty tomes on film aesthetics for restoring the integrity of the dancer's space after Busby Berkeley's crane shots had reduced choreography to aerial botany. In a sense, Astaire was to Berkeley as Renoir was to Eisenstein. Of course, this analogy is a dreadful oversimplification, but it serves to save space on dead theory for the sake of live observation.

The peculiar charm of the Astaire–Rogers musicals does not derive, in my opinion, from any Bazinian integral-space aesthetic but from the extraordinary alchemy of the musical interludes. Hard-boiled Hollywood producers of the period marveled at the chemistry of the Astaire–Rogers team. Alone, Astaire was a skinny guy with a receding hairline and with about as much sex appeal as Neville

Chamberlain. Miss Rogers was a gum-chewing blonde out of a
chorus line from a hosiery counter and with about as much class as
Stella Dallas.

Yet as soon as these two bickering mediocrities went into their
dance, they were invested with an aura reserved for the screen's gods
and goddesses. Astaire's seductive grace in motion together with Ginger's gracious compliance in response demolished all the Puritanical
defenses of the Production Code. The release was only symbolic, of
course, but it was and is exhilarating just the same. The lilting Lubitsch musical with the Continental charm and rhymed couplets was
going out just as Astaire and Rogers were coming in, but the back-
stage musical, the cross-eyed at the microphone radio spectacle and
the hoop-skirted operetta were still riding high. The stylish economy
of musical expression in the Astaire–Rogers romances remained the
exception that proved the rule. Later in his career Astaire had no
trouble finding better dancers (Cyd Charisse, Vera Ellen, Barrie
Chase, Leslie Caron) better singers (Judy Garland, Nanette Fabray,
Jane Powell) and even better pictures, but he never regained the
solitary pre-eminence he enjoyed in the Thirties. The stylish Metro–
Minnelli–Donen–Kelly–Walters–Sidney musical renaissance of the
Forties and early Fifties exploited Astaire's extraordinary talent, but
this talent seemed only a part of larger conceptions. Ginger Rogers
hit her peak in the forties, shifting from musical blonde to dramatic
brunette.

The frustrating problem with musicals is that talent is more important than genius. Of the many talents that collided so memora-
bly in the Astaire–Rogers cycle, perhaps the most notable are the
corps of composers led by George Gershwin, Jerome Kern, Cole
Porter and Irving Berlin. The stench of satire is so oppressive in our
land that melodious standards like "The Way You Look Tonight"
and "A Foggy Day" may not be adequately appreciated. I don't
know. I may be culturally paranoiac. It seemed to me that Fellini's
use of the Rodgers and Hart "Blue Moon" in 8½ did more for 8½
than for "Blue Moon," but then again that bit of cultural jingoism
might just reflect the prejudice of one who would rather sing an off-
key duet of "Blue Moon" with a lovely girl at three o'clock in the
morning on a Gotham street than ride in triumph through Persepo-
lis.

THE SPECTACULAR: *HAWAII*

Hawaii has to be seen to be disbelieved. Fred Zinnemann was fired from it, and George Roy Hill was nearly fired, and Zinnemann was much the luckier of the two. Nine million people have allegedly perused the 946-page novel by James A. Michener, the successor to Edna Ferber in the big business of best sellers with social significance, historical sweep and domestic decorum. *Hawaii* or *Giant* Texas. Julie Andrews or Elizabeth Taylor. The wife can never desert her husband, be he Max von Sydow or Rock Hudson, bigot or bully. By the same conformist convention, the lover must fade away with ill-grace, be he Richard Harris or James Dean. Actually, the last person liberals want to liberate is the harried housewife and martyred mother. Otherwise, the screenplay by Dalton Trumbo and Daniel Taradash preserves Michener's vulgar virtuousness on Race Prejudice and the despoilment of the Noble Savage. *Hawaii* comes out forthrightly, if a bit belatedly, against the intolerance of Bible-thumping fundamentalism, the acquisitiveness of American capitalism and the Kiplingesque smugness of White Imperialism. Unfortunately, Michener is even weaker than Ferber when it comes to finding dramatic correlatives for his simple-minded sloganeering. The whole movie is less dominated than domineered by the oppressive omnipresence of Max von Sydow's fanatical Abner Hale. An alumnus of the Ingmar Bergman repertory company, von Sydow is one of the most ridiculously arty hoaxes ever perpetrated on Hollywood. A cross between Ray Bolger and Bert Lahr in physique and physiognomy, von Sydow should make an ideal Ichabod Crane before being shipped back to Sweden for less ridiculous roles. Between reciting from fortune cookies in *The Greatest Story Ever Told* and wreaking havoc in *Hawaii*, the sullen Swede has become the most inexplicable punishment inflicted on moviegoers since the late George Arliss. All through *Hawaii* this reviewer kept hoping for Ingmar Bergman's seven seals to rise out of the surf and drag von Sydow across the seas back to Scandinavian soul-searching. Alas, the Hawaiian climate is too warm for seals, and even the sharks seem to disdain von Sydow.

Despite location shooting and a multimillion-dollar budget, *Hawaii* doesn't really look like Hawaii. The whole shebang resembles nothing so much as an old Dorothy Lamour sarong saga of the South Seas. Not a good one like John Ford's *The Hurricane* but a standard one like *Aloma of the South Seas*. There are echoes too of a mid-Fifties Metro monstrosity like *Green Dolphin Street*, notably in the contrived courtships of incompatible characters, not to mention suspenseless shipboard storms. In *Hawaii*, particularly, it seems ridiculous to worry about Max von Sydow and Julie Andrews not reaching Hawaii in a movie called *Hawaii*. Nevertheless, the passage through the Straits of Magellan is so splashy that one wonders idly when movie producers are going to learn that spectacle is not an end in itself.

Curiously, there is not a single shot of surging surf or period surfboarding. Several years ago Julie Newmar confided to Earl Wilson and the readers of the New York *Post* that she wanted to ride a surfboard naked in the film version of *Hawaii*. There is some nakedness in *Hawaii* but strictly of the *National Geographic* dance-you-innocent-pagans-dance variety, and that's pretty old stuff. Robert Flaherty's *Moana* in the Twenties and F. W. Murnau's *Tabu* in the early Thirties didn't even need a revision in the Production Code to bare a few breasts. Now when Julie Andrews takes off all her clothes, then and only then can we reasonably expect the Mongolian hordes to storm the Radio City Music Hall.

The oddest thing is that *Hawaii* has its defenders. There are those who seem to confuse sourness with substance, as if most movies are too sweet and syrupy for the sophisticated palate. Hollywood has certainly favored the happy ending over the years, but that is too much of a 50–50 proposition to justify the charge of sentimentality. Your hero can live or be killed. Your romantic team can come together or separate. In each instance, the negative resolution in and of itself is more sentimental than the positive resolution. Endings are basically conventions derived from an arbitrary tradition. A British New Zealand western called *The Seekers* gained nothing in conviction or verisimilitude by having all its pioneer protagonists slain by the aborigines. This switch ending was more stupefying than refreshing. Similarly, Abner Hale's grotesque dodderings at the end of *Hawaii* are no more profound than similar dodderings in *Goodbye Mr. Chips*. Abner Hale has behaved monstrously and destructively for three hours only to be commended to our mercy and compassion in the last minutes of our ordeal. The only thing Hale has going for him in the script is his longevity and lack of land-greed. He has brought misery to everyone, particularly his frail wife, whom he virtually kills off after making her endure needlessly the most painful agonies of childbirth. He has inflicted God on a sailing schooner by persuading the captain to cast books by Richardson, Smollett and Defoe overboard as a sacrifice to God's alleged seagoing wrath. He has smashed native idols and imposed guilt on the guiltless, unhappiness on the happy and cruelty on the kindly. He even curses a child to gain converts to Christ. Not that Hale's hatefulness matters particularly in a movie in which none of the characters ever comes to life except as a spouter of slogans. In this context, Hale is merely a nauseating nonentity, a minuscule monster stinging his victims with the petty poisons of nasty Puritanism. Once the balance sheet is completed, Abner Hale's aversion to private property makes him as sympathetic as Stalin.

THE THRILLER: *THUNDERBALL*

Thunderball is less interesting as a film than as a phenomenon. Bing, bing, bing, bing, four Bonds in a row, and each one making more money than its predecessor. There has never been anything quite like it in the commercial history of the motion-picture medium. Pictures have made more money than the Bonds but not on such a steady escalator upward. There was *Birth of a Nation*, but that was a momentous social and aesthetic event. There were Chaplin, Pickford, Valentino, *et al.*, but they were individual personalities, and there is nothing to indicate that Sean Connery has made it on his own. *Marnie* and *The Hill* gained some grosses with his name, but not all that much. It is Connery as Bond and Bond as Connery that is the issue here. Nor can we cite Al Jolson picking up box-office steam with *The Singing Fool* after *The Jazz Singer* because the technological revolution of sound was involved there. Nor is it the spy genre. The Bond spoofs and imitations have not done particularly well, and I am willing to bet that *The Spy Who Came in from the Cold* will turn out to be a box-office disappointment. There is something here that goes beyond sociological analysis. The Bond movies are a triumph of merchandising and advertising, and even their aesthetic mediocrity works in their financial favor. If any of the Bonds had been particularly good, the others would stand out for their inferiority. It is better for the series that each sequence is consistently inferior. What I find mystifying is that some of the reviewers managed to like *Thunderball*. Bosley Crowther even put *Thunderball* on his ten-best list. The humor got to him. Sample Bond humor: Bond shoots a harpoon into someone's chest and then remarks: "I think he got the point." And they say *What's New Pussycat?* is sick? Some more Bond lines: depositing a dead girl on a night-club table: "Would you mind if she rests here? She's dead."

Some of the reviewers chortled over the mink mittens Bond used to stroke a girl's back. All in all, I counted about eight laughs in the movie and one burst of applause when Bond told the villainess he had derived no pleasure from their sojourn between the sheets. This in no way seems sufficient entertainment for a two-hour-plus movie. Normally, I would predict that the fifth Bond will slip commercially, but I said that about the fourth, and I have been proved wrong. When and where will it all end? Producers Salt and Broccoli, or whatever their names are, probably figure the Bond craze will go on forever, and maybe they are right.

The pity of it is that *Thunderball* is a disgrace to a genre I happen to love. I recently saw Fritz Lang's *Spies* for the first time and am looking forward to the Modern Museum's reprise of Hitchcock's *Secret Agent* later this month. These are both beautiful, clever, personal works with finesse and feeling, qualities completely lacking in the department-store-dummy world of James Bond. Even the villains have been deteriorating in the series. From Joseph Wiseman in *Dr. No* to Lotte Lenya and Robert Shaw in *From Russia with Love* to Gert Frobe and his caddy in *Goldfinger* we have reached zero in *Thunderball* with a blackmail plot filched from Fu Manchu and a bevy of undistinguished, indistinguishable bikini models who set a new low for the series. On the plus side, *Thunderball* is more vicious than *Goldfinger*, with less of Bond's castration complex hovering in the background, but *Goldfinger* had more of an edge with Honor Blackman and Shirley Eaton.

The strangest thing about *Thunderball* is the inordinate time spent underwater. I haven't seen so much fishy-eyed footage since *World Without Sun*. One or two images of fleets of skindivers in mortal combat is about as much phantasmagoria of the future as I care to enjoy. The rest of the time is concerned with how many different ways a man can be made to drown underwater. On this level of audience appreciation, this reviewer is obliged to confess that he is no skindiving enthusiast, either direct or vicarious.

Does the audience like *Thunderball*? Probably to some extent. After all, even the reviewers like it. I don't like it, and I don't recommend it. Like all the Bonds, it is cluttered up with useless gadgets devised for the clumsy adventures of its hero, and Bond is the clumsiest, stupidest detective in all the annals of crime. Next to Bond,

Fearless Fosdick is a figure of classical grace and Mike Hammer a mental giant. The Bond films telegraph every last turn of the action so that Bond can always be fifteen minutes ahead of the villains.

Still, the Bonds are not the worst bonanzas I can imagine. There is no cant in them and very little solemnity. There are also random moments of beauty in the orgiastic spectacle of violence and death. Bond obviously derives more ecstasy from strangling a man than embracing a woman, and the plot is only a pretext to conceal the fact that Bond limits his inspired improvisation to killing rather than making love. That is because all women are alike in Bond's world, but no two murderous antagonists are the same. Yet Bond is not even a convincing killer, and so the audience is let off the hook. If there is one scene that sums up the Bond ethos it is the one in *Thunderball* where Bond and his girl friend dive deep behind some rocks to make love in full view of the fish. They are out of sight for a moment, and suddenly the water is steaming with air bubbles, and the audience giggles appreciatively at the childishly smutty subterfuge which is both unbelievable and unnecessary besides. It almost makes one miss the hygienic high jinks of Esther Williams.

cock's deliberate downgrading of the distaff members of his cast: Dany Robin's weepy wife, Claude Jade's boringly beaming daughter and Karin Dor's undramatically sensual creature of desire.

But with all its blemishes and drawbacks, Hitchcock's *Topaz* is a haunting experience, both inspired and intelligent, convulsive and controlled, passionate and pessimistic. At its best, *Topaz* undercuts its own premises with unexpected glimpses of the most saving of all human graces: perversity and humor. In an age when love is me chandised like soap, a little cultivated dislike seems refreshingly ci lized.

COMEDY: ROLE PLAYING AND PARADING

Dwight Macdonald and Pauline Kael, dedicated classicists that they are, have devoted recent articles to denunciations of such recent comedies as *Morgan!* and *Georgy Girl*. Mr. Macdonald is more sweeping and scathing than Miss Kael, but their conclusions are strikingly similar. Modern movies, particularly comedies, are singularly disorganized in form, chaotic in content and generally messy. Mr. Macdonald is particularly upset by the disconcerting jumble of comic and serious elements. Miss Kael, ever sensitive to campus currents, finds it ominously significant that *Morgan!* is rapidly approaching the legendary level of the collegiate vogue of *Catcher in the Rye* and *Lord of the Flies*.

There is a lot wrong with *Morgan!* and *Georgy Girl*, but I question the assumption, implicit in the Macdonald–Kael arguments, that a classical comedy tradition ever existed in the cinema. Even the frothiest farces of the late James Agee's Golden Age of Comedy tended toward an uneasy mixture of laughter and sorrow. Aside from Chaplin's controversial slapstick tragedies and the terribly traumatic humiliations of Harold Lloyd on the social ladder, there is now a greater awareness of Buster Keaton's gloomy gravity anticipating Godot and the little matter of the chairs lent by the Marx Brothers to Ionesco.

If *Morgan!* and *Georgy Girl* ultimately fail as works of art, it is through excessive calculation rather than extreme disorganization. Both films congeal their fetching vaudeville turns in conceptions of satirical-sentimental Jell-O. Karel Reisz, erstwhile throw-up-in-the-kitchen-sink realist of *Saturday Night and Sunday Morning*, finds himself floundering in a *nouvelle vogue* fantasy in which King Kong meets Karl Marx. Only David Warner's truthfulness as the frightened Morgan and Vanessa Redgrave's compassion as the wife save the film from a mendacious modishness. Yet the biggest effects are derived from the self-conscious role playing of the principals: Vanessa Redgrave's Jane tentatively tapping her chest in compliance with David Warner's Tarzan who is closer to Jung than the jungle; Warner's eyes gleaming at the flick of a switchblade; Vanessa's stand-up riotousness in a sports car, her pose affecting by its very awkwardness. Where the film goes wrong is in its facile equation of human tenderness and animal spirits. Karel Reisz' academically metaphorical montage tends to detach him from any emotional involvement with his characters whom he exploits more than he expands. Locking Morgan up in the loony bin merely constitutes a clinical cop-out. If Morgan were sane, the world would be mad. By making Morgan mad, Reisz can disengage his direction from any personal commitment to Morgan's anti-social antics. Yet it is when Morgan is most gratuitous and irresponsible that he becomes a culture hero in the Salinger–Golding tradition and not because modern youth is disorganized but because the modern world hardly offers any orderly alternative.

Similarly, *Georgy Girl* is most effective when Lynn Redgrave, Charlotte Rampling and Alan Bates are parading as Ringo Starr never imagined in *A Hard Day's Night*. Bates: "What you got under that robe?" Redgrave: "Cost you threepence." The fast, bold reading of this repartee makes the character superior to the plot. When Redgrave and Rampling stage an impromptu strip-club interview without missing a beat, they establish a rapport that calls for a more charitable managing of the *ménage-à-trois* than the movie will give us. The German Catholics at the Berlin Film Festival roared with laughter at the scene in which Lynn Redgrave wheels a baby carriage away from the sputtering James Mason (sadly wasted in a Wilfred Lawson-type role) with the loudly put-on line: "I told you the pills wouldn't work." The execution of the scene is copied directly from the I-am-a-whore exchange between Julie Christie and Dirk Bogarde in *Darling*, but the conception dates back to the prurient days of Shirley Temple in *Kiss and Tell*. The maternal sentimentality of the film becomes obscene when it persists in making the non-maternal character (Rampling) *persona non grata* simply because she doesn't fit into the film's ugly-duckling fantasy. The ul-

timately naïve nastiness of *Georgy Girl* probably explains its good
notices from normally prud h reviewers.

Thus both *Morgan!* and *Georgy Girl* are merely counterfeits of
contemporary self-consciousness. The fun and games go only skin
deep; the same old drearily conformist formulas lurk beneath the
surface. Life is real and life is earnest, and escapist fantasies are
either insane (*Morgan!*) or immoral (*Georgy Girl*).

By contrast, *What Did You Do in the War, Daddy?* and *Dead
Heat on a Merry-Go-Round* are movies that display the courage of
their lack of convictions. Future historians will note the contemporary vogue for long shaggy-dog titles reflecting much of the perfo-
rated prose of the period. The titles reflect also very coherent visions
of very stylized realities, and both movies display as personal a stamp
as any movie by Godard or Fellini. Contrary to most of the daily
reviewers, I find *Daddy* much more felicitous an achievement than
Dead Heat. *Daddy's* director, Blake Edwards, gets genuine belly
laughs whereas *Dead Heat's*, director, Bernard Girard, is content
with tentative chuckles. Both movies, nevertheless, tend to be
underrated because of their genre disguises—*Daddy* as a military
farce, *Dead Heat* as a big-caper comedy thriller. If Blake Edwards
has gotten the worst of it critically, it is because there are people
who still believe that World War II was no laughing matter. Edwards has been directing movies for about ten years, and this is not
the first time he has been charged with bad taste. From *Breakfast at
Tiffany's* to *The Great Race*, Edwards has shown the ability to stare
at the most outrageous gag with a straight face. Quite often, he takes
old gags beyond the point of no return. When Leo McCarey sent
Cary Grant bursting into Irene Dunne's innocent recital (*The Awful Truth*, 1937), he mercifully cut away from Grant's moment of
maximum humiliation. When Edwards borrowed the gag for *A Shot
in the Dark*, Peter Sellers went careening across the room, out the
window, and splash down into the river. The gag was thus transformed by exaggeration and magnification into a comic-cosmic disaster. In *What Did You Do in the War, Daddy?* Edwards borrows
the old bit about the drunk thinking he is going up the stairs
when he is actually going around the stairs. When Audrey Hepburn
pulled it in William Wyler's *Roman Holiday* (1953), it was charm-

ing. When Dick Shawn pushes it in *Daddy*, it becomes an outrageous exercise in manic determination.

On a certain level, *Daddy* is one of the dirtiest movies ever made. The anal-phallic imagery of tunnels, graves, spears, bayonets, not to mention an infinite variety of digital signals, is so richly integrated into the festive decor that the snout of a tank gun begins to look ominous in a way only King Kong could have fully understood. On another level, Blake Edwards has managed to convey some of the excitement of make-believe-bang-you're-dead movie-making. All war movies are fake in one way or another. *Daddy* is a fake war movie in which fakery is the style of expression. The Americans, the Italians, the Germans play their fantasy roles in a swirling, confetti-strewn carnival of cynicism and opportunism. Even when Dick Shawn becomes Dracula in drag, the boisterousness of the comic style blasts the smut out of the wit. Good taste is usually associated with tact and restraint; Edwards is one of the rare directors who seems to succeed with excess. However, a closer look at his style reveals an ambiguousness toward his subject. However much his military characters wallow in the trough of the absurd, the military virtues of courage, discipline and honor remain intact. Edwards is serious, but never smug, and unlike *Morgan!* and *Georgy Girl*, *Daddy* is never more serious than when all its characters are playing games.

Dead Heat on a Merry-Go-Round goes even further than *Daddy* in fashioning a world in which every character is his own *metteur-en-scène*. Writer-director Bernard Girard makes his debut with *Dead Heat* a disconcerting interlude of irrelevancy. James Coburn, a relatively straight actor in *Daddy*, is the driving force of *Dead Heat*, and a perpetual mystery. He is first encountered in the group psychotherapy ward of a prison that does not look like a prison. He gets his parole by seducing a lady psychiatrist, the first of many conquests en route to a caper. Coburn, an actor so off-beat he makes Lee Marvin sound classically cadenced, spends the whole film doing various imitations, none of which is effective, convincing or even strictly necessary. The only big laugh in the script comes at that point when one of his more elderly female victims reports to the police that her seducer wore a truss. The implications of this "joke" are rather chilling. For no good reason, Coburn played his role of serious-minded

Bircher to the hilt. Why? Simply because the play's the only thing
that counts. Coburn and his curiously dilettantish confederates rob a
bank in an airport on the day the Soviet Premier arrives merely because of the irony implicit in the situation. This is one caper in
which no one bothers to count the loot. It doesn't matter. The wife
Coburn abandons is inheriting seven million dollars, but this would-
be retributive climax doesn't work on the screen. Coburn wouldn't
have passed up his masquerade for seventy million. Economic motivations are no longer of any consequence. Criminality is merely a
pretext for the actors, the characters and the director to present life
as a perpetual parade of pretense.

Girard tends to play it both ways with the humanist critics by
providing some easy satire of State Department protocol in a criminal context. The movie is marred also by curiously intense shots of
anti-Soviet pickets too passionate to fit into the frivolity of the passing parade. These political fanatics seemed to have come from another planet or at least an older tradition. More significantly perhaps
are the death motifs lurking around the edges of Girard's role-
playing fantasy. No one is actually killed in the movie, but one of
Coburn's mock professions involves the transportation of coffined
corpses across the country, another is termite-exterminator (shades
of *Crazy Quilt*), and there are striking, completely unmotivated
shots of a hangman's noose and a lifelike, deathlike mannequin.
Daddy and *Dead Heat*. Hardly the noblest enterprises of our time,
but perhaps more indicative of our giddy hysteria than we care to
admit.

ANIMATION

The critical and commercial success of *Yellow Submarine* in America (after relative indifference in England) has given movie animation a new lease on life. Or at least so it seems to the average viewer unfamiliar with the feverish activity in film graphics since World War II. Of the 125 feature-length cartoons produced around the world since 1917, close to 100 have been produced since 1945, but none, it seems, with the universal mass appeal of Walt Disney's *Snow White and the Seven Dwarfs* (1938), *Dumbo* (1941) and *Bambi* (1942), three of the most frighteningly traumatic film experiences ever inflicted upon helpless children, but popular nevertheless with supposedly protective parents. Disney's anthropomorphic animals and flipped-out parental figures (particularly the Witch that torments Snow White) may never be surpassed in the unconscious projection of basic Freudian imagery. Disney's art, such as it was, was emotionally red hot in relation to its audience. *Yellow Submarine*, by contrast, is cool, collected and eclectic to the extreme—in short, more of a snob film than a sob movie.

"Movie critics have been having a field day," art critic Emily Genauer ruefully remarks, "(but in the field of the visual arts, not the movies) with *Yellow Submarine*. Their reviews of the new Beatles film . . . have been peppered with references to: Arshile Gorky, Andy Warhol, Robert Rauschenberg, Saul Steinberg, Aubrey Beardsley, James Thurber, Dr. Seuss, Kate Greenaway, Walt Disney, art nouveau, psychedelic art, comic strips, and, almost as an afterthought, Heinz Edelmann who is credited in the movie's program with having designed it."

Not to be outdone in art-gallery one-upmanship by rank outsiders, Miss Genauer cites additional influences "even more direct than those cited: Robert Indiana, Bridget Riley, Richard Lindner, Lyonel

Feininger, Rene Magritte, Paul Klee, and Frank Stella."

Previously Renata Adler had hailed Yellow Submarine as "beautiful, soft, and rich, drawing its inspiration from almost every cultural source outside of literature: Art Nouveau, Steinberg, Mandrake; Arshile Gorky, stencils; breakfast cereal boxtops; Warhol and Rauschenberg screens; Christmas wrapping paper; traffic signs; Advent calendars; beach toys; Mad Comics; Big Little Books (where one used to be able, by flipping the corners of the pages, to stage a little movie of one's own); cut-outs; playing cards; Alice; miniature golf courses; medical textbook diagrams; Op polka dots; penny arcades (particularly pinball machines); King Kong; Flash Gordon; Prince Valiant; decal transfers; poster buttons; Pooh; kites; the Little King; the Golden Books; radar screens; Little Orphan Annie; crossword puzzles; alphabet soups; particularly the rebus (the kind of puzzle in which a combination of word, pun, and lettering yields a meaning)."

Such explosions of elucidation aside, Yellow Submarine remains something of a freak phenomenon in our popular culture to the extent that its success is due less to its visual imagery than to the melodious songs and mythic psyches of the Beatles, a quartet of nonconformist folk heroes hitherto rendered more effectively by their rousing record albums and Richard Lester cut-up movies (A Hard Day's Night, 1964; Help! 1965). Actually, the Beatles had very little to do with the conception and creation of Yellow Submarine beyond supplying the appropriate music, lyrics, and copyrights, and making one very brief appearance in the filmed flesh. Even the speaking voices of the Beatle drawings are not those of the Beatles themselves but belong instead to four anonymous Liverpudlians with a talent for sounding like the Beatles. Still, it is difficult to believe that the large audiences patronizing Yellow Submarine represent a commercial resurrection of the animated, frame-by-frame film, financially dormant since the decline of the Disney Empire and the fall of the big studios. Take the Beatles away from Yellow Submarine and all that is left, box-office-wise, is an overpriced hunk of animated cheese. But thanks to these very same Beatles, the creative condition of animated cinema has been suddenly and unexpectedly illuminated.

"The success of Yellow Submarine is the best thing that's hap-

pened in our field," John Hubley insists, "since Mr. Magoo bumped
into Gerald McBoing Boing." Hubley himself, perhaps the most
prestigious name in American animation, represents in his own career the steady drift of movie cartoons from the peanut gallery of
cute animal slapstick to the art gallery of cutting adult satire. Hubley
had already collaborated on the art design of such Disney classics as
Snow White, Pinocchio, Fantasia (Rites of Spring Sequence),
Bambi and Dumbo before serving from 1941 until 1945 with the Air
Force, under whose auspices he turned out several award-winning
training shorts. Then, in 1946, came Brotherhood of Man, a co-
production of UPA (United Productions of America) and the
United Auto Workers Union, a film Hubley describes as "the major
breakthrough from the Disney tradition because these characters
were simpler, more expressive, not so cute."

Hubley subsequently directed for UPA Robin Hoodlum, Rag
Time Bear (the first of the Magoos), Gerald McBoing Boing and
Rooty-Toot-Toot. Since leaving UPA in 1952, Hubley (in collaboration with his wife Faith Hubley) has worked on such relatively individualistic projects as Adventures of an Asterisk, Harlem Wednesday, Tender Game, Moonbird, Children of the Sun, Of Stars and
Men, The Hole, The Hat, The Cruise, Tijuana Brass Double Feature, Urbanissimo, Windy Day and, most recently, Zuckerkandl, a
whimsical yet savage satire on those who preach blissful hedonism
and political disengagement, hardly the kind of material that would
have concerned Mickey Mouse.

Nonetheless the ghost of Walt Disney still haunts even the artiest
animators if only as someone to react against. UPA, for example,
came into being as a result of a strike of animators at the Disney
Studio in 1941. (Disney apparently carried over the laissez faire
economics of Mickey Mouse and Donald Duck into his industrial
relations.) But the studio system that Disney pioneered has per-
sisted even in non-capitalistic countries simply because of the sheer
drudgery involved in making graphics move on the screen. The most
realistic cartoonist of the so-called Disney school may be required to
produce twenty-four different drawings for each second of screen-
time, corresponding to the twenty-four frames per second of the
sound movie camera and projector. A ten-minute cartoon may con-
sume as many as 14,400 different drawings, a ninety-minute feature-

length cartoon more than 125,000 separate illustrations. By contrast, the live-action cinematographer can twiddle his thumbs while the camera records reels and reels of "reality." Indeed, an Andy Warhol can eat his lunch while his tripod-planted camera grinds away at the spectacle. But an output of thousands of drawings necessitates a collective if not assembly-line operation. Over the years Disney had devised such time-saving devices as the division of foreground and background on separate layers of transparent celluloid so that the usually stationary backgrounds can be used again and only the moving parts—lips, fingers, eyes, feet, etc.—need be redrawn; the tilting of drawings to indicate movement without redrawing; and the use of xerography to reduce the purely reproductive demands on draftsmen.

Anti-Disney animators have fostered even greater economies by substituting elliptical stylization for exact realism, thereby getting away with four drawings a second whereas previously twenty-four were necessary. Thus the Disney flow has been replaced by the UPA jerk in the trend away from realistic movement. Also the style has been simplified both in the foreground (less verisimilitude in the figures) and in the background (less color and more line to the decor).

Hubley estimates that in the heyday of UPA, the Magoo and Mc-Boing Boing cartoons could be turned out for about $25,000 apiece in contrast to the $35,000 for the Metro ("Tom and Jerry") and the Warners ("Bugs Bunny") equivalents. Unfortunately, the UPA economies were not sufficient protection against a shrinking theatrical market, and the collective entity that was once UPA is now no more though its influence on animation was incontestable. Animation, like cinematography generally, is too expensive an art form to support its more individualistic expressions with any degree of consistency.

One of the problems peculiar to the film animator is the subordinate role imposed upon him almost since the beginning of cinematography. Whereas the painter still lords it over the photographer in the still realms of art, animated cartoons have generally been marketed merely as chasers for live-action feature films. "When the cinema was being invented," Ralph Stephenson observes in his book

Animation in the Cinema, "it was the graphic artist's work which first came alive. Almost the first movements on a screen were those of the silhouette puppets of China, Java, and Turkey, imported to Europe as *ombres chinoises,* and, superficially, their black and white shapes resemble and might seem closely related to the chiaroscuro of the photograph. Nevertheless there is a fundamental difference between the two images, the one is a hand-made picture, the other, although subject to artistic control, a chemical reproduction."

Stephenson goes on to trace the evolution of *ombres chinoises* into "Lotte Reiniger's charming silhouette films created by scissors, black paper, and frame-by-frame filming." Even before the invention of cinematography, there were attempts at animation through such devices as the zoetrope ("life-wheel"), the phenakistope ("deceit-look"), and praxinoscope ("action-look"), all nineteenth century gadgets that simulated motion through revolving and reflecting colored strip cartoons.

The most important of the early animators was Emile Reynaud, who combined the principle of praxinoscope with a projector in 1882, and by 1892 was presenting public performances of pictures painted on strips of celluloid at his Théâtre Optique in Paris, and all this more than fifteen years before Winsor McCay's *Gertie the Dinosaur* made its American appearance. Reynaud's ambitious animation was soon engulfed by the greater facility and verisimilitude of the live-action cinematography turned out by Lumière, Méliès and their American, British and French competitors. Reynaud's particular movie martyrdom took the form of his dumping his equipment into the Seine in 1910 and dying in a sanitarium in 1918.

If Reynaud had survived commercially, it is conceivable that animation might have developed independently of cinema proper and might thus have achieved its art-gallery gloss much sooner. Instead, animated cartoons drew most of their early inspiration from newspaper and magazine cartoons and comic strips while Picasso and Matisse were moving into new areas of abstraction. Thus we see the very individual French cartoonist Emile Cohl pooling his talents with the American comic-strip illustrator George McManus (*Bringing Up Father*) to produce a screen character called "Baby Snookums" (1912–1914). Other cartoons in the silent era were *Mutt and Jeff, The Katzenjammer Kids, Krazy Kat, Popeye, Barney Google,*

Casper the Friendly Ghost, Koko the Clown, Bubbles and that Mae
West of cartoon creations, Max Fleischer's Betty Boop, the first and
last cartoon character to suffer the censor's shears—that is until
Muriel, the wrapper-dropping sultry cigar, raised ad-agency temperatures along television row in the Fifties.

As a result of severing its ties with its graphic roots, movie animation was literally colorless in the Twenties. But there were compen-
sations in the visual inventiveness of that era's prankish pen-and-ink
men, so many sorcerer's apprentices who were not above dumping
their creations back into the inkwell (on screen) to show who was
boss of the creative process. Since animation was merely the caboose
on the express train of film history, animators had to wait for the
rest of the film industry to rediscover sound and color. Ultimately, it
was Walt Disney who guided animation past the sound barrier in
1929 with The Skeleton Dance.

Meanwhile, an avant-garde tradition of sorts has evolved out of
the varied forms of non-realistic cinematography—puppetry (Jiri
Trnka), pinboards (Alexandre Alexeiff), semi-abstract lines (Robert
Breer), collages (Stan Vanderbeek) and just about everything from
stop-action live photography to celluloid-scraping (Len Lye, Norman McLaren). If animation is taken to be everything in cinema
except live-action photography, it is more pervasive than most
people realize. King Kong, for example, succeeds mainly on the level
of the foot-high miniature of the monster being animated to mythic
proportions, a form of puppetry actually pretending to real-life realism. Even Max Steiner's moving background music for Kong has
been defined by Oscar Levant as "Mickey-Mousing," a Hollywood
term for especially close synchronization of music and image. Most
film credits at the beginning of feature films qualify as animation,
Saul Bass being one of the most conspicuous artists in this form. Indeed, a French critic devoted almost his entire review to Bass's end
credits for Around the World in 80 Days in terms of their appropri-
ateness to Jules Verne, and then dismissed the film itself in one sentence as a "tedious prologue." It can be argued also that the opening
credits of the Hubleys for Up Tight surpass in graphic expressiveness
all that follows and that the cartoon sequences in The Charge of the
Light Brigade evoke the Victorian era more effectively than do the
live sequences. From a certain viewpoint, 2001: A Space Odyssey is as

much a concept of animation as is *Yellow Submarine*. Even certain forms of live-action cinematography intersect animation either through trick editing (the Sennett Chase) or trick frame-by-frame posing (Norman McLaren's *Neighbors*). Hence, movie animation is a much larger subject than its commercial prominence would indicate, and subject to a confusing proliferation of categories. The fact remains that animation, despite all its guises, changes and challenges, is unlikely ever to supersede the live-action feature film in the public's esteem. Indeed, the more "artistic" animation becomes, the less it seems to satisfy the deep urge for myth in the audience.

A case in point was a 1968 cartoon carnival billed as "New York's First International Festival of Animated Film," at City Center from November 26 to 30. There were works from Canada (2), Poland (3), Finland, Great Britain (3), Portugal, Germany, Czechoslovakia, Italy, Yugoslavia (2), USA (3), Holland and Japan, indicating the international range of animation activity, much of it state-supported. Three of the entries were out-and-out television commercials in which form presumably transcended content, the rest a mixture of abstraction (Rene Jodoin's *Notes on a Triangle*, Stefan Schabenbeck's *Reign of Numbers*), political allegory (John Halas's *The Question*, Miroslaw Kijowiev's *Cages*), art satire (Jiri Brdecka's *Why Do You Smile, Mona Lisa*, Herbert Kosower's *Faces*), and gloomy fantasy (Zofia Oraacewska's *The Thirteenth Lamb*, Franz and Ursula Winzensten's *Dust*). Viewed as a whole, the program was somewhat depressing to watch and almost impossible to recall in retrospect. Also so terribly genteel, cerebral and well intentioned that this viewer felt an overwhelming desire for a "Tom and Jerry" —any "Tom and Jerry." Sado-masochist the "Tom and Jerry" cartoons may be, but they do manage to keep you awake.

Ralph Stephenson tells the story (in *Animation in the Cinema*) of Frank Lloyd Wright's visiting the Disney studio, noting the rough sketches of the final polished cartoon drawings, and observing (to an unappreciative Disney) that the rough sketches would look more interesting on the screen than the polished drawings. It is clear from Stephenson's point of view that Frank Lloyd Wright has all the best of this anecdote, and indeed John Hubley's *Moonbird* is all rough sketches on the screen, hence more modern in showing the creator's hand rather than the creature's reality. Still, there are other ways of looking at the situation beyond the eternal self-congratulation of modern animators.

Ernest Pintoff, one of the leading luminaries of UPA, has moved into live-action cinematography without a qualm. "Graphics simply do not reach as many people as drama does." That much is obvious even to observers without Pintoff's options, but why? Here, I think, Ralph Stephenson and other apologists for animation begin from a false premise in tracing their "art" all the way back to the caves in Altamira where man first attempted to depict life and motion in graphic forms. True, this Altamiran thousands of years ago may have been the first animator, but his relation to reality was direct rather than oblique, representational rather than abstract, sacramental rather than satiric. If he had found a camera in the cave, he would probably have abandoned his strenuous murals on the spot. As the late André Bazin observed, the fundamental impulse of the earliest graphic art is to immortalize the mortal and eternalize the temporal, to stop the flow of life into death, to honor the surface as well as the soul of reality.

Consequently, live-action cinematography retains the most essential social motivations of art with such facility that the art of the animator will always seem to enclose reality in whimsical quotes. This is not to say that animation lacks widespread respect for its technical achievements, but rather that animated films will never be worshipped for illuminating the sacred mysteries of the human condition. Animation requires an extra layer of sophistication in the audience, and this extra layer makes the audience response more cerebral than visceral.

The tendency nowadays in animation circles is to downgrade genre cartoonists like Tex Avery and Chuck Jones in favor of the satiric cartoonists now flourishing on both sides of the Iron Curtain. Indeed, the Hubleys boast that their cartoons are free of violence, at least of the physical variety. The tone of moral superiority implied in this boast can become very wearing when repeated in hundreds of supposedly non-conformist cartoons from Zagreb to Tokyo. The mistake animators make is the same mistake so-called experimental movie-makers make—that is, each artist assumes that he is making the only statement against the grain when, in actuality, thousands of colleagues are working in the identical direction to make up the new conformity.

It might be argued that the traditional cartoons' chase-and-bang formats delve more deeply into the audience's mythic unconscious than do liberal, humane, smugly overcivilized cartoons. Who can say that children might not be better served by animated representations of life as a violent struggle than by intimations of life as a liberal parable? The truth, of course, lies somewhere in between. As there have been brilliant cartoons in the modern mold, so have there been brilliant cartoons in the traditional mold. It might be noted that Disney's Goofy sports series in the Forties was probably a high-water mark of athletic satire in any medium. Also, Max Fleischer's feature-length *Gulliver's Travels*, though vulgarizing the Swiftian original, was nonetheless a sincere preachment against war.

It might be noted in conclusion that the animated cartoon is invading the art gallery at a time when the art gallery is rediscovering (via Rauschenberg and Warhol) the mythic potential of comic strips and other popular graphics. Modern animation has as its major social task the recapturing of the mass audience lost since the collapse of the big studios. It might be desirable for some form of direct intervention to take place (as it has in France) whereby theaters are either encouraged or required to show animated films and other short subjects as part of their regular program. There is no easy solution, however, to the eternal conflict between mass taste and coterie art. That animation has survived at all, in view of its enormous economic problems, augurs well for its future prospects.

SCIENCE FICTION: *THE FORBIN PROJECT*

The Forbin Project represents the most up-to-date variation of the old monster movies, particularly *Frankenstein* (actually mentioned in the script as the key to the spiritually presumptuous scientist-protagonist Forbin), *King Kong* (in which sympathy is sentimentally transferred from man and his infernal machines to a beast innocently enraptured by beauty) and *The Golem* (an unearthly creature that served as the avenging conscience and creation of the Jewish ghetto). Other aspects of *The Forbin Project* may remind you of *The Sorcerer's Apprentice* from *Fantasia*, the Doomsday Machine from *Dr. Strangelove*, the computerized voice from *Alphaville* and, most strikingly of all, the harried HAL from *2001: A Space Odyssey*.

Nonetheless, the screenplay by James Bridges from the novel *Colossus* by D. F. Jones comes up with some wrinkles of its own as it postulates a world suddenly dominated by two autonomous computers, one American (Colossus) and one Russian (Guardian). For a time Forbin (Eric Braeden) and his Russian counterpart Kuprin (Alex Rodine) attempt to control the computers they have created, but no human being is a match for the monsters in tandem, and mere people are reduced to being victims or slaves of a superior though inhuman intelligence. Joseph Sargent directs all the actors in that dull, deadpan, repressed, ho-hum Houston style that Stanley Kubrick brilliantly anticipated in *2001*. Gordon Pinsent's President of the U.S.A. and Leonid Rostoff's First Chairman of the U.S.S.R. are so colorlessly cool on the hot line that they make the computers seem bubbly by comparison.

The horrible thing about *The Forbin Project* is how casually inevitable it all seems. Why *not* turn the world over to the computers?

I'd much rather listen to Colossus croaking out its instructions than have to listen to Nixon and Agnew explaining the subtler points of the Cambodian campaign. We have now entered a new era not only in our politics but also in the context of our political satire. Through the Kennedy–Johnson years there was a kind of simplistic intolerance of the gap between what politicians practiced and what they preached, even between what they practiced and what they really felt. Hence, Lenny Bruce built a popular comedy routine around Lyndon Johnson's laborious effort to learn to say "nigra" instead of "nigger," as if Johnson's regional heritage were more important than his political actions. As it happened, Johnson put through more civil-rights legislation than the more charismatic FDR and JFK put together. But that didn't really matter. Now we have a President who has probably never said "nigger" in his life but who enjoys listening to "Welfare Cadillac" and calls college protesters "bums." And perhaps Spiro Agnew is funny, but it is beginning to hurt too much to laugh. It was much better in the old days when the liberals in power were too insecure in their position to strike back at the professional purists and innocents of the Left. Even now in this hour of dire Constitutional peril, Jerry Rubin links arms with Spiro Agnew to denounce Kingman Brewster, and it isn't really funny or even deliciously ironic anymore but just plain desperate. The world as we know it may be dying before our eyes, and we seem completely helpless. It's not just one particular system that is collapsing but every social contract man has ever conceived. No version of Marxism or anarchism can halt the deterioration of our environment and the brutalization of our culture by the sheer mass of mankind. And it doesn't seem to matter who pretends to be President—Nixon, Johnson or Liberace. Events cast a larger shadow than can be attributed to the follies of those in high places, and politics has become as much a decadently bourgeois luxury as aesthetics.

Consequently, my traditionally humanistic arguments against *The Forbin Project* (and Kubrick's 2001) now seem increasingly irrelevant. I have always tended to sniff suspiciously at the sentimentalization of brutish innocence at the expense of human irascibility. I have always been turned off by so-called "humane" types who actually prefer dogs to other human beings. Indeed, a recent poll of humane-society members in England showed that the great majority favored the retention of the death penalty for human beings.

But now alienation and anomie are taking such a psychic toll of our social instincts that we may indeed become indistinguishable from the mechanisms we monitor. This seems to be one of the subsidiary points of *The Forbin Project*, especially when Forbin and his comely assistant Cleo (Susan Clark) try to fool Colossus by pretending to be lovers, and then actually become lovers in very stiffly performed scenes that resemble nothing so much as the shy, excessively self-aware exhibitionism of computer dating. But when Colossus "tells" Forbin that he has poured too much vermouth into a martini, the audience is conditioned (in the most charming way imaginable) to surrender to a mechanistic world of pure reason on the screen if only as a respite from the increasingly mindless chaos everywhere else. Moviegoers of the world, surrender yourself to *The Forbin Project!* You have nothing to lose but your *Angst!* Forget Cambodia, and leave the driving to Colossus!

And while we remain in this mood of apocalyptic anguish, I must report that I recently paid another visit to Stanley Kubrick's *2001* while under the influence of a smoked substance that I was assured by my contact was somewhat stronger and more authentic than oregano on a King Sano base. (For myself, I must confess that I soar infinitely higher on vermouth cassis, but enough of this generation rap.) Anyway, I prepared to watch *2001* under what I have always been assured were optimum conditions, and surprisingly (for me) I find myself reversing my original opinion. *2001* is indeed a major work by a major artist. For what it is, and I am still not exactly enchanted by what it is, *2001* is beautifully modulated and controlled to express its director's vision of a world to come seen through the sensibility of a world past. Even the dull, expressionless acting seems perfectly attuned to settings in which human feelings are diffused by inhuman distances.

However, I don't think that *2001* is exclusively or even especially a head movie (and I now speak with the halting voice of authority). For once, the cuts in the movie helped it by making it seem less perversely boring for its own sake. The cuts also emphasized that the greatness of the movie is not in its joints and connections (the literary factor) but in the expressive slowness of its camera movements (the plastic factor) and the distended expansiveness of its environment (the visual factor). I am still dissatisfied by the open-ended abstractness of the allegory, not to mention the relatively conventional sojourn in psychedelia. Nonetheless, 2001 now works for me as Kubrick's parable of a future toward which metaphysical dread and mordant amusement tiptoe side by side. Even on first viewing, I admired all the stuff about HAL literally losing his mind. On second viewing, I was deeply moved by HAL as a metaphor of reason afflicted by the assaults of neurotic doubt. And when his rectangular brain cells were being pulled out one by one, I could almost feel the buzzing in my own brain cells as they clung ever more precariously to that psychic cluster I call (quite automatically) ME. I have never seen the death of the mind rendered more profoundly or more poetically than it is rendered by Kubrick in 2001.

I believe also that 2001 gains immeasurably by being projected on a flat wide screen rather than on the distorted curve of Cinerama. On a flat screen, 2001 is seen more clearly as Kubrick's personally designed tableau. On a curved screen, the miniatures and the simulations seem more trivially illusionist and cartoonish. 2001 is concerned ultimately not so much with the outer experiences of space as with the inner fears of Kubrick's mind as it contemplates infinity and eternity. As the moon shots should have demonstrated by now, there is absolutely nowhere we can go to escape our selves.

THE WESTERN: *ONCE UPON A TIME IN THE WEST*

Once Upon a Time in the West opened originally in 1969 in a two-hour-and-forty-five-minute version, out of which Paramount gouged about half an hour after a few first-run engagements. Especially grievous are the cuts of the first confrontation between the man with the harmonica (Charles Bronson) and "Cheyenne" (Jason Robards) and of the death scene these two men share when all the accounts have been squared. And now the problem of print restoration for the purists seems as insurmountable as it has been these past fifteen years for George Cukor's *A Star Is Born*, the best parts of which were snipped out in the early days of *its* run. One would think that the wealthy Judy Garland enthusiast who paid a small fortune for the shoes Judy wore in *The Wizard of Oz* might better expend his money and energy on restoring the small bits of humor and pathos in her best screen performance.

Fortunately (for my viewing purposes), the complete print of *Once Upon a Time in the West* is still circulating in Europe though dubbed into French, Italian and who knows what else, the catch being that *Once Upon a Time in the West* is basically an English-language production, perhaps too basically English and not as nuanced and idiosyncratic in its dialogue as it might be, but I don't think even a Buck Henry–Terry Southern script would make Sergio Leone's westerns fashionable in New York, a city so feminized in its tastes that the only cowboys that make money are those who ride at midnight far from the lone prairie. However, I myself cannot claim to have been among Sergio Leone's earliest admirers. I didn't like his first Clint Eastwood movie at all, and I never even reviewed his next two although I liked them much better. My only excuse is that he seems to have improved as he has gone along, and *Once Upon a*

Time in the West I consider his masterpiece even more than *The Good, the Bad, and the Ugly*, which is actually more efficient if less ambitious. Indeed, after seeing *Once Upon a Time in the West* once more, I am convinced that Sergio Leone is the only living director who can do justice to the baroque elaboration of revenge and violence in *The Godfather*.

Once Upon a Time in the West begins with a gunfight at a train station shot as a low-angle panorama of western wasteland psychology and ends after another shoot-out near a railroad in construction with a last shot of a high-angle panorama of western expansionist history. With authenticated American actors like Henry Fonda, Jason Robards, Charles Bronson, Jack Elam and Woody Strode, *Once Upon a Time in the West* is Leone's most American western, but it is still dominantly and paradoxically European in spirit, at one and the same time Christian and Marxist, despairing and exultant, nihilistic and regenerative. In the very beginning, Strode, shortly before he is to be gunned down, feels some drops of water falling on his forehead as he is framed in close-up on the frescolike wide screen. He places his Stetson on his head so that it will receive the water between its camel-like humps, and then shortly thereafter drinks the water from the Stetson in a gesture so ceremonial as to make the hat seem like a holy chalice. After this portentous, implacable technique, Leone leaves no way out for his characters. It is kill or be killed, and so it is with close to thirty identifiable victims, including all the male leads except Bronson. Nonetheless *Once Upon a Time in the West* unfolds across the screen in time and in space with all the mellowness and majesty of such great westerns as *The Searchers*, *Rio Bravo* and *Seven Men from Now*. Especially enjoyable is Ennio Morricone's extraordinarily melodious score, but at its most melodious it never extends beyond the emotional range of Leone's editing of eagle-eyed expressions interspersed with a circular orchestration of screen space.

Why then has *Once Upon a Time in the West* not been more joyously received in America even by aficionados of the genre? For one thing, its plot is oddly obscure even in the original long version. The elaborate double-crosses that mark the relationship of the ruthless railroad tycoon (Gabriele Ferzetti) and his hired gunslinger (Henry Fonda) are never adequately described or explained. Jason

Robards' "Cheyenne" character functions much of the time as a
fateful herald for the final confrontation between Bronson and
Fonda, but, curiously, "Cheyenne" is the only character in the
movie with biographical and psychological self-awareness in those
moments when guns are not blazing. He is the only character in the
movie to be seen in the behaviorally realistic processes of eating and
shaving, but ultimately he seems to have lived with mysterious des-
peration only to die in a grotesque accident, but he dies with the
heroic dignity of undignified self-awareness, and it all seems right
somehow as if the fusion of Leone's forms and feelings had overcome the improbabilities of what in other hands would have been a
turgid narrative.

There are a great many reasons why *Once Upon a Time in the
West* should not be a good movie. We have been told that Italians
and other furriners should not meddle in a distinctively American
art form. But actually Leone is no farther away from the legends of
the American West than the Florentine Renaissance painters were
from the Crucifixion, and if film is even partly a visual medium,
Leone's vision is as valid as anyone else's. Indeed, Leone has succeeded in making what is essentially a silent movie with aphoristic
titles for dialogue. All the dialogue could be eliminated from the
movie, and we would still have been shown all that it is essential to
know about the obsessive concerns of the characters. We would
come to understand Claudia Cardinale's role as the bearer of water,
life and continuity to the civilization of the New West. We would
see that around the edges of the Bronson–Fonda confrontation is
the fashionable leftist flourish of the Latino revenging himself on
the Anglo, but only around the edges. At the core of the confrontation is not the politics of a revisionist genre but the mythology of a
poetic parable, and how fitting it is that the aging prairie liberalism
of Fonda's features should be foredoomed by a revenge plot of awe-
somely fraternal dimensions. Even so, Leone takes no chances with
his archetypes. Fonda's *hubris* cannot be curbed merely for past ex-
cesses. In the course of the movie itself, he and his long-coated
henchmen must be shown exterminating an entire family down to a
small child as an expression of big business at work overcoming obstacles at whatever cost to moral values. And we must see again and
again (without any dialogue) the dreamlike re-enactment of the

traumatic experience of Charles Bronson's revenge-seeker with the harmonica so that all the violence and all the close-ups may finally fit into a harmonic pattern of the feelings of loss we can never forget or even endure until we have transformed them into the poetry of fables and fantasies. And the western is above all fable and fantasy, as the desire for revenge is childish and fruitless. And Leone has understood fully that in setting out with his hero to learn to kill, he has learned instead that he has come this way only to learn how to die.

The gunfights themselves partake of Leone's penchant for the circular staging of the corrida. At one point Bronson actually extends one foot forward as if to execute an intricate maneuver with a cape, but this is the West, and history comes out of the barrel of a gun, a dynamic truth Leone emphasizes with his intercutting of locomotives thrusting out of cavernous gun barrels. *Once Upon a Time in the West* is perhaps the exception to the rule that the best films come out of nationally nuanced cinemas without cross-dubbing and international financing. But it is so glorious an exception that the rule can never seem quite so rigid again.

THE DECLINING WEST

The western film has counted among its admirers such diverse personalities as Jean Cocteau and former President Dwight D. Eisenhower. In the latter instance, many political analysts correlated the self-righteous posture of American foreign policy during the Eisenhower years with the Manichean conventions of the western genre. Since we were the good guys and the Russians were the bad guys, the moral purity of our actions could never be questioned even when our beloved sheriff was caught snooping at the villain's hideout, and, to the consternation of many, was not devious enough to disclaim responsibility. The world, we were told after the U-2 fiasco, had become too sophisticated, too treacherously ambiguous and relativistic for the simple faith of a man from Abilene, itself a focal point of frontier legends. The fact that everything came out right in westerns did not imply that everything would come out right for the West. When cartoonists reduced Tolstoy's swirling historical forces to *High Noon* confrontations between an American lawman and a Soviet badman, analogy of six-shooters and H-bombs became ominously prophetic in the violent context of the western. Yet, somewhere in our collective unconscious, in the history of our race, we felt the stirrings of heroic fantasy as the bewildering complexities of the modern world suddenly dissolved into the image of a lonely rider silhouetted against the horizon, the evil of the world arrayed against him, but to no avail. Part of us would always ride with him, that better part of us hidden in our paunchy souls and behind our Walter Mitty façades.

The most endearing quality of *The Western* by George N. Fenin and William K. Everson is its deadpan documentation of our nostalgia. For the most part, the authors are content to fill the gaps of our memory and experience, allowing each reader to make his own links without undue prompting. A pioneering work of prodigious scholarship, *The Western* traces the evolution of an art form on its own terms and for its own sake. By simply recording the striking mutations of the western in sixty years of development, the authors have established an organic conception of their material. The weight of detail both in the text and in 150 evocative illustrations serves to counterbalance previous notions of a monolithic genre. Every thesis seems to generate its antithesis. William S. Hart and Realism is supplanted by Tom Mix and Showmanship. The Indians evolve from antagonists to protagonists. The women undulate from Victorianism to Freudianism and ultimately, the authors fear, to Kinseyism. The virile representations of John Wayne and Gary Cooper are debased by Frank Sinatra's cowardice in *Johnny Concho* and Marlon Brando's narcissism in *One-Eyed Jacks*. General Custer is a megalomaniac in one film and a martyr in another. Billy the Kid and Jesse James run the gamut from juvenile delinquents to populist avengers.

If these theses and antitheses of *The Western* have not been dialectically synthesized, it is because the two authors provide us with a double vision. From their individual writings in film periodicals, it is clear that they are involved here less in collaboration than in amalgamation. Fortunately, their separate styles alternate from chapter to chapter rather than from paragraph to paragraph. In what amounts to an interdisciplinary partnership, Mr. Everson tends to be the historian and Mr. Fenin the sociologist. While Everson tells us what the western has been, Fenin tells us what it should have been. Everson's tone is nostalgic, fatalistic, almost antiquarian. Fenin's tone is liberal, constructive, almost Messianic. What they share is affection and enthusiasm for their subject, and it is fair to assume that both subscribe to this concluding prognosis: "There will always be an audience for the Western, for the Western represents romantic adventure and idealism, achievement, optimism for the future, justice, individualism, the beauty of the land, and the courage and independence of the individuals who won the land. It is in the Western that the American discovers himself again as one of the descendants of a people who knew how to work hard, who knew how to fight, who were prepared to die. This is all in contrast to the padded world in which the American so often finds himself today; the land is a little bit further away, and the day of the horse has passed."

It follows that the authors would dedicate their book to William S. Hart, "the finest Western star and director of them all, and the best friend the West ever had." Hart had lived through many of the experiences he later enacted, notably as a trail-herd cowboy in Kansas and once as an innocent bystander in a Sioux City gunfight between a sheriff and two badmen. From 1915 through 1925, Hart established a relatively realistic western hero in opposition to some of the overcostumed dude types of the period. Significantly, Hart was in his forties when he began his career, and his gnarled maturity gave his westerns a pessimistic fin-de-siècle quality which enhanced the nobility of his character. It is this weary nobility, what the French call *Grandeur et Servitude*, which has invested the western with emotional and intellectual resonance. In recent years such aging actors as John Wayne, James Stewart, Gary Cooper, Henry Fonda, Randolph Scott and Joel McCrea have upheld the dignity of the Hart tradition against gun-happy juveniles and Method neurotics.

The stature of the western as an art form must take into account the visual qualities of its landscapes. Here, where literary criticism becomes inadequate, the cultural problem of the cinema becomes most acute. The prestigious arts of our time have lost a sense of Place, and the western is as much a Place as a Time. The majestic vastness imposes limits on the presumption of its inhabitants, and eventually dictates an anti-power mystique for the genre. Curiously, it is the European critics, rather than their American counterparts, who have grasped the aesthetic implications of the western landscape. One French critic, for example, made a detailed visual analysis of an American western in terms of the paintings of Poussin and Delacroix. One cannot imagine such an ambitious cross-reference in an American publication. Our niggardly criticism may arise from an excess of specialization, a suspicion of the profundity of pleasurable art, or simply a facile hatred of *kitsch*. Whatever, the cause, any book on the cinema seems to require an elaborate cultural defense before it can be enjoyed. But snobbery aside, *The Western* is an eminently enjoyable book.

My favorite chapter is concerned with the costuming of western characters over the years. It goes almost without saying that one picture on this subject is worth a thousand words, and the illustrations here provide a hilarious accompaniment to the graphic text. To look at the absurd tassels which adorn Roy Rogers is to realize that if clothes do not entirely make the man, they certainly determine the function of the western hero. The short-lived experiment of John Wayne's suspenders in John Ford's *Stagecoach* indicates that Hollywood cannot always impose its will upon the public. The recurring moral tonality—white for the hero, black for the villain, with horses to match—was spectacularly reversed by Hopalong Cassidy in a jet-black outfit portending a dire fate for his adversaries. All in all, an uneasy compromise has been effected between the functional and the ostentatious. If the dudes have departed, they have not yet been replaced by the prairie proletariat.

The authors might have treated modern variations on the western with an appropriately adventurous spirit instead of invoking Hart's austerity at every turn. Sex is probably here to stay in the western, and we might as well get used to it. Moreover, in its increasing pastness, the western may be entering a Proustian era in which memory transcends adventure and symbol replaces spectacle. One can appreciate Mr. Everson's nostalgic recollections of the stunt-men and second-unit directors who staged the cavalry charges, range wars and Indian massacres of yesteryear, but their day has passed, and this does not necessarily mean that the western has regressed. Yet what is most important about *The Western* is that its authors have reminded us of a fundamental deficiency in modern man's imagination given as it is to abstraction, generalization and what F. H. Bradley has called, "the ballet dance of bloodless categories." *The Western* makes us see again what we have seen so often and have never really noticed—the visual configurations of our myths, our legends and our dreams.

THE THIRTIES: *THEY SHOOT HORSES,*
DON'T THEY?

They Shoot Horses, Don't They? has finally come to the screen thirty-four years after the publication of Horace McCoy's classic wouldn't-that-make-a-wonderful-movie novel. I read the novel myself back in the Forties and I have been busy casting it ever since. Nowadays it would be hard to improve on Jane Fonda as Gloria, Michael Sarrazin as Robert, Susannah York as Alice, Gig Young as Rocky, Red Buttons as Sailor, Bonnie Bedelia as Ruby, Bruce Dern as James, and Allyn Ann McLerie as Shirl. All things considered, I'm glad the movie was made even after a thirty-four-year delay. Director Sydney Pollack, scenarists James Poe and Robert E. Thompson and producers Irwin Winkler and Robert Chartroff have brought *Horses* to the screen with considerable intelligence, sensitivity and affection, and they have avoided needless flourishes of stomach-churning pseudo-realism. John Green's subdued potpourri of pop music is particularly tasteful in its avoidance of the temptations of self-parody.

But thirty-four years is a long time just the same, and when the picture started on a lyrical note of horses and rural America and childhood and lost illusions and the credits not even completed I began to worry that they were about to mess up my movie and so I began to kibitz the writing and direction. First I wouldn't have illustrated the last line of the movie. The visual stuff, however beautifully photographed in slow motion, makes the reading of the line itself superfluous. What everyone remembers about the line from the novel is its marvelously apt incongruity. Either do the line without the visual horses or do the horses without delivering the line.

My next worrisome moment came when the dance-marathon contestants were lined up in a gaudy torture chamber on the Pacific

Coast. Susannah York's ultra-refined Jean Harlow imitator looked at first glance like a parody of the Glenda Farrell floozie in *Dames at Sea*. For her part, Jane Fonda made her first entrance with frizzed hair and tough talk reminiscent of Barbara Stanwyck in her *Baby Face* period. Oh-oh, I thought, high camp on the late, late show. Perhaps, the Thirties are beyond serious restoration after all.

Then I began to worry about the overly explicit ex-post-facto ironies in the dialogue. (Happy days are here, again, folks, and, as President Hoover tells us, prosperity is just around the corner.) Gig Young's smooth-talking Rocky the promoter seemed too sympathetically satanic as the diabolist ex marathon. Hence, his final confession of being a financial as well as spiritual swindler falls flat as dramatic revelation and serves instead as halfheartedly existential ritual in order to trigger (literally) the ultimate violence.

Also, the characters take on a doomed look from the very outset, and the very modern plot-killing flash-forwards drain away the last possibility of suspense in the ongoing action. Still, the seaside dance hall succeeds as a symbol fully as much as it failed in *Oh What a Lovely War*. Nothing kills a symbol more effectively than stripping away its realistic raiment. Because the dance hall is so palpably real in *Horses*, it reverberates with all the symbolic resonance of the Pacific Ocean pounding under the floor. The Pacific functions on so many levels for American writers as the fatal frontier beyond which only the great, cold silences lurk that Horace McCoy's choice of locale can never cease to evoke intimations of mortality and morbidity.

And finally there are the dancers themselves, slower and slower and slower, from the dance of love to the dance of death, the girls degenerating from clinging vines to clutching serpents, the men watching the last shreds of their manhood peeling off with shame and fatigue. I was moved, then shaken by the beauty and genius of Horace McCoy's metaphor. Two people, male and female, circling endlessly around a dance floor, the girl, tough and scared and vulnerable, spitting out "Christ" as an epithet at every new evidence that God did not exist. (Jane Fonda and Michael Sarrazin transcend the trashy romanticism of their portentously underdeveloped characterizations.) In the last stages of the marathon with death hovering everywhere, the survivors make us rejoice for all those Thirties families that hung together through the incredible squalor of the period. *They Shoot Horses, Don't They?* is joyous entertainment even though or perhaps because its joy is the joy of despair, the only decent mood we can feel as we enter the Seventies.

IV.
POLITICS

BIRTH OF A NATION, OR, WHITE POWER BACK WHEN

The Paris Cinemathèque recently screened D. W. Griffith's *Birth of a Nation* in connection with Lillian Gish's arrival in the city for a lecture, and so I decided to take another look at this fountainhead film in the history of the medium. Classic or not, *Birth of a Nation* has long been one of the embarrassments of film scholarship. It can't be ignored in even the most basic curriculum, and yet it was regarded as outrageously racist even at a time when racism was hardly a household word. What to do? One academic solution is to honor Griffith's contributions with a screening of *Intolerance*, itself an act of alleged atonement on Griffith's part for any bad impression fostered by *Birth of a Nation*. Anyway, the Old Left film historians have always insisted that it was *Intolerance* and not *Birth of a Nation* that inspired Eisenstein, Pudovkin and the other Russians to make their montage masterpieces, and since the cinema attained its ideological-aesthetic peak with *Potemkin*, we were told further, *Intolerance* could be safely studied as a relatively primitive influence on *Potemkin*. The fact that *Intolerance* was as much a popular failure as *Birth of a Nation* was a popular success carried little weight with the left-wing revisionists. "Popular" merely meant "commercial" in the lexicon of Marxist film history, and everyone knew that commercial success in the cinema usually involved the manipulation of the ideologically innocent masses by the evil exploiters.

My own attitude toward *Birth of a Nation* and *Intolerance* is one of reluctant respect without great affection. I much prefer the Griffith of *True Heart Susie*, *Broken Blossoms*, *Way Down East* and even *The White Rose* to the Griffith of the monumental superproductions o 1915 and 1916. Not only do I have an ingrained bias in favor of small, personal visions to big, social spectacles; I feel also that Griffith was more at home (literally and figuratively) with domestic details than with cosmic configurations. Indeed, there is more of eternity in one anguished expression of Mae Marsh or Lillian Gish than in all of Griffith's flowery rhetoric on Peace, Brotherhood and Understanding. Another factor in my not booking *Birth of a Nation* and *Intolerance* for my classes is the three-hour running time of each picture, a rather long stretch for a silent movie nowadays, particularly when no musical accompaniment is provided. Henri Langlois, super-purist that he is, never has music played at the Cinemathèque for silent films, a position I consider illogical to the extreme in that silent movies were always accompanied by music, and *Birth of a Nation* in particular was released with an elaborate score for the guidance of its exhibitors.

The pioneering marvels represented in *Birth of a Nation* and *Intolerance* present an increasingly more troublesome challenge to the film lecturer. The more we get to know about the period from 1896 to 1915, the more subtly ambiguous Griffith's position becomes in terms of easily identifiable technical and stylistic contributions. Also, the neo-antiquarianism of Welles and the *nouvelle vague* directors has taken from Griffith some of the patina of his pastness. Griffith's editing, for example, is not nearly as sophisticated as film histories would have us believe, certainly not by the surrealistic standards of Eisenstein. Griffith's artificial masking and iris framing is fairly primitive next to Eisenstein's functional framing in *Strike* through which the dynamic movements of machinery and architectural forms vary the visibility ratios on the screen. Or so we thought until Welles reintroduced the iris dissolve as an expression of nostalgia in *The Magnificent Ambersons* in 1942 and Ophuls reinvented artificial masking and framing in *Lola Montès* in 1955 to make CinemaScope more supple, and Godard expressed his fleeting narrative instinct with an iris fade-out in *Breathless* in 1960. With everything again possible, nothing seems antiquated, Griffith least of all, and if the criteria for Griffith's shot sequences seem relatively literary and theatrical next to Eisenstein's, who is to say that "literary" and "theatrical" are necessarily pejorative expressions in this period of more flexible film aesthetics?

On the level of content, however, *Birth of a Nation* was an infinitely more influential political event than either *Intolerance* with its well-meaning abstractions and sentimentalities and *Potemkin* with its for-export-only exhortations to revolution. Indeed it was naïve for Griffith to imagine that the platitudinous generalities of *Intolerance* could ever atone for the plastic specifics of *Birth of a Nation*. The best that could be said for Griffith was that he was not fully conscious of all the issues involved in his treatment of Reconstruction after the Civil War. Certainly, Griffith could not have been overly sensitive to the absurdity of casting his blackest black villains with whites in black face while showing authentic negritude in the ranks of the Reconstruction extras. Hence, we have blackness itself (apart from the "loyal" Mammy and Tom black-face servants) as an index of social and sexual presumption, and the hero gets the inspiration for the Ku Klux Klan robes from watching white children frighten black children with white sheets representing the ghosts that were to make a whole generation of Negro screen comics roll their eyes in abject fear and ritualistic servitude. But I am describing the visual Manicheanism of Griffith's racism in mere words, black type or print on white paper, a medium in which "black" and "white" are in themselves equivalently colorless sensations to the eye. To witness whiteness and blackness on the screen is to witness the birth of a color taboo that has not been shattered to this day. Griffith aggravated the problem by thrusting the coyest of coy Victorian heroines into the most sordid situations a Southern sentimentalist could imagine. Curly-haired child-women who resisted their own upper-class sweethearts suddenly became the prey of uppity blacks, and the poor innocents either fainted with lascivious modesty or jumped off cliffs with commendable honor. It is as if an army of black Uriah Heeps were unleashed on an array of Agneses meant for the snobbish fantasies of a Dickens and nowhere else. Griffith, like Dickens, had no adult conception of social organisms and class structures. Unlike Gance and Eisenstein, Griffith relied more on a theory of character than a theory of history. What happened after *Birth of a Nation* was in many ways more dispiriting in its hypocrisy than the racist shock of *Birth of a Nation* itself, and even so-called progressives were not immune to this hypocrisy.

*   *   *

Birth of a Nation opened officially at the Liberty Theatre in New York on March 3, 1915, preaching peace at a time when most of the world was at war. President Woodrow Wilson, who honored the film with an unprecedented screening in the White House, is reported to have remarked, "It is like writing history with lightning." At that, Wilson's blurb came under the heading of noblesse oblige, since Griffith's titles for Birth of a Nation quote Woodrow Wilson the historian on more than one occasion for historical evidence of the evils of Reconstruction. Wilson, born a Southerner, like Griffith, was a liberal Democratic President in an era when most of the Negro vote, North and South, went to the Republicans virtually by default. Hence, there is no reason to believe that he felt unduly menaced by the race riots in Northern cities or the political protests from such lingering abolitionists as Jane Addams and President Charles E. Eliot of Harvard.

Unfortunately, the outcries against Birth of a Nation served merely to drive racism underground without confronting the specific issues involved. By arguing that Griffith was being unfair to Negroes, the white liberals succeeded in preventing any sequels to Birth of a Nation, but they failed completely and perhaps deliberately to counter the impact of Birth of a Nation with a positive picture of the Negro on a scale comparable to Griffith's negation of negritude. For decades, Southern theater owners exercised veto power over the slightest intimation of black-white miscegenation, and this veto power was never seriously challenged even by supposedly Stalinist-swimming-pool-Hollywood screenwriters of the Thirties and Forties. The Left was always good for a few pickets to protest racial slurs in Gone with the Wind and Song of the South, but there never seemed to be any countering scripts to restore sexual dignity to the Negro. Indeed, liberal tolerance was counterproductive to the extent that it blocked out any consideration of race-sex taboos as potentially harmful to the Negro race. Even Birth of a Nation has failed to receive the detailed analysis it deserves because the liberal and Left activist prefers to dismiss the entire film as a distortion and thereby evade the politically dangerous issues involved. If it isn't true, nice people will say, why discuss it at all? The answer is of course that a work of art need not be true for it to be deeply felt and fervently believed.

Marxist critics have been particularly handicapped in this particular controversy by their reluctance to open the Pandora's box of sexual mythology. To argue, however, as Griffith does, that no black man can ever aspire to any white woman goes beyond the boundary of political partisanship into racial taboo, and taboos must be broken at least metaphorically before they can poison the body politic. Certainly out of all the stories that have unfolded on the American continent, Griffith himself could have found some black-white version of *Broken Blossoms* if he had been truly sincere in his professed desire to atone for *Birth of a Nation*. But though there were many movies on the forbidden loves of whites and Orientals, whites and Indians, not to mention the intramural taboos among whites themselves, there were no movies until very recently to romanticize even one example of black-white miscegenation from the millions that must obviously have occurred. *Birth of a Nation* not only upholds the lily-white mythology of the Aryan Southland; it imputes to Thaddeus Stevens (alias Stoneman) sordid sexual motives to explain his vendetta against the defeated Confederacy dear Abe Lincoln wants only to caress and forgive. Thus the ghost of Lincoln is allied with the formidable cultural presences of Griffith and Wilson in a blanket condemnation of black arrogance. Significantly, the uppity mulatto maid who seduces Stoneman merely by baring one of her shoulders is played by a white actress in black face. The effect of black face in white-oriented iconography is to emphasize the treacherous incongruity of darting white eyes and daggerlike white teeth. And the use of black-face performers makes blackness itself a state of being so inferior that blacks themselves are incapable of interpreting and communicating its inescapable baseness. Hence, an American screen tradition is born in *Birth of a Nation* to the effect that no authentic black man younger than Bill "Bojangles" Robinson will ever place his hand on the flesh of any white woman older than Shirley Temple. This taboo has remained in force for so long that even as late as 1957 Joan Fontaine was deluged with poison-pen mail for merely holding hands with Harry Belafonte in *Island in the Sun*, and only recently a TV functionary admitted cutting a bit of television tape in which Petula Clark was shown touching the presumably still untouchable Belafonte.

Curiously, *Birth of a Nation* has gained more ambiguity over the years than its professed bias would indicate. Mae Marsh, in particular, seems more than the conventional victim of black lust. Even by Griffith's outraged Victorian moral standards, Miss Marsh's fierce virgin overreacts hysterically to every emotional challenge until, finally, she is doomed not so much by the relatively restrained black-face pursuer who keeps insisting that he merely wants to talk to her as by her own increasing inability to cope with all the demands made on her feelings. Mae Marsh and Lillian Gish are brilliantly directed by Griffith because he believed in all their Victorian-American affectations as sublime manifestations of white womanhood, and he could not bear to see them buffeted about by the disorder represented by Reconstruction. His small-town–agrarian vision of the world is intellectually inadequate by any standard, but there is no point suppressing *Birth of a Nation*. It marks not only where we were but where it's still at. And it remains to be answered on the screen in its own terms, not by Marxist metaphors of the class struggle.

Z

Z turns out to be a reasonably effective entertainment based on the real-life-and-death case of Gregory Lambrakis, a Greek pacifist leader slain foully in Salonica in 1963 almost as if Edmond Rostand's Cyrano de Bergerac had written his obituary back in 1897: "Behold me ambushed—taken in the rear— / My battlefield a gutter—my noble foe / A lackey with a log of wood! . . ." The title of the film (and of the novel by Vassilis Vassilikos from which Jorge Semprun's script was adapted) refers to the first letter of the Greek word for "He Lives" (Zei) found on walls all over Greece after the assassination. The Conservative Karamanlis government fell shortly after the judicial scandal surrounding the Lambrakis conspiracy, and the Center-Left government of the late Georges Papandreou came to power only to be removed from office by an arbitrary act of King Constantine, who was in turn deposed and exiled (though not formally dethroned) in 1967 by a cabal of colonels acting as a ruling junta. I mention these facts of recent history in order to restore some historical perspective to the Lambrakis Affair. As it is, the people behind Z have attempted to establish a direct causal link between Lambrakis and the junta, much as if an American film-maker had attempted to establish a direct link between the assassination of Bobby Kennedy and the accession of Spiro Agnew. Such links, if they exist at all, are less historical than allegorical. And it is as allegory rather than history that Z is being hailed here in America. How could it be otherwise when a predominantly French all-star cast shoots a film about Greece in Algeria? Inevitably, the specifics of a historical situation are blurred over in the name of universality. Not that I am quibbling here over the mechanics of adaptation. Indeed, the movie is in many ways more restrained in its use of addled agit-prop than the book, itself a remarkable literary hodge-podge of Eric Ambler and Clifford Odets.

What I object to most in Z is its pretense to the suspense of a thriller merely as a means of keeping the audience in its seats for a straight dose of manipulative propaganda. The problem begins with the book, a polemical-poetical semi-documentary mixing facts and fictions in such a self-serving way that art appeals to journalism and beauty to truth whenever any criticism is made. It is to Vassilikos' credit that he has been exiled by the current regime and his book banned, but the fact remains that no American writer could get away with such crude caricatures of the bourgeoisie as the following overheard conversational excerpts: "Where did you have that dress made?" "At Kouka's. And yours?" "In Athens, at Thalia's." "It's a dream!" "Thank you." "The psychiatrist told her she'd work out her troubles with Vallium." "You know, I'm on a new diet. I've lost six pounds in a week." "Impossible." And all the while, of course, "Z" is dying on a bloody street.

Vassilikos uses his novel to preach the New Politics in Greece. This means that Greece should break away from NATO, restore ties with Communist countries to the north and east and devote monies now wasted on armaments to social reconstruction. One dimension of the novel lost in the geographical abstractness of the movie is the social and political tensions between Salonica and Athens. (Vassilikos even manages a delicious joke on the provincial defensiveness of the Salonica Film Festival.) The novelist's bias is so systematic that it serves as a class-conscious discipline. At the bottom layer of Salonica society are the dregs and drabs employed by the fascists for criminal ends. The middle classes (excerpted previously) pretend that nothing has happened and blindly support the regime. A mixture of decent idealists from all classes are then left to combat the pervasive evil of the militaristic Minotaurs in their tangled labyrinths of intrigue.

Vassilikos seems ambivalent about Communists. For the most part, they are presented as right-wing hallucinations. The military men are mostly former Nazi collaborationists and inveterate anti-Semites. (This latter ideological aberration is noticeably lacking from the movie, possibly in deference to the tenderer sensibilities of the movie's Algerian hosts.) At one point, however, Vassilikos expresses through one of his characters an ideological impatience with the centrist government of the late Georges Papandreou. This is an important point to keep in mind. The entire Lambrakis affair unfolded in the context of bourgeois democracy, that same bourgeois democracy so scorned and derided by both Left and Right in Greece and America. An independent investigator of conservative convictions (Jean-Louis Trintignant) pursues the truth wherever it leads him, high or low, Right or Left. This creature of conscience is actually a sentimental hangover of an allegedly old-fashioned liberal tradition. On this occasion he has served to discredit the mountebank militarists, but, to be genuinely free, he would have to exist within a free judiciary not now in existence in any non-democratic Left regime on the face of the earth. (Whatever may be said about Havana and Hanoi, they do not remotely qualify as havens of *habeas corpus*. And the members of the Algerian junta might question themselves and their own Colonel Boumedienne about the extraordinarily illegal detention of the late Moise Tshombe and the present whereabouts of Ahmed Ben Bella, their first President.)

Purely as a movie, Z bears a strong resemblance to Costa-Gavras's previous all-star thriller *The Sleeping Car Murder* and has much the same cast: Trintignant, Yves Montand ("Z"), Charles Denner, Jacques Perrin and the substitution of Irene Papas for Simone Signoret. Both movies are fun, but *The Sleeping Car Murder* was more consistently superficial and hence less pretentious than Z. Costa-Gavras has tried to keep "Z" alive throughout the film by flashback images of Yves Montand, but Trintignant's indefatigable investigator comes to prevail even over the iconographic imagery of Montand's martyrdom. By contrast, Vassilikos kept the investigator a relatively shadowy figure in the book all the better to illuminate the legend of Lambrakis. Where Costa-Gavras and Jorge Samprun miscalculate most grievously is in their planting tantalizing suggestions about "Z," his wife (Irene Papas) and his supporters and then not following up these suggestions with any political or psychological insights. Z is thus overburdened with red herrings as a murder melodrama and yet undersupplied with dramatic details for its political characters. Whereas the book tapered off into disillusion and despair, the movie proper ends on a note of comic triumph, and then plasters on the depressing postscripts of modern history.

What then is the moral of Z? The conservative Karamanlis has fallen. The King and Queen and Queen Mother have been exiled. And political conditions in Greece are worse than ever from any reasonably liberal point of view. As allegory, Z is self-deluding and hypocritical. But audiences will like it. Why? Not because they will be traumatized by Lambrakis as a kind of Greek Bobby Kennedy. Not because they will be brainwashed by the massive bad faith of the French Left. But because there lingers in all of us an unsatisfied thirst for justice and fairness and truth and moral heroism, and these are precisely the qualities Jean-Louis Trintignant's fearless investigator demonstrates in Z.

THE MOVIE TASTES OF THE MIGHTY

President Richard M. Nixon may not be quite the cinephile his recent press notices would seem to suggest. Or so we are led to believe by a recent *Variety* follow-up to the news stories in which Mr. Nixon reportedly plunged straight from the screening room into the practice of statecraft. First there was the Cambodian caper supposedly inspired by a viewing of *Patton*, and then the analogy between good old frontier justice in a John Wayne western like *Chisum* and the kookier kind represented in the trial of Charles Manson, a man the President branded as a murderer without due process. Even at the time of the two news stories it struck me that the President was going far afield in current movies to find justifications for his actions and attitudes. And now *Variety* has confirmed my worst suspicions with this list of films screened for Mr. Nixon since he assumed the Presidency: *The Sound of Music, The Man in the Gray Flannel Suit, Swiss Family Robinson, The Bridge on the River Kwai, Flower Drum Song, Marooned, The Odd Couple, Quo Vadis, War and Peace, Sunrise at Campobello, West Side Story, Cat Ballou* and *Dr. Zhivago*. Hardly a list of films resounding with relevance. Furthermore, daughter Tricia is apparently in charge of booking although the systematic exclusion of all X-rated product may reflect the all too visibly inhibiting presence of Billy Graham. Hence, unless the President sneaks off by himself to catch such conversation pieces as *Easy Rider, Bonnie and Clyde, The Graduate, M*A*S*H, Catch-22* and *Oh What a Lovely War*, he is effectively insulated from what a great many of his countrymen are looking at these days. Not that even *Patton* and *Chisum* are as ill-conceived as the Presidential decisions they are supposed to have influenced. Once more and this time on the highest level of power, we are confronted with the problem of the viewer seeing in a movie precisely what he wants to see in it, no more, no less.

Normally the cinematic preferences of political leaders are more piquant than profound. Thinking back, I can recall that Franklin D. Roosevelt once said some kind words about Jean Renoir's *Grand Illusion*, but I have a feeling FDR's rhetoric was influenced more by the propriety of Peace as a subject than by the pleasure he found in the movie. I remember also his enthusiasm for "Amos 'n Andy" on the radio and his weariness with "Home on the Range" as his "favorite song." Mrs. Roosevelt provided a more honest reaction, as always, by reacting instinctively against a harrowingly clinical documentary on childbirth with the observation (recorded by John Grierson) to the effect that childbirth should have more joy associated with it.

Winston Churchill's favorite movie was *That Hamilton Woman* and/or *Destry Rides Again*. Of the latter movie, Lord Beaverbrook is said to have remarked: "The image of Marlene Dietrich standing in her black stockings on a bar singing 'See What the Boys in the Back Room Will Have' ranks with the Venus de Milo." Marshal Tito's favorite film is *The Petrified Forest*, and no one seems to know why exactly. Josef Stalin loved not the revolutionary montage classics of Eisenstein, Pudovkin and Dovjenko but rather a simple-hearted Russian musical called *Volga Volga*. Ike liked westerns, especially *Shane*, and he was also a prodigious reader of pulp westerns, a predilection that separated him from the more cultivated admirers of the movie genre. I never remember Jack Kennedy being associated with moviegoing in any conspicuous way. He seemed always to be on too much of a reality kick to require the mediation of the silver screen, and rumor has it that he preferred to date the movie goddesses in person.

Even Hitler's tastes did not always seem to run true to form. His favorite opera was *Die Meistersinger*, the least morbid of Wagner's works, the least obsessed with blood, death, immolation and revenge, all presumably Hitlerian motifs. One of his favorite novels was C. S. Forester's *The General*, a very ironic account of the career of a British general on the Western Front during the First World War. Forester's general butchered his troops by the tens of thousands in a stupidly conceived offensive, and then, as the Germans were successfully counterattacking, he mounted his horse and, in a burst of prescience, realized that if he sensibly retreated he would be regarded ever after as one of the defeated ones and he would be whispered about and mistrusted because the stench of failure would follow him everywhere, and so he spurred his horse forward and led his men back to more dismemberment and death, and he himself was blown off his horse, and his leg was shattered, but his foolishly heroic charge did earn him the honor of rank and respect in a Bath chair till the end of his days. And that was all Hitler took away from *The General:* the heroism and the honor, not the stupidity and the horror. But that is the way with obsessive personalities as they bore in on multilayered works with laser beams of neurotic concentration. From the very top to the very bottom of any social structure, it is what people bring to movies that determine what they get out of them. Hence, the fruitlessness of all censorship and sociological speculation on audience impact.

It must be added that George C. Scott's Patton and John Wayne's Chisum are more complex and ambivalent than the dubious politics they have been invoked to justify. And even at their worst, movies have not yet become as barbarously polarized as our politics. There are now at least Two Americas whereas there is still only one Cinema. Still, as long as the Two Americas do not break out into violently uncivil warfare, the situation could be worse. If I said in Russia about Brezhnev half of what I've said in America about Nixon, I would be clamped into an insane asylum for "tests" before I could say "Ivan Ivanovich." Which is to say that America is still America even though we are stuck with a leader who prefers to treat the Presidency more as an ordeal than as an opportunity and who whines more than all the current crop of movie anti-heroes put together, anti-heroes incidentally he seems destined never to see on the screen if Tricia has her way.

CATCH-23

Catch-23: *Catch-22* is a bomb. A bomb, not a bombshell. It is never as funny as the funniest moments in *Dr. Strangelove* and *M*A*S*H*, nor as charming as the most charming moments in *The Graduate* and *Butch Cassidy and the Sundance Kid*, nor as originally nihilistic as the most originally nihilistic moments in *How I Won the War* and *Les Carabiniers* and even the overabused *Zabriskie Point*. As a movie, *Catch-22* tends to evoke rather than express the college bull-session caricatures and oh-brother-where-art-thou polemics of Joseph Heller's novel without any of the compensating energy and intricacy and institutional insidiousness with which the cardboard intrigues were presented on the printed page.

It is as if Buck Henry's screenplay (or at least that part of the screenplay that survived the reportedly ruthless editing of Mike Nichols) were to be considered merely the synopsis for a novel deemed too universally beloved and admired to require any full-scale enactment on the screen. Hence, the movie dispenses with not only half the characters in the book but, more injuriously, with almost all the obsessional power struggles of petty bureaucrats. We are given General Dreedle in the oversized dimensions of Orson Welles, but we are denied General Peckem altogether. Colonel Cathcart (Martin Balsam) and Lieutenant Colonel Korn (Buck Henry) operate in terrible (almost interchangeable) tandem in the movie with none of the competitive backbiting they display in the book. Gone entirely are the brassy, literary, nervy mail clerks and paperwork parasites who labored night and day to subvert their superiors. Gone also are the middle-brow literary references to T. S. Eliot and Washington Irving and Dostoevski.

Even worse is the movie's insistence on stripping away every last vestige of Heller's satiric sociology. Thus the characters become increasingly disconnected as the movie goes on and on and on into the void of secondhand abstractness. With few exceptions, the acting is too broad and self-satisfied to get laughs from even the most culturally intimidated audience. Anthony Perkins is the most notable exception by getting inside the tortured shell of Chaplain Tappman and managing to function with absurdist anguish as the genuine man of God resisting the bogus religiosity of the military. On the same level is Bob Newhart's cameo gem as the relentlessly retiring Major Major, and just a few notches below is Austin Pendleton's Katzenjammer Kid foil to Orson Welles's General Dreedle. (It is a measure of the movie's excess strain that Mr. Welles, the broadest actor, literally and figuratively, in creation, seems comparatively subtle in the context of Catch-22.) Alan Arkin's interestingly troublesome interpretation of Captain Yossarian cannot be faulted on any technical deficiency in the actor but rather in the conceptual dilemma of the whole project. Yossarian, part protagonist and part poltergeist, part lucid raisonneur and part loony rebel, has insurmountable problems in making the transition to the screen where he must serve as the audience's point of view to satisfy the essentially subjective, even solipsist and faintly Felliniesque style of Mike Nichols. And Arkin has the same problems as a movie actor that Yossarian has as a movie character. As a consequence, Catch-22 itself emerges in 1970 as a movie with more problems than pleasures.

Having thus concluded my movie-reviewing functions as taste consultant and market researcher, I feel free to discuss Catch-22 as a fascinating cultural phenomenon of our time. I certainly wouldn't want to keep anyone from seeing the movie even if I could. After all, most of my favorite flicks have been bombs of one kind or another. Docks of New York, Design for Living, Angel, Holiday, Bringing Up Baby and Cluny Brown were all bombs, as were Vertigo, The Magnificent Ambersons, Shoot the Piano Player, Contempt, The Sun Shines Bright, Seven Women, Day of Wrath, Gertrud, The Rules of the Game, The Golden Coach, Oharu, Once Upon a Time in the West and, lest we forget, the late, great Max Ophuls' Lola Montès, a movie for which my irrepressible rave review still draws a steady supply of poison-pen mail. Indeed, lost critical causes seem to have constituted the major part of my career and the politics of perversity the major share of my rhetorical reflexes. When the audience goes one way, you can trust at least part of me to go another. Part of me, but not all of me.

There is another part of me that chomps on a big cigar and sits in a talent office with a casting couch and tells people whether they have it or not. This Sammy Slick character sits in a movie house where *Lola Montès* is playing and can tell that Martine Carol's pathetically accessible courtesan doesn't really grab New Yorkers and that poor old Max really bombed out this time simply because his art is too beautiful to be borne.

But this is not the way I feel about *Catch-22*. Whereas Ophuls tried to give his audience more than they expected, Nichols tries to punish *his* audience by giving it less. It is partly the old snobbish syndrome of Mike Nichols posing as Michelangelo Nichols, and how many guffaws have you gotten lately from the Sistine Chapel? The old Nichols–May routines? Forget them. These tap dances of talent have nothing to do with the grand ballets of which true genius is capable. And there is another side to Nichols, the side that shows itself in the tears that fill his eyes at screenings of *8½* and *Le Bonheur*. Indeed, Nichols was so moved by *8½* that he fired veteran cinematographer Harry Stradling from *Virginia Woolf* for remarking that he (Stradling) thought that Guido (of Fellini–Mastroianni in *8½*) was a "shit." God help you if you don't cry in synch with Mike.

But suddenly something happened to the aura around Mike Nichols. He was no longer either Mike Nichols or Michelangelo Nichols but, after the fantastic grosses of *The Graduate*, nothing less than Cecil B. DeNichols. Single-handed, he had changed the entire industry. He had the magic touch, the Midas touch; he was tuned into the new, the young, the daring. He might have argued once that good movies could be made for less than a million dollars. Now he himself was getting a million dollars and throwing his weight around and puffing himself up to be canonized on the cover of *Time* and cracking jokes with Joe Levine about what a loser Carroll Baker was, and, all in all, setting himself up as an irresistible target for the great American pastime of kicking someone when he's up. How easy it is, after all, to hate an intelligent young man with his own private airplane. Even Bernie Cornfeld, the playboy pasha of I. O. S., could scarcely be less lovable than Mike the New Mogul of Movies.

But history, that faithless whore, has played a cruel trick on *Catch-22* by making Mike Nichols' heartfelt (though derivative) technique look pointlessly poetical. All revolutions run the risk of devouring their own rhetoric, and radical revolutions most of all. Yossarian may have anticipated the Swedish sanctuary for war resisters but little else in the increasingly polarized politics of our time. The masks are all gone from the monsters. Nixon, Mitchell and Agnew don't even pretend to be idealists. You can't spill the beans on their villainies and then step back for a superior snicker at their expense. They'll gladly trade you the last laugh of parody for the last trump of power. What once seemed on the campuses to be Yossarian's commendable instinct for survival may strike today's rebels, real and vicarious, as a contemptible insensitivity to the struggle.

It must be remembered that although *Catch-22* was first published in 1961 its spirit was very much of the mid-Fifties, when it was being written, in that savagely somnolent era of the silent generation. Heller's satiric vision was sour Fifties puking on hitherto heroic Forties. Nichols and Henry on Heller is absurdist Sixties sanctifying sour Fifties on heroic Forties. Thus we are three degrees of stylization (and almost three decades) removed from the original subject. And it shows, especially in the movie's treatment of Forties women, Paula Prentiss and Susanne Benton coming on so freakish as to make Betty Boop look positively Botticellian. As for the Italian hookers impersonated by Olympia Carlisli and Gina Rovere, only the modish misogyny of "serious" movie-making can explain why Nichols couldn't get something better and more sensual for a $15 million production. Even the Heller novel made a stab at sensuality now and then in amid the satire, but the movie prefers to treat girls as functions of militaristic freakiness à la Strangelove. Nichols and Henry even pay tribute to Kubrick's *2001* with a burst of the Strauss Zarathustra keynote (*vide* also *The Strawberry Statement*) when Arkin first spots the slut of his life on a Roman street, but the girl is not very pretty at all, and the effect is thus not a joke on genuine desire but on feigned horniness.

On the whole, the Roman scenes are peculiar even as savage parodies on the American military presence in Italy in World War II. There were relatively few Hollywood movies on the Italian campaign, and even fewer on the Italian girls. Rossellini and the other

neo-realists pre-empted the field in the middle and late Forties with
self-serving caricatures of the American soldiers as gum-chewing vul-
garians. Even in the novel, the passages of brutal America raping
gentle Italy came over as mildewed Alfred Hayes ("You've got Michelangelo, baby, but we've got General Motors.") And so it's hard
to tell what the movie is really about in its sullen *Walpurgisnacht* on
a Roman street, except possibly as an allegory on Vietnam out of left
field.

Still, it is not only history that has led Nichols and Henry astray
but also the relentless temptation of Brechtian distancing and Fel-
linian dreaminess and Kubrickian dourness. By trying to be the ultimate film, *Catch-22* ends up not being even a very good movie. But
then neither is *M*A*S*H* nor *The Graduate* the ultimate film, and
the relentless search for the ultimate film is one of the unhealthiest
trends in recent years. I hate to see hordes of people lining up for
one picture on the Bloomingdale Belt and no one lining up for the
picture next door. In this all-or-nothing, rags-or-riches atmosphere,
the fiscal giddiness that attended the filming of *Catch-22* takes on
the appearance of Russian roulette. Spend $5 million or $15 million,
but if you don't click with the hit-herd audience, the total investment goes down the drain. The studio system, or at least what's left
of it, cannot abandon its old habit of seeking guarantees of success.

Hence, we are told quite solemnly that Elliott Gould is a great
star and that his name on a marquee will by itself draw millions of
breathless fans into the movie houses. You take Dustin Hoffman
(out of *The Graduate*) and Mia Farrow (out of *Rosemary's Baby*)
and you put them together in *John and Mary* and you make as much
money as *The Graduate* and *Rosemary's Baby* combined. Right?
No, wrong. Well then, the chemistry between Dustin and Mia
wasn't as strong as the chemistry between Dustin and Jon Voight in
Midnight Cowboy. Well then, if it's all-male teams they want, Sam,
why not team up Dustin with Robert Redford and Paul Newman in
something we'll call "The Midnight Graduate and the Sunflower
Freaks" with a yoot-oriented script from my nineteen-year-old
nephew at Stanford and a back-up polish job from Ring Lardner, Jr.
(He's so full of self-pity after Cannes, he'll take anything.) But wait,
Sam, didn't I read something in a *Saturday Review* symposium
about big stars being out and creative people being in at the "new"

Hollywood (and if we're not new Hollywood I'd like to know who is). Let's pull all the money we can borrow on gilt-edged talents like Neil Simon (*The Out-of-Towners*) and Mike Nichols (*Catch-22*). Give them everything they want, and fire all the rest of the dead-beats.

Between the time that Mike Nichols began work on *Catch-22* and the time it was ready for release, a great many things happened. The Vietnamese war became the Indo-Chinese war. The body count of slaughtered blacks in Southern schools was interrupted by a quad-ruple execution of white youth at Kent State. And $250 billion of stock values were wiped out on the Big Board, causing many radical causes to founder for lack of funds. Knee-jerk nihilism seemed in-creasingly irrelevant in a world determined to die given half a chance. The nutty spectacle of Mike Nichols and Buck Henry glee-fully bankrupting a major studio in search of their muse across several continents suddenly seemed trivially self-indulgent. *Catch-22* took too long to make, not merely for its timeliness but also for the traditional turnover aesthetic of movie-making, the perpetual polish-ing of careers by constant activity until effortless professionalism eventually yields deeper personal meanings in the style of the story-telling rather than in pretentious mannerisms extraneous to the story.

Catch-22 is ultimately not my kind of movie because it puts on airs of being the only movie around. It was Paramount's gamble and Nichols' that *Catch-22* would indeed seem like the only movie in town, and yet at least part of the pleasure one derives from this movie (and all others) is the network of iconographical cross-references in the performances of Perkins, Welles, Newhart, Arkin, Pendleton, *et al.* from all the other movies in which they've ap-peared. Moviegoing is as much a context as a contest, and if I have contributed to a feeling of absolutes with my somewhat ironic invo-cations of pantheons and old masters, I apologize. My appreciation of pantheon directors is a function of my attending all the directors and seeing all the movies I possibly can. Nichols is not without tal-ent, and I still have fond memories of *The Graduate*. It strikes me, however, that the Hoffman–Bancroft assignation scenes draw their comic bite from the wit and timing of the old Nichols–May con-frontations and that Hoffman and Bancroft almost resemble Nichols and May. Also, Nichols, both in *Virginia Woolf* (Burton superb, Taylor, Segal and Dennis so-so) and *The Graduate*, seems an unusually subjective director. In fact, his fiercely aggressive first-personality betokens a fatal lack of otherness in his directorial personality. Finally, it must be acknowledged in all fairness that none of the faults of *Catch-22* can be attributed to that most abused of all contemporary screenwriters, Terry Southern. But after *Candy* and *Catch-22*, Buck Henry had better be careful that he doesn't take Southern's place as the scapegoat for the current malaise over the screen's increasingly boring audacity.

ZABRISKIE POINT

Michelangelo Antonioni's long-awaited *Zabriskie Point* had its first New York press screening at 8 p.m. on Thursday, February 5, 1970, at the Coronet Theater. Audience reaction seemed to range from mixed to negative, but I didn't really want to talk about the movie until I had sorted out my immediate impressions, and so I ducked the opportunity to gather gut reactions in the lobby à la Nathalie Sarraute. My review deadline for *The Voice* is normally Friday afternoon for the following Thursday's issue, which is usually on the newsstands by Wednesday afternoon. But because I had to leave on Friday morning for a wedding in Virginia, I pushed my deadline forward to Monday morning.

It is now Sunday afternoon, February 8, 1970, as I sit staring at my docile typewriter keys. I have been thinking about *Zabriskie Point* all weekend, on the plane from New York to Richmond and on the plane back, in cars and in cabs, in the city and in the country, in fog and in smog, but particularly in the placid company town of Franklin, Virginia, the most prominent features of which are three towering chimneys (the kind that are always tilted expressionistically in industrial documentaries) belching black, white and gray columns of smoke into the coughing clouds. I may never revisit Franklin, and hence I may never be able to separate my impression of the town from the image of its smoke streams. Mine is an outsider's vision of Franklin, a superficial view for a novelist or a dramatist or an essayist, but not necessarily for a painter or a sculptor or a photographer. It would seem that there is one standard of experience (and research) for the arts of the mind and another for the arts of the senses. Film-making draws from both realms, and thus what bores the mind may please the eye, and what offends the eye may stimulate the mind.

Zabriskie Point, an outsider's view of America, is as much a delight to the eyes as it is a disappointment to the mind, or at least to
that part of the mind that relishes complications and consumma-
tions in its dramatic entertainments. Antonioni is at his best in the
first hour when nothing happens and in the last ten minutes when
nothing matters. In between he gets bogged down with two callow,
inexpressive protagonists (Mark Frechette and Daria Halprin) who
make love, not sense. Mark Frechette was reportedly discovered at a
bus stop in Cambridge, Massachusetts, shouting at a man who had
thrown a flower pot at a quarreling couple. He is described in the
program notes as a twenty-year-old sometime carpenter, an occupa-
tion that in this context resounds with a quasi-Biblical solemnity and
foreboding. He is inertia itself, having mastered the nonactor's trick
of masking thoughts and nonthoughts alike behind the slit-eyed
mask of a poker face. He cannot read adequately even the few la-
conic lines dredged up from the desert sands of Death Valley by the
collective efforts of Antonioni, Fred Gardner, Sam Shepard, Tonino
Guerra and Clare Peplo. Daria Halprin displays an interesting bodily
frame for the camera to photograph, particularly across the shoulders, and there is a slight spark in her eyes and teeth, but her face is
hopelessly uncoordinated for any expression of emotion beyond the
most rudimentary, and she tends to walk like a camel on a cobble-
stone road, hardly a disgraceful deficiency for a nineteen-year-old
anthropology student at Berkeley. Together Mark and Daria (for so
also are they called in the film) fail to achieve even the rapport of
their shared awkwardness. They are as dead psychologically as their
desert decor is dead metaphorically, and Antonioni must have
sensed their inadequacy at an early point in the production, or why
else would he have gone to such unprecedented lengths to establish
visual correlatives for the most basic human emotions? For Daria to
simulate tears at Mark's death, it is thus necessary for Antonioni to
drench her with the twisting drippings of a granite grotto. And when
Mark himself is finally trapped by California police as he attempts
to land the small plane he stole for a joy ride, Antonioni diverts the
audience's attention from the human confrontation between non-
conformism and police authority to an aerial view of police cars con-
stricting the free movement of a grounded metal bird painted over
with the psychedelia of peace and flowery passivity. Mark's spirit,

such as it may have been, flows out of his clumsy body into the metal metaphor of his aerial/Ariel aspiration. And that's all there is to his youthful, disorganized, ultimately impotent rebellion.

For her part, Daria can only stand idly by while Antonioni's camera passes through her for his final explosion of America's Pop canvas into the spiritual shrapnel of materialism. For Antonioni, *Zabriskie Point* is a different kind of blow-up, not the magnification of art into truth but the disintegration of America into trash, and not just America but indeed the increasing muchness of matter everywhere, and all kinds of matter, even, or perhaps especially, books.

Almost half a century ago Lev Kuleshov performed an experiment with a relatively expressionless close-up of the great Russian actor Ivan Mozhukhin. Kuleshov intercut this same close-up first with a shot of a plate of soup, then with a child playing with a teddy bear, and finally with an old woman lying dead in her coffin. (Some French film historians have garbled the experiment by substituting a shot of a nude woman for that of the child with the teddy bear in Kuleshov's montage series.) The point of the experiment was that audiences of that time were allegedly deluded into thinking that Mozhukhin had masterfully changed his expression from hunger to joy to grief in response to the three situations when actually it was merely the juxtaposition of shots that created the illusion of an actor's performance. This hoary anecdote (reported initially by Pudovkin) has been used by directors for decades as proof that they don't need actors, and Daria's mental explosions of an Arizona chalet are perhaps the most spectacular substitution of a director's vision for a player's persona in the history of the cinema. But it doesn't really work or satisfy once we get back, as we must, to the player herself. It is at that moment that we feel the fatal rupture in *Zabriskie Point* between a brilliant documentary and a bedraggled drama. If people have to be used at all, they have to be good. Bad people can be transcended, they can be sublimated, they can be overshadowed, but they still flaw every foot of film in which they appear.

Still, *Zabriskie Point* is a film not to be missed. And yet, of all of Antonioni's films, it is the only one that does not require a second viewing for the resolution of its ambiguities. The main trouble with *Zabriskie Point* is that there are not enough levels of signification.

Even *The Red Desert*, hitherto the most aesthetical of Antonioni's works, contains plot nuances that require repeated viewings to clarify. The anecdotal material in *Zabriskie Point* is too slight to hang together believably. We never believe that Daria could ever serve as a link between muddled Mark and Rod Taylor's Lee Allen, a genially omnivorous land speculator with more skyscraping and glass-partitioned camera angles than lines of dialogue or discernible human feelings. The opening sequence of white radicals rapping with Black Panthers, and subsequent intimations of pig-panther rituals of violence, extend the film without enriching it. The two main characters are so unencumbered by psychological development that we are always left free to peer at the background for Antonioni's choice of American Gothic with which to embellish his fable. Antonioni's viewpoint throughout is that of the interplanetary visitor descending on the American West with more curiosity than compassion, but with far more compassion than contempt.

Audiences may be somewhat let down from the lurid expectations inspired by rumors of right-wing repression. (Conspicuously absent from the film is the "Fuck You America" that Daria was supposed to have scrawled on the desert sands for Mark's aerial appraisal.) The scenes of communal lovemaking are there in some measure, but they operate merely on a symbolic level,—that is to say, as imaginary sociological extensions of the coupling of Mark and Daria. The skin is all there, but not the dramatic certification or pseudo-documentary simulation of Today's Youth on the Rampage. And never has Antonioni's depiction of lovemaking been so arid and listless. From the biological orientation of sex in *La Notte* and the chemical orientation of sex in *The Red Desert*, Antonioni has descended to the geological orientation of sex in *Zabriskie Point*, gradually sanding over the fleshy substances into the deathlike mineral constituencies of the dust and rock of Antonioni's American landscape.

As an American, I am not offended by Antonioni's apocalyptic vision of our supermarket civilization. It is his misfortune, however, that he has not provided facile fantasy figures with which his art-house audience can identify in its voluptuous isolation from the Great Silent Majority. If only Dustin Hoffman or Jon Voight or Jack Nicholson or Arlo Guthrie or even Peter Fonda had been joy riding over the Mojave Desert in a flying bike, *Zabriskie Point* would be this year's box-office bonanza and next year's subject for sociological essays. Unfortunately, Mark Frechette is endowed with so little charisma that even Antonioni seems to spend most of his time avoiding him. When Mark passes a sandwich counter on his way to make a telephone call, Antonioni cuts away from the call to some luscious red tomatoes about to be seduced by a hero sandwich. Indeed, Antonioni's relentless aestheticism dilutes his ideological impact at every turn. If he had photographed the Nazi death camps, he would have found the most beautiful compositions available for that sort of material. This absurd dilemma of a *Vogue* photographer with a Marxist overview is Antonioni's curse and glory. It makes me enjoy *Zabriskie Point* more than I really respect it, but I can't help thinking that I belong to a minority of a minority in the pleasure I derive from dynamic visual forms for their own sake. Without pleasing performances, zippy dialogue and an unspoken complicity with the guilt-ridden but oh-so-comfortable affluence of America, Antonioni's art must carry *Zabriskie Point* single-handed, and that may not be enough to pay the rent in Culver City. But no one who takes cinema seriously can afford to pass up this latest canvas from the palette of the Michelangelo for our own time and our own medium.

THE STRAWBERRY STATEMENT

I have no particular quarrel with Jack Newfield's comments on *The Strawberry Statement* carried in *The Voice* of June 25, 1970, and I make no special brief for the film though I am not turned off by it quite as much as other people are. The main problem with the movie is that it started out with no plot and tried to compensate with an excessive number of camera angles. But one of Newfield's points intrigued me, and I assumed he must have gotten his information from the horse's (or Leo the Lion's) mouth. According to Newfield, the original ending of *Strawberry Statement* showed the male protagonist (nicely played, incidentally, by Bruce Davison) actually killed by the police. The allegedly new ending and allegedly on James Aubrey's orders shows Davison frustrated and brutalized by the police in a series of stop-motion freeze frames on his way to aid his girl friend (very ultra-professionally played, incidentally, by Kim Darby). Newfield complains also that the movie tries to placate right-wing audiences by showing students roughing up the gendarmes before the final bust and that the protagonist is shown with a picture of the late Bobby Kennedy in his room, whereas in the book James Simon Kunen proclaimed himself a supporter of Eugene McCarthy. On a more aesthetical level, Newfield criticizes the crudity of the pop-music background, and proceeds to wonder aloud how *The Strawberry Statement* could possibly have won any prizes at Cannes.

Without having been at Cannes, I would imagine that *The Strawberry Statement* was somewhat overrated because no other country in the world would allow its film-makers comparable freedom to denounce domestic institutions and policies. The French can criticize the Greeks, and the Italians can criticize the French in Algeria, and the Russians can criticize the Chinese, but scathing self-criticism is relatively rare in the goldfish bowl of high-budgeted movie-making. That Metro-Goldwyn-Mayer should have lent its corporate resources to what is, after all, the most pro-student, anti-cop movie ever made anywhere should at least be a cause for rejoicing among pro-student and anti-cop people. But if Newfield's reaction is a reliable criterion, such is not to be the case. *The Strawberry Statement* is not to be commended for going 90 percent of the way, and it struck this observer as almost sickeningly pro-student, but condemned for not going the final 10 percent into the funeral parlor of political martyrdom in commemoration of the student slayings at Kent State.

We are back again in the familiar political terrain of all or nothing, dump the Hump even if it means getting Nixon, and let's get a pure-peace candidate on a fourth slate in 1972 to make sure that Nixon is re-elected even if we're not sure that 1976 won't see elections replaced by a royal referendum supervised by Billy Graham and George Gallup. And as we're carted away to concentration camps, we can speculate about what might have happened if Bobby Kennedy had lived and Franklin D. Roosevelt had lived and Che had lived and, above all, if we had lived instead of spending all our time in the fashionable cemeteries ascribing virtues to the dead they never displayed when they were alive.

I agree with Newfield that something doesn't ring true in *The Strawberry Statement* but I would draw up an entirely different set of particulars to explain my objections. First of all, the book was set in Columbia and concerned very real people like Mark Rudd and Grayson Kirk and, of course, James Simon Kunen. The biggest chunk of the book is concerned with what happens to Kunen after the big bust, and the book as a whole comes out piecemeal as a marginal, somewhat skeptical memoir. (Bruce Davison's personality captures much of the wholesomely skeptical flavor of the book, and I liked Kunen's cameo appearance in the film.) The movie is set in some anonymous institution in the San Francisco Bay area without being either Berkeley (the historical continuity of radicalism) or San Francisco State (the sudden eruption of black power with muscle). Why? The book makes no sense apart from the uniquely incestuous power relationships at Columbia University and throughout Manhattan Island. Also, Newfield is well informed enough about the book to know that its author is still very much alive and with us, and so how could the movie ring more true if his alter ego on the screen were to be killed by the cops? The book is about Columbia, and no student was killed at Columbia in the police bust. The book is not about Kent State or South Carolina or Mississippi or San Francisco. It is about Columbia and New York. I don't say that *The Strawberry Statement* would have been a better movie if it had been set at Columbia even to the point of showing us Mark Rudd in glorious Technicolor. But it would have been a more intelligent movie if it had at least made a stab at recapturing James Simon Kunen's revolutionary in the rye as he found himself an instant celebrity on the malicious media we all hate so much even as we are powdered by the make-up man.

There is no doubt, however, that a great deal of tampering has gone on with the movie. Most spectacular of all, perhaps, is the excision of the fellatio simulation under the severe gaze of a Che poster, a sequence that so convulsed Cannes that the director himself (Stuart Hagman) told a press conference that he was having second thoughts about the episode. As the scene was described to me, a girl (not the one played by Kim Darby) apparently comes down (below the screen) on our hero, and all we see really are his eyes becoming glazed. I wonder why the scene was cut? Is it that fellatio and revolution do not really mix? Or is it that the juxtaposition of sensual pleasure with the iconography of Che Guevara might be considered ideologically incorrect if not downright sacrilegious? I don't know, and, frankly, I don't care. As Alfred Hitchcock once told one of his brightest stars, who had burst into tears of temperament, "It's only a movie, Ingrid."

THE GREAT WHITE HOPE

The Great White Hope was considerably overpraised as a play, partly as a reflex reaction to its roaring out against racism in America and partly as a testimonial to the alleged vitality of so-called regional theater, a largely mystical entity which double-domed theater pundits were pushing last year as a form of cultural decentralization to purify bad old Broadway. For whatever reason, Howard Sackler's drama managed to garner the Pulitzer Prize and the New York Drama Critics and Antoinette Perry awards for 1969. Sackler himself wrote the screenplay, and Martin Ritt directed the movie with what, at times, amounts to Famous Players fidelity to the stage production.

But suddenly the spell seems to have been broken. No longer do masochistic movie reviewers diagnose their own discomfort as another instance of Hollywood hacks betraying the divine drahma. No indeed. They go right back to the source of the trouble, and to hell with the Pulitzer Prize and the New York Drama Critics and the Antoinette Perry puffs. Howard Sackler wrote a bad play, which was badly performed, and almost everyone was taken in by it, or at least pretended to be taken in by it.

Why? Well, when James Earl Jones as Joe Jefferson alias Jack Johnson beats his chest like a tom-tom and rumbles out his basso profundo challenge to a guilt-ridden white liberal audience, it is admittedly difficult for that audience to avoid looking with glazed eyes beyond the stage to the ugly realities outside. The old problem of extracting the ethics from aesthetics bedevils the brashest reviewer whenever the race problem is raised. It is so easy to be misunderstood. So easy and so dangerous. Hence, any reasoned judgment of The Great White Hope becomes almost impossible in the wild oscillation between extreme critical caution (racism is always relevant) and extreme critical bravado (racism is the last refuge of thesis drama).

Howard Sackler's tactics in treating the shameful story of Jack
Johnson's ordeal as World Heavyweight Champion from 1908 to
1915 may be rationalized as Marxist and/or Brechtian, but even so,
the treatment of the central character and his milieu is neither coherent or consistent. I don't go along with the current criticism of
Sackler and Ritt for not letting the movie tell it exactly like it was
(the time-honored realism argument). The Great White Hope is
much more a race movie than a fight movie, and so be it. The
trouble is that Sackler and Ritt move from an overly explicit exposition of the basic problem to an increasingly vague development of
that problem's effect on the black champion and his white mistress.
Dramatic psychology is sacrificed, almost absent-mindedly, to racial
mythology. And thus as I have watched both play and film, I have
found my attention wandering from the awkward histrionics in
front of me to the more complex historical presences lurking behind
stage and screen.

The best writing I have ever read on the subject is the late John
Lardner's two-part article in The New Yorker of June 25 and July 2,
1949, entitled "The White Hopes." Earlier that year Joe Louis had
retired from the heavyweight championship in an atmosphere of relative good will, racially speaking. Indeed, Lardner pegged his articles
on the contrast between the Johnson years and the Louis years.
Whereas Louis proposed and effected a match between the two
men, both black, whom he considered best qualified to fight for his
title, Johnson was subjected to a steady stream of white hopes without ever being consulted. Lardner was very careful, however, to qualify the contrast in periods with the observation that Louis might
have had less trouble in Johnson's time than Johnson did, and Johnson more trouble in Louis' time than Louis did. And it is well that
Lardner provided this qualification, for with the advent and mis-
adventures of Cassius Clay–Muhammad Ali, the relevance of Jack
Johnson becomes more painfully pointed. Ali, like Johnson, has
been everything that Louis was not in his championship years—arro-
gant, proud, boastful, stubborn, ostentatious, even a bit sadistic beyond the functional demands of his profession.

But there are crucial differences as well between Ali and Johnson.
Ali is more overtly political, even factionally political, than Johnson
ever dreamed of being. Johnson's greatest offense against public

opinion in the early 1900s was his open preference for white women. Lardner even quoted Johnson first hand on the subject: " 'I didn't court white women because I thought I was too good for the others, like they said,' he told me one day in the 1930's, when he was working as a sideshow attraction at Hubert's Museum, on West 42nd Street, a few years before he died in an automobile accident. 'It was just that they treated me better. I never had a colored girl that didn't two-time me.' "

Sackler's script glosses over the multiple connotations of Johnson's self-professed womanizing by caricaturing the villainous faithlessness of Joe Jefferson's black wife while idealizing the crusading fidelity of his white mistress. (Johnson was actually married three times, his second wife, white like his third, having committed suicide.) By making Johnson more relentlessly monogamous, Sackler deflects the audience's attention from the internal feelings of the characters most concerned to the external pressures of a racist society. But all around the edges of the drama there are dissenting murmurs—a Black Power prophet here (Moses Gunn), a massah-dear mammy there (Beah Richards), little dribs and drabs of racial dialectics which evoke more complexities than they explain. With one eye on the black theoreticians and the other on the theater parties, Sackler balances off the bloated rhetoric about white devils with an Odetsian Jewish fight manager called with endearing condescension "Goldie" (Lou Gilbert).

James Earl Jones acts Joe Jefferson with the loftily liberal knowingness with which Paul Robeson once played the Emperor Jones. On stage, Jones acted by fits and starts, and his voice lacked expressive resonance. He lurched about more with the inexorability of a golem than with the grace of a fighter. So much so that he had made me completely forget the interestingly disciplined performance he gave as the bombardier in Dr. Strangelove. But I remembered that performance when I saw him go into the malignantly self-mocking rendition of Uncle Tom in the movie version of The Great White Hope. The effect is still too broad, too theatrical, in fact, but it is the kind of theatricality that belongs more on the screen than on the stage. Jones is at this point more a stirring presence than an accomplished actor, and he is not up to the kind of Brechtian role playing and commenting that the Sackler script calls for, and, besides, the great contribution of D. W. Griffith to the cinema was not montage (and certainly not race relations) but rather the development of a privileged sanctuary for the actor to express his most intimate feelings with the most delicate gestures. *The Great White Hope* represents a long step backward to the days of Italian divas like Lydia Borelli who waved their arms frantically in a show of emoting. But I think Duse herself would have asked her director for a more oblique camera treatment of the dreadful scene in which James Earl Jones is asked to heave with Herculean sorrow over the soggy corpse of Jane Alexander.

The Great White Hope does not exaggerate the rampant racism of American life between 1908 and 1915, a period in which Jack Johnson was both persecuted and prosecuted for being too uppity. Indeed, the evidence of racism is so overwhelming that Howard Sackler's play and screenplay run the risk of incurring the intellectual sin of obviousness. Some subjects, in and of themselves, are too morally one-sided for the dialectical demands of drama. What is one to say on the most literal level about the Nazi death camps or apartheid in South Africa beyond cease and desist we pray you or lest we forget.

Unfortunately, Sackler's attempt to avoid the curse of cant results only in psychological obfuscation and ideological confusion. All the sound and fury of James Earl Jones's performance, and all the whimpering and whining of Jane Alexander's, never gets us any closer into the core of their drama together as a doomed couple. Martin Ritt's Philco Playhouse staging of the indoor scenes is so unimaginatively three-wallish that we never feel either privacy or intimacy.

Ultimately, Sackler's politicalization of the subject subordinates the sensuality of a fact to the rhetoric of a right. A self-mocking joke about sunburn across the color line is boomed beyond the bed and across the footlights so that we can all laugh too comfortably about the absurdity of discrimination. And all the time the character of Joe Jefferson is kept in the limbo of innocence betrayed. By the time the white devils of the fight game, our shameful surrogates historically and allegorically, have completed their conniving, Joe Jefferson has been battered into a bloody hulk beyond good and evil, beyond irony and ambiguity, beyond edification and catharsis.

However, *The Great White Hope* raises other questions that are never even considered, much less answered, in Sackler's one-issue presentation. Jack Johnson was a fighter, a man of violence, a professional inflicter of pain on other men. The spectacle of one man hurting another is, under any circumstances, morally ambiguous. The enjoyment of this spectacle is even more dubious. I am happy that Ali vindicated himself after being wrongfully and hypocritically stripped of his title, but I cannot rejoice that Jerry Quarry required eleven stitches to close the cut over his eye. I have not reached that stage of ideological commitment that would enable me to regard Jerry Quarry as any less human than Muhammad Ali. (I wince even when I see old fight films of Max Schmeling being demolished by Joe Louis in their second fight.) No man is an island apart from me, and no man's pain can leave my own conscience painless. It is not that I wish to ban boxing or anything like that. It is simply that boxing, like all other sports and wars and competitions, is more fact than fable. Some people win and some people lose, and afterward the commentators draw the appropriately moralistic conclusions, which are, more often than not, the most rancid of rationalizations. If Joe Namath throws five touchdown passes, hurrah for the swinging singles, and if Fran Tarkenton throws five touchdown passes, hurrah for Sunday school and clean living.

The late John Lardner observed in his *New Yorker* articles that the four best fighters of Johnson's time, apart from Johnson himself, were Sam Langford, Joe Jeannette, Sam McVey, and Harry Wills, all blacks, and hence racially ineligible to qualify as white hopes and indeed challengers of any kind. Johnson himself rationalized his reluctance to take any of them on with the frank admission that the meager gate would not be worth the major risk. Langford, Jeannette, McVey and Wills were so good, in fact, that they seldom received the opportunity to fight any white pugs, and on the rare occasions they did they were strongly urged by the all-powerful white promoters to avoid delivering knockout punches.

This extraordinarily unfair situation would seem to be a thing of the past. Whatever your politics, Ali and Frazier are both black, and it would seem that in the fight game we have come a long way in rewarding pugilistic talent regardless of race, but I say "seem" advisedly because it is quite clear that the white race has farmed out the heavyweight championship to what it considers the lowest orders.

For all the vaunted violence of American life, few parents above the subsistence level encourage their boys to dream of becoming heavyweight champions of the world anymore. The lower East Side Odetsian sagas of the Jewish or Italian boy who must choose between his violin and fame and fortune no longer have the slightest sociological underpinning. Max Baer was the last of the credible Jewish heavyweights, Marciano the last of the Italians, and Quarry could be the last scrappy Irishman to be a contender. Middle America prefers the controlled violence of pro football, and there is where the crunch is still felt, not so much on the Johnson–Ali level of recognizably superlative talent but on the Langford, Jeannette, McVey, Wills level of either intermediate or indeterminate talent.

But by being too stark and too abstract and too allegorical, *The Great White Hope* actually distracts us from the refinements of current cruelties by wailing too loudly about the rawer brutalities of another time. In this one respect, however, the film improves on the play by substituting the late Chester Morris' quietly manipulative fight promoter as a reasonably realistic white presence for the blustering, bellowing, bigoted poet laureate of white supremacy embodied by George Matthews on the stage. Morris reminds us as Matthews did not that reasonableness is the most pernicious aspect of and attitude to racism. Still, Lardner's oblique treatment of the racism in the Johnson years is more persuasively critical of White America than all of Sackler's flat-footed forensics.

For one thing, Lardner contoured his articles around the crooked contortions of the fight racket, and thus provided a left-handed parody of capitalistic exploitation. As it was, the white hopes themselves were so many lambs led to the slaughter, sometimes literally as well as figuratively. Maimed, mangled and mutilated to the roar of the crowd, they took on the role not so much of the glorious matador as of the gored bull. And for all their sufferings, they usually ended up being swindled by the system. Jack Johnson was part of that system, and he was accustomed to the fast shuffle and the double cross. On one occasion, according to Lardner, Johnson was fighting Stanley Ketchel, a much lighter man, both skinwise and weightwise, under a gentleman's agreement that no knockout punches would be attempted. When Ketchel rared back and floored Johnson with a fully swung white hand, the champion, in Lardner's words, "recognized the blow as sincere to the point of treachery. He was used to double crosses, and had had signal success in frustrating them. Rising, he hit Ketchel in the face so hard that the middleweight's lips were impaled on his teeth. He was unconscious for an hour."

The Johnson–Ketchel fight is not even fictionally referred to in *The Great White Hope*, even though it is this fight that persuaded Jack Jeffries to come out of retirement for the purpose of upholding the honor of White America. I did happen to see the Ketchel fight on film some years ago as part of a television series, and I was most struck by the period defensive style with which Johnson fought the fight. He seemed the last of the great classical fighters as Dempsey was the first of the great modern fighters. The point is I did feel the patina of pastness settling on his reputation and upon an era in which men thought nothing of fighting for twenty, thirty and forty rounds.

As corrupt and brutal as boxing may be, it does have its own logic and nuance, and the James Earl Jones King Kong characterization of Johnson is somewhat unfaithful to the ironic fact that Johnson depended more on speed and guile than brute strength. And this adds a further complication to the problems Johnson (and Ali) have had with certain segments of the bloodthirsty public. Great defensive fighters simply do not bleed enough. They also don't take enough chances with their opponents, nor score as many clean pow! bam! knockouts. Thus, Jim Corbett was never really as popular as John L. Sullivan, nor Gene Tunney as Jack Dempsey; nor Ezzard Charles and Floyd Patterson as Jersey Joe Walcott and Rocky Marciano. By contrast, with Johnson and Ali, Joe Louis created in the ring the atmosphere of a jungle in which at any moment the hunter might be brought down by the hunted, and this is what fight fans all lust for, a sense of mystery, suspense and danger, not a neat night's work accomplished with the monotonously rhythmic thrusts of a left jab on a slower man's skin tissue. Ali, like Johnson before him, does a neat night's work and is not about to let himself get marked up to satisfy the blood lust of the ringside ghouls.

The Great White Hope doesn't go into any of these questions possibly because to do so would mean raising moral questions of an absurdist order such as why do Mafia chieftains discriminate against blacks in the recruiting of gunmen. Hence, ring action is kept to a minimum so as to allow more time for the rhetoric of racism, and every time James Earl Jones blows up on stage or screen we are encouraged to believe the cause is invariably racial persecution untainted by any innate meanness of spirit. This overloading of sympathy I find incredibly naïve. Indeed, a little more meanness would have made the character infinitely more believable and his plight infinitely more moving.

Curiously, the movie does finally venture out into a still disputed historical terrain that the play avoided like the plague. In short, did Jack Johnson actually throw the championship fight to Jess Willard in Havana in 1915 or was he legitimately defeated by a younger, stronger fighter? The play strongly implies, as Johnson did himself in what was described by Lardner as a somewhat fanciful autobiography, that the fight was indeed so much of a tank job that it splashed under the hot Havana sun. The movie is more ambiguous. Sackler suggests (in both versions) that some sort of deal was arranged on the Mann Act conviction. If so, Johnson was double-crossed again because he finally served out almost his entire sentence. Lardner suggested more plausibly that the deal entailed money and film rights to the tune of at least thirty thousand dollars.

Last year, a compilation of fight films entitled *The Legendary Champions* professed to prove that the controversial still photo of Johnson apparently shielding his eyes from the hot sun as he was being counted out created a misleading impression that was corrected by the motion-picture footage of the fight long unavailable to the American public because of the fear of race riots. The motion-picture footage shows Johnson's legs (drawn up in the still photograph) slowly sagging down till they were flush with the canvas. But it must be recorded that Lardner himself never considered the evidence of the still photograph conclusive evidence. We may never know what actually happened on that racist afternoon in Havana, but what little we do know is infinitely more interesting and complicated than Howard Sackler's shrill simplistics would indicate.

GAWKING AT THE GEEKS

The geek in carnival parlance is a performer sunk so low that he will entertain morbid audiences by eating the head of a live chicken for a bottle of booze. As it happens, *The Groupies* is a film that treats girl camp followers of rock groups as if they (the girls) were geeks. And not only the girl camp followers but the even more pathetic gay groupies of San Francisco. No opportunity is missed to make groupies seem creatures of grubbiness and grotesqueness. A Swiftian close-up of false-eyelash plucking here, a rear-view shot of a skinny groupie squatting in a dirty bathtub there, unimaginatively foul language everywhere and the slightest sense of compassion nowhere. Consequently, audiences can gawk and giggle at the groupies without any problem of identification or recognition. Those are not human beings up there on the screen, but geeks, freaks, fiends, gargoyles spewed out by our pop-rock-cock culture like sewage spewed out by our cities into our waterways.

Not that *The Groupies* is much of a movie even by the generously permissive standards of rock-group revues. More often than not, the studiously nervous camera of co-directors Ron Dorfman and Peter Nevard gets in the way of their musical performers, particularly Joe Cocker, the splendid spastic who requires stable medium shots to render his convulsive art most effectively on the screen. The other rock entertainers seem to confuse percussive repetition with poetic rapture, and even Joe Cocker was far more rousing in *Woodstock* than he is here in *The Groupies*. Still, the rock performers around whom the groupies somewhat murkily gravitate do manage to retain a certain amount of dignity. They at least have their music to turn to when the menacing microphone of Dorfman and Nevard becomes obscenely obtrusive. Indeed, frame after frame of *The Groupies* is so amateurishly violated by the illusion-destroying microphone that this electronic instrument provides a phallic fillup of its own in a film that is ostentatiously phallic without being erotic. But the intrusion of the microphone serves also to reinforce the impression that the contrivers of *The Groupies* were interested less in psychological exploration than in psychotic exhibitionism. Far from concealing their microphone and camera, Dorfman and Nevard point them like weapons at their attention-starved subjects. But like Pilate on his cynical quest for truth, they do not wait around long enough for an answer, nor even long enough for a pattern of personality to emerge. And, of course, no hard and fast factual information is supplied to place the footage in some sort of psychological or sociological perspective. Who are these groupies, and where do they come from, and what are their families like, and how old are they really, and how do they differ from the more reserved rock fans (like that marvelously skeptical black girl in one of the last scenes)? There are no answers to these questions in *The Groupies*, and there is no compensating spectacle to take up the slack. Stylistically, Dorfman and Nevard hover between the boring impassivity of Andy Warhol and the dynamic superficiality of Russ Meyer, and they achieve the worst of both worlds with a movie as visually boring as *The Chelsea Girls* and as intellectually superficial as *Beyond the Valley of the Dolls* with neither Warhol's compassion nor Meyer's dynamism ever balancing the aesthetic accounts.

My first instinct is to denounce *The Groupies* as the nastiest movie of the year, a murkily photographed slice of Spiro Agnew cinema at least three years out of date and the latest demonstration of ripping off the pop-youth scene with calculated contempt. Unfortunately, *The Groupies* is less an isolated instance of messy moviemaking than a reflection of the increasingly immoral voyeurism of contemporary movie-making in the so-called realistic mold. And as the voyeurism increases in scope and intensity, so does the exhibitionism. I am sure the makers of *Groupies* had no trouble persuading people in the movie to sign releases. Indeed, many of the girls most ridiculed and reviled by the microphone and camera preen themselves as if they were embarked on the road to fame to fortune. One girl has gotten herself up almost as a darker-haired double of Lee Remick and another as a dry run for Shirley MacLaine. A third, popping up late in the proceedings, would give Barbara Hershey and

Lauren Hutton fairly stiff competition in the pouty-pretty-putting-one's-thing-together sweepstakes. But even these favorably endowed creatures are befouled by the banality and obscenity of the film-maker's attitude toward them. Thus the most beautiful girl in the movie ends up seeming boring and stupid simply because there is no attempt to probe beneath the pat phrases of her peer group. The less pretty girls are treated with even greater cruelty, though I am sure that they are too dazzled by the glare of publicity and notoriety to mind the loss of dignity and privacy. But that isn't the point. There is an implied moral commitment in film-making even to people suffering from self-hatred. We are not morally entitled to shoot a person who says he wants to die, and neither is a director morally entitled to degrade a person who wishes to make a fool of himself. A great many people in our society are apparently willing to sacrifice their dignity and privacy for relatively little money and publicity. Alex de Renzy alleges in *A History of the Blue Movie* that a steady procession of hippie couples in San Francisco eagerly volunteer to perform in his professionally photographed stag movies, and de Renzy demonstrates the results with equal eagerness. Curiously, he displays less contempt, cruelty and condescension toward his subjects than Dorfman and Nevard display toward theirs. But then, de Renzy, unlike Dorfman and Nevard, is posing neither as a serious artist nor as a social conscience. He's not really moral either, but at least he doesn't pretend to be smugly superior to his material.

THE CAREER OF A CENSOR

"Being a censor," Jack Vizzard tells us in the very first sentence of his memoir, See No Evil, "is like being a whore; everyone wants to know how you got into the business." After the back-slapping geniality of this beginning, we are treated to a series of rowdy anecdotes, the punch lines of which were until very recently verboten on the silver screen Mr. Vizzard helped police with the Production Code. Indeed, the code itself (usefully reprinted at the end of the book) specifically forbade the use of the word "whore" under Article V (Profanity). Thus from the outset Mr. Vizzard's ribald recollections attest to the abiding hypocrisy of all censorship.

Not that Vizzard was exactly a censor in the most inquisitorial sense of the role. Mandated by neither civil nor ecclesiastical authority, he was for almost a quarter of a century more the self-imposed superego of the movie studios themselves, their willing instrument of self-flagellation designed to escape the unknown and untested perils of statutory regulation. Vizzard himself does not so much defend self-censorship as rationalize it as the least of many evils ranging from anarchy to theocracy. Time and again he finds himself caught in the middle between the libertarians and the Legion of Decency, but as much as he professes his own moderation he always ends up sounding ridiculously smug and repressive.

Particularly outrageous is his recollection of an encounter between the Code office and Charles Chaplin over the scenario for *Monsieur Verdoux*:

It was the Code contention that the dialogue clouded the distinction between right and wrong. "These speeches," we stated, "indicate what purports to be the inconsistency of applauding those who kill in war as great heroes and, at the same time, condemning to death those who murder." Latent in this line of reasoning, too, was the sentimental argument that the murderer himself was the product of injustice, having been forced to kill in order to raise the money to support his needy household.

Chaplin retorted that we were indulging in a philosophical question, not a moral one. He doubted that anyone, including the devisers of the Production Code, could determine exactly what is right and what is wrong. "The Dialogues of Plato have struggled with that question."

With such arguments did Chaplin dig his grave as a would-be intellectual. He left behind him an image of a smallish man, brisk as a cricket. with beautiful silvery hair, and somewhat sensual lips—but stubborn, as only a person with limited academic resources is apt to be, and, in his style, narcissistic.

It takes a certain ignoble eminence to be able to look down on one of the greatest artists the cinema has produced as an ill-educated insect. It is hardly surprising that Vizzard's favorite Hollywood people were the foul-mouthed studio executives with whom he established a kind of big-city-machine-melting-pot Jewish-Jesuitical understanding against the anarchic artists on the lower level of the Hollywood pecking order. But no producer, not even the late, unlamented Harry Cohn, seemed to be more foul-mouthed than Joe Breen, the most censorious of all the self-censors and the man who almost single-handedly put Mae West out of business, destroyed the subjective gangster movie genre of *Scarface, Little Caesar, Public Enemy, Quick Millions,* etc., drastically reduced the erotic élan of James Cagney and Jean Harlow and made movies second-class entertainments by denying them the relative freedom of books and plays. Breen and his cohorts could not have done all their damage without the assistance of a film industry too craven and too greedy to risk the loss of a single customer on the altar of artistic freedom. And when the Production Code finally did collapse, it was more desperate greed than belated emancipation that enabled Albert Finney in *Tom Jones* and Sean Connery in *Goldfinger* and Melina Mercouri in *Never on Sunday* to do in the Sixties what Cagney, Harlow and West had been forbidden to do in the Thirties.

Even through the late Sixties, however, Vizzard continued to think in the company way, particularly when Michelangelo Antonioni had the audacity to insist on the right of final cut for *Blow-Up:* "The film is not Antonioni's," Vizzard insists. "Surely it bears his signature. But that is what he has sold. He is, to put it plainly, not anything else but a contractee. Had he, in a spurt of altruism, put up his own money, as well as his time and his talents, then he would be completely at liberty to gamble with his very own product. But when he is only surrogate for the resources of others, then it is pompous to attribute to him the prerogatives of ownership. The Executive, which is the proxy for the investor, has every right to exercise quality controls either directly or through designees, and this is properly called 'self-regulation.' "

By this line of reasoning, Vizzard would have undoubtedly upheld the right of Pope Julius II to alter Michelangelo's contracted labors on the Sistine ceiling. After all, neither Michelangelo, then or now, was so altruistic as to put up his own money. Vizzard and his entire order of self-righteous fixers thus emerge as mere minions of what was once Hollywood's corporate state.

My first instinct is to consign this book to the shelf containing the collected wisdom of Spiro Agnew, but, ultimately, its disarming disingenuousness makes it recommended reading for today's yes-but libertarians like Dr. Spock, who, while defending the right of political dissent, would like to see some restraints placed on nudity, obscenity, pornography and all forms of supposedly non-political permissiveness. But once the censors are let loose, as they were in Hollywood back in 1934, they will inevitably employ sexual modesty as a shield behind which the status quo may be rigidly protected. No more movies like *The Liberation of L. B. Jones* with intimations of corrupt policemen. No more miscegenation: "Production Code: Article II. (sex) 6. Miscegenation (sex relationship between the white and black races) is forbidden." Jack Vizzard has unwittingly performed a service for those libertarians, unlike Dr. Spock, who believe that all freedoms are indivisible.

V.

ODES AND OBITS

JOSEF VON STERNBERG (1894–1969)

The death of Josef von Sternberg followed a long period
of enforced inactivity in his chosen profession. A legend resurrected
in his own lifetime, Sternberg was a frequent guest of festivals, museums, universities and other embalming institutions. But there were
no calls from the studios, and all the dream projects of his late years
were effectively aborted. The unpublished writer, the unsold
painter, the uncommissioned sculptor, the unsung composer may all
be discouraged by neglect, but their output is still physically possible. By contrast, a film director cut off from financing is like a king
in exile, a creature dependent for his very functioning more on politics than on poetics.

Sternberg stood Hollywood on its head between 1927 and 1932.
These were the golden years of his Paramount Period: *Underworld*
(1927), *The Last Command* (1928), *The Docks of New York*
(1928), *The Blue Angel* (1930), *Morocco* (1930), and *Shanghai
Express* (1932), the most beautifully photographed body of work in
the history of the cinema. These were works that depended less on
literary or theatrical tricks than on stunning visual images floating
across the screen as if from an expressionistic director's dream. Scen-
ery, props, even bits and pieces of cloth, net and confetti were transformed by Sternberg's extraordinary flair for lighting and composition into self-contained worlds of mystery, ambiguity, sensuality and
joyless revelry.

Then suddenly the box-office magic was gone. Beauty was out and
brashness was in. The last two Dietrich films von Sternberg directed
for Paramount, *The Scarlet Empress* (1934) and *The Devil Is a
Woman* (1935), may seem like dazzling exercises in ironic splendor
today, but back in the Great Depression audiences stayed away in
droves from what the critics denounced as von Sternberg's unforgiv-

able self-indulgence. Sternberg and Dietrich parted company, each scrambling for survival in a world that, amid bread lines, had tired of cake. But in all the years after von Sternberg was never allowed to forget that he had served as a stylish Svengali to Marlene Dietrich's luminous screen image.

It is to Sternberg's credit that he never bent his style to the winds of fashion. His last film—*Anatahan*—is as delirious, obsessive, romantic and personal as his first—*The Salvation Hunters*. Indeed, among all the twenty-six movies he directed between 1925 and 1953, we need not search for slumbering allegories of Man and God and Life, but rather for a continuous stream of emotional autobiography focused on the dilemmas of desire that torment men and women eternally.

What seems astonishing today in any systematic retrospective of his career is the subtlety and lucidity of the feelings he expressed in even the wildest melodramas. The obituaries reported that Sternberg had suffered a heart attack ten days before his death and that he had entered a hospital in Los Angeles without notifying friends. One cannot help recognizing in this final melodrama of his life some of the unobtrusive grace and gallantry exhibited by the doomed protagonists of his films.

HAROLD LLOYD (1893–1971)

Even at his peak Harold Lloyd had neither Keaton's sublime serenity nor Chaplin's passionate poetry, but he was often funnier than either just the same. Lloyd was the man in the crowd, on the subway, in the elevator, at the office. He was the country boy who made good in the city less through inspiration than perspiration, and the skyscrapers from which he so often dangled expressed not only the upward mobility of his aspirations but also his morbid fear of falling back into the herd below. Ambition glinted in his glasses along with a wistful yearning for approval. Whereas Chaplin's balletic tramp struggled for survival and Keaton's saintly acrobat searched for the ecstasy of equilibrium, Lloyd's white-collar Everyman strained for success on the American Plan. It follows that though with Chaplin and Keaton we feel that we shall never see their like again, Lloyd's spiritual facsimile is an even-money bet to turn up at the next convention of the Shriners, the Rotarians or the Elks.

Lloyd's golden age was almost exclusively in the silents. From *Grandma's Boy* to *Speedy*, Lloyd fulfilled the wildest success fantasies of the so-called Jazz Age. He was less effective in the sound era, and even the very special farcical gifts of Leo McCarey (*The Milky Way*) and Preston Sturges (*Mad Wednesday*) were unable to resurrect Lloyd as a comic favorite. Audiences of the Thirties were somewhat baffled and put off by this zany optimist with more energy than charm. Still, Lloyd is hardly the only comedian who failed to cross the sound barrier. Keaton's fall was even more precipitous, and Langdon virtually disappeared. As Otis Ferguson remarked at the time, the comic tasks of the sound film were taken away from the stylized clowns of the silent era and passed out to a passel of realistic bit players. Nonetheless, Lloyd's fall was only partly technological.

His comic type simply became obsolete after the Crash. The aggressive values he had embodied in the giddy Twenties seemed downright irresponsible in the hungover Thirties. Besides, a certain loss of resilience was inevitable in a comic persona exposed in over a hundred and thirty movies from the administration of Woodrow Wilson through that of Harry Truman. As it is, *The Freshman* seems as fresh and funny today as it must have seemed back in 1925 when college football knighthood was still in flower. And there is no better barometer of immortality than the earnest laughter of revival audiences. As we laugh, Lloyd lives.

THAT HAMILTON WOMAN

I have seen *That Hamilton Woman* some eighty-three times at last count, and that doesn't include free television viewings. That is to say that on eighty-three separate occasions I plunked down coin of the realm for the privilege of watching Vivien Leigh and Laurence Olivier impersonate Lady Hamilton and Lord Nelson in history, Emma and Horatio biographically, Viv and Larry iconographically. By any reasonably objective standard of aesthetic worth, this admission should come under the heading of Confessions of a Misspent Youth. The first question that suggests itself is why; the second how. I shall try to answer the second question first. Between 1945 and 1952 New York possessed an unusually large number of film revival houses, a much larger number, in fact, than today. Of course we movie buffs lacked movies on television back then, but we more than made up for it with a far-flung network of memory shops spread all over Manhattan. For some reason, *That Hamilton Woman* was always available somewhere or other almost invariably on a double bill with a turgid Merle Oberon vehicle entitled eponymously *Lydia*. (I once even went so far as to see *Lydia* all the way through, but most of the time I would catch only the last few moments with Oberon, Joseph Cotten and Alan Marshall in grotesque old-age powdered-white make-up reminiscing about lost and forgotten loves.) In those days the Forty-second Street houses concentrated on oldies rather than nudies, and it was possible to catch "classics" like *Scarface* and *Street Scene* without undue fuss or fanfare. Nowadays I pass any number of Spanish ethnic theaters, sexploitation passion pits, television studios and supermarkets with a twinge of nostalgia for the happy hours I spent there in my improvident high-school and college days.

I was seventeen years old in 1945, and for the first time in my life

I had enough money in my pocket to indulge my moviemania. During the Depression I had been brought up, like most people, to walk in on double features and walk out after someone nudged you with that unmistakable this-is-where-we-came-in nudge. I found it unthinkable when I was a kid to see a movie more than once. Once you saw how the plot came out, what was there left to see? Even through most of high school I was more a bookworm than a movie bug. Indeed, I was such a compulsive reader that I would think nothing of reading two or three novels in a night. In 1943 I decided to go for the top academic honors in my class, and I stopped going to movies entirely. Not that I had been going to movies all that often even before 1943. In moviegoing, like everything else, I was a late starter, but once I started on anything—chocolate sundaes, sex, detective stories, basketball, crossword puzzles, chess, bowling, and you name it—I became crazily compulsive. I was a nut about elections and conventions, almost every form of spectator sport, newspapers, comic strips, not to mention the normal compulsions of the human male. And so it was relatively late in my voyeuristic life that I first discovered and was then devoured by the exquisitely aesthetical logic of the union of Vivien Leigh and Laurence Olivier. It may have been a childish infatuation on my part, but it was hardly a childhood infatuation. Back in 1939 I had managed to miss both *Gone with the Wind* with Vivien Leigh's dazzling green eyes and *Wuthering Heights* with Laurence Olivier's romantically ironic voice. I then compounded my ignorance and innocence by missing both Vivien Leigh's ladylike whore in *Waterloo Bridge* and Laurence Olivier's brooding aristocrat in *Rebecca*. And finally in 1941 I managed to avoid *That Hamilton Woman*. Needless to say, the disastrous Leigh–Olivier production of *Romeo and Juliet* in 1940 on the Broadway stage passed me by completely. Thus I was seventeen before I saw Vivien Leigh in *Gone with the Wind* and eighteen before I saw Laurence Olivier in *Henry V* and on the stage as Oedipus, Hotspur, Shallow, Puff and Astrov. I saw *Gone with the Wind* twenty-six times and *Henry V* a dozen, and I filled in on everything about my dream couple before and after their legendary if not mythical union. I began listening to theatrical gossip around Columbia University and once heard that Alfred Lunt and Lynn Fontanne were patronizing toward the Oliviers at a Bundles for Britain benefit after the *Romeo and Juliet* fiasco, and I have loathed the Lunts to this day for their slight.

What then was the extraordinary appeal of *That Hamilton Woman* to me? It's a rather sketchy rendering by any standard, and Olivier spends most of the movie with a patch over one eye and an otherwise ravaged countenance. The Battle of Trafalgar is boring as those things go, but as is so often the case with a movie by Alexander Korda, a certain care, a certain charm, even a modicum of wit creeps into the pageantry and the passion. It's nice the way Alan Mowbray says of Vivien Leigh's loose-living Emma that the pattern of her youth has been "lower and lower, and up and up." Anything spoken with a British accent seemed just that much wiser in those days.

One of Miklos Rozsa's lushly imperial scores (as opposed to his lyrically insane scores for *Spellbound* and *The Lost Weekend* and *The Killers*) cannot be underestimated as one of the factors in making me see *That Hamilton Woman* so many times. "Favorite" movies so often coincide with favorite scores. And to this day I can hum the score to *That Hamilton Woman* upon request. The contrived flashback structure of the story also contributed to the cyclical quality of the film so that it seemed eternally renewed from the moment in the beginning when a slatternly Vivien Leigh is trying to steal whiskey from a Calais wineshop to the moment when Heather Angel asks her what happened then, after, and Vivien replies there is no then, there is no after, and we are back in the beginning, she and I, numbed by the loss, but prepared to begin again at the very next screening.

Winston Churchill once hailed *That Hamilton Woman* as the greatest film he had ever seen, but Alexander Korda never exploited the quote because of fear of giving offense in the midst of Britain's fearful struggle against the Nazis, and later Churchill asked Korda why he hadn't used the quote in his advertising, and Korda explained, and Churchill said stuff and nonsense and the only reason he had made the statement was to help Korda at the box office. Still, I can see why an old imperialist like Winnie would love the film. After Lady Hamilton's first encounter with Horatio Nelson, she suddenly feels frivolously uninformed about world events, and she asks her husband Lord Hamilton (the aforementioned Alan Mowbray) to explain the background of the Napoleonic Wars. Mowbray takes her to a globe of the world and starts spinning it with the observation "All through history there have been men who have tried to destroy what other men have built." At one screening a group of Columbia eggheads began giggling at this bit of instant history, Marlborough Tory style, and I had to admit that Mowbray had overstated the case for the British Empire, but this had nothing to do with the enchantment of that magical moment when Olivier's Nelson says to Leigh's Emma, "People don't believe that there can be friendship between a man and a woman," and Vivien Leigh smiles with twinkling complicity: "Do you?" and Olivier slowly smiles back, his curling lips very slowly, very awkwardly creasing his cheeks, as he acknowledges for all time the precious privilege of being admitted to the arms of a beautiful woman with a marvelously grown-up sense of humor. On October 17, 1947, I was hit by a truck on my way back from a screening of *That Hamilton Woman* in a Greenwich Village theater. I was laid up in St. Vincent's Hospital for three months, and when I got out I had my own battle scars from the Battle of Trafalgar. I kept seeing *That Hamilton Woman* even after the accident, and I gradually realized that I had invested so much of my life up there on the screen that some day I would have to tell others what it had been like, and now I have in a way, but I have only scratched the surface, and there is more, much more to come. But I am sure that Nelson and Lady Hamilton have stolen my love by cleverly concealing their vulgar, reactionary personalities behind the façades of Laurence Olivier and Vivien Leigh, or Larry and Viv, as their intimates like Noël call them.

JUDY GARLAND

The agonizingly downward trajectory of Judy Garland's later life and career ended with her death (from an overdose of barbiturates) in the early-morning hours of June 22, 1969. She was forty-seven years old, but many of her mourners still wept over the little girl who had first sung "Over the Rainbow" in *The Wizard of Oz* more than thirty years before. To others Miss Garland's voice had always been larger than life and louder than art. Like Helen Morgan and Edith Piaf, she had somehow institutionalized her sorrows in a singing style that was tremulous, emotionally demanding, sometimes rasping and scraping in its plea for sympathy and understanding, and yet as often intuitively precise in its grasp of a lyric or feeling. It is not the least of the virtues of Mel Tormé's book (*The Other Side of the Rainbow*) on the late star that it helps bridge the chasm between those who remember her as Judy and those who regard her as Miss Garland.

The author was not there at the end; nor had he been in at the beginning. His life intersected Judy's in that period from May of 1963 until February of 1964 when he functioned as (in his own words) "Special Musical Material Writer and advisor on a CBS venture called 'The Judy Garland Show' (or, as one wag put it, 'The Noble Experiment')." Though Tormé's account is not overly encumbered with literary sensibility, it communicates a casual intimacy with its material from the inside out. Actually, the book does triple duty as biography (Miss Garland's), autobiography (Mr. Tormé's) and reportage (the ins and outs and ups and downs and rantings and ratings of a network television series). Tormé never presents himself as the ubiquitous, anonymous and invisible observer in search of the true Judy Garland but rather as a not so innocent bystander with his own ego on the line. Adding a note of poignancy to his memoir is his grown-up acceptance of the fact that whereas his subject had over-drawn on her talents he had never fully cashed in on his own.

Far from executing a Freudian fandango over a corpse, he never probes or pries into Garland's garish past. Indeed, he seems bored when she keeps bringing it up herself and even advises her not to rehash her old troubles with L. B. Mayer in front of a presumably indifferent public. And by not being excessively clinical and porten-tous, he manages to build up suspense over the impending disaster, not so much as to when or why it will occur but how.

Tormé himself continues to function inside the system that both made and mangled Judy Garland, and thus he hardly qualifies as an objective or even neutral observer of that system. Never questioned, for example, is the nebulous logic of the CBS network in pitting "The Judy Garland Show" against "Bonanza" on a winner-take-all bid for national ratings. The recent history of the medium is replete with instances of sophisticated shows being swamped in Trendex terms by cornpone attractions. (It probably all began when Law-rence Welk drove "The Show of Shows" off the video screen even as Sid Caesar, Carl Reiner, Howard Morris and an army of profes-sionals were doing scathing satires on the folksy amateurishness of the Welk show.) Hence, even if Judy Garland had attended all her rehearsals in a reasonably sober state after a good night's sleep and had put forth her most brilliant efforts for "The Judy Garland Show," there is still no guarantee that she would have bumped "Bo-nanza" in the ratings, nor even that the aura of sloppiness and scandal that surrounded her did not attract more viewers than were to be won over by mere polish and professionalism.

But being an insider has advantages as well as disadvantages, and not the least of the advantages here is an absence of moralizing cant in the treatment of show-biz celebrities. The author is remarkably generous in his assessment of others and, as a result, imparts gravity and dignity to the most embarrassing squabbles, most notably the running battle over Tormé's loss of status in appearing on screen as Judy Garland's personal voice conductor after having been lured to his behind-the-screen duties by a promise of guest shots for his own velvety foghorn of a voice. It may seem silly to an outsider (but not to Tormé) that so many grown men spent so many wee hours of the morning on Judy Garland's Dawn Patrol to hold her hand in the night and reassure her that this time she was really coming through the rainbow to confound all the old ogres at Metro who had pumped her full of pills and doubt and self-hatred and, as their final legacy, made her an ogre in their own image, pathetically power-hungry and plaintively resentful that her revenge, like all revenges, had come too late to end her sleepless nights.

The very title of the book makes it sound as if the author were out to get his own back at the expense of a beloved star. Nothing of the kind. Mel Tormé's book is a knowledgeable and lucid tribute to its subject in the spirit if not in the scope and genius of Sigmund Freud's tribute to Leonardo da Vinci. By confronting Judy Garland in her most monstrous moments and still being moved enough by the little girl behind the mythic persona to let bygones be bygones, Mel Tormé affirms the size of her talent more convincingly than any mindless claque ever could.

VI.
ARTS AND LETTERS

THE DOSTOEVSKY GAME

Samuel Astrachan's *The Game of Dostoevsky* is peopled exclusively by an assortment of literary gamesters, designated collectively as the Wolgamuts, who assemble in a Riverside Drive retreat overlooking the Hudson River and the New Jersey Palisades. These spatial cues evoke the academic background of Columbia University, to which the author refers with Russian reticence as "the University of Y" in New York City. An expanded Wolgamut version of Monopoly establishes that most of the players earn between six and fifteen thousand dollars per annum, most of them receiving additional small incomes from investments. The individual names of the Wolgamuts —Edgar Hope, Max Wise, Luther Halverson, Victoria Harm, Donald Marwel, Emily Marwel, Jane Robinson, Chester Mawr, Lucian Whittier, Charles Rizzo, Simon Parr—contain their share of allegorical overtones, and the customary obsessions, perversions and addictions are assigned, often with apparent aimlessness, to this field of eight men and three women: ten Gentiles and one Jew (Wise), not to mention at least one homosexual (Mawr).

The revelatory possibilities of Monopoly are quickly exhausted, to the point at least of establishing the ancestral shrewdness of Max Wise, a curiously masochistic projection of Sam Star, the tortured protagonist of Samuel Astrachan's highly regarded and quasi-autobiographical first novel, *An End to Dying*. The Wolgamuts are then initiated into the Game of Dostoevsky, a board operation in which the roll of the dice lands a player on one of the Seven Deadly Sins, thus prompting a confession in the name of some fictional character. A Grand Inquisitor judges the aptness of the confessions by granting or withholding Grace Cards, used to absolve players from future obligations to confess. During the introductory sessions, Astrachan begins computing his literary logarithms through one of

his characters: "Edgar made a mental note that Dostoevsky would
not do as a context. English novels would be best, the kind of books
in which the characters' sins are not explicit beyond a certain point
and thus are open to inference." The Wolgamuts soon settle, quite
wisely, on Henry James's *The Tragic Muse* and Jane Austen's *Pride
and Prejudice*.

But by then it is already cruelly apparent that the author is ill-
equipped to bring off this dangerous stunt in double-entry bookkeep-
ing. The graceful gestures under pressure of the invoked Jamesian
and Janean characters only help to expose the awkward affectations of Astrachan's puppets. For all its tastefulness, the book reminds us that the greatest novelists play for the highest stakes and
that there is nothing really at stake in the Game of Dostoevsky—
neither life, nor death, nor love, nor hate, nor success, nor failure,
nor careers, nor reputations, nor morals, nor values, nor even Monopoly money. Not only are the Wolgamuts too complacently satanic for their confessions to carry any weight; they are paralyzed
dramatically by a lack of immediate purposes and points.

Nothing crudely irrevocable happens beyond the ambiguous dis-
appearance of the pulp-writing, marijuana-smoking Luther Halverson, and two almost ritualistic intrusions of Negroes from the
Harlem Valley as a breed of fabulous felons out of a LeRoi Jones
play. Even when the author is describing a spectacle as outrageous as
an intersexual flogging frolic in a sauna bath, and with as much Bohemian bravado as he can muster, the effect of the description is to
muffle the action within the padded walls of stuffy, painless, bloodless fantasy.

If I have not discussed the author's dramatis personae in greater
detail, it is because he has fabricated biographies without creating
characters. The lack of genuine contrast and conflict, the absence of
gaiety and humor, and the remoteness of the characters from their
environment, all contribute to the sterile abstractness of a childless,
parentless, neighborless, almost classless world. The Wolgamuts
pipe out their personal paradoxes from a single, stereophonic sensibility and are differentiated as arbitrarily as bootleg whiskey poured
out of one jug into different brand bottles. Even if the author had
succeeded in executing his undeniably ambitious conception, the

aesthetic guardians of the Novel might have questioned the incestuous relation of a story to a seminar. Things being what they are, however, it must be reported that the Game of Dostoevsky will never replace Monopoly.

RICHARD GILMAN

Richard Gilman's new collection of writings, *Common and Uncommon Masks* (*The Confusion of Realms* was published only last year), continues the self-examination of a sensibility in search of a subject. *Common and Uncommon Masks*, an uncommonly turgid title for a book of brisk insights, contains seventy-four of the author's pieces (most relatively short), a refreshingly candid introduction and an invaluable index. What is both disconcerting and disarming about Mr. Gilman is that he seems to have become a drama critic almost in spite of himself.

"Still, though my interest in drama grew," Gilman writes of his earlier intellectual evolution, "I had no special incentive to write about it, except for some passing references in my other work. By the end of the fifties I was writing literary criticism and reviews for various publications, most frequently for *Commonweal*. One evening James Finn, the magazine's literary editor, asked me down for a drink and took me entirely by surprise with the question, Would I like to be their drama critic? I told him, which he of course knew, that I had no background in theatre, had nothing but an amateur perspective on it, and he replied that the editors liked my mind and writing and thought these better qualifications than any sort of presumed expertise."

And indeed there is nothing wrong with Gilman's mind and writing in *Common and Uncommon Masks*. He writes well and thinks clearly and argues persuasively. What is at issue is the intensity of his involvement with theater and with the grinding routine of reviewing. Gilman frequently cites as his high-minded antecedents such immortal journalists as Shaw and Beerbohm (though even the *Police Gazette* drama critic claims a kinship with Shaw and Beerbohm), Stark Young and George Jean Nathan. It may be argued that Gilman possesses their rigorous standards but certainly not their professional stamina.

Shaw is of course a special case, but Beerbohm and Nathan were stage-door dandies in comparison to the culturally fastidious Gilman. A mere six years of reviewing plays for *Commonweal* and *Newsweek* seem to have left Gilman more embittered than Beerbohm was after a dozen years with the *Saturday Review*, or than Nathan was after more than half a century on the firing line. "The only effect I could discern," Gilman writes of his ordeal, "apart from the few minds I might have taught to see drama a bit differently, was that I had gained a reputation for being sour, hypercritical, an outsider ranting against the party to which he hasn't been invited."

In an age when criticism seems to be flowering more richly than creation, Gilman's utilitarian criteria for his craft seem beside the point. Teaching a few minds "to see drama a bit differently" is as much as the greatest drama critics can reasonably expect for their labors, and even Shaw could not claim any final victory over the Philistines. In a piece entitled "The Necessity for Destructive Criticism," Gilman asks rhetorically and triumphantly: "And in which of our playhouses are the revivals of Sydney Grundy, Jerome K. Jerome and Arthur Wing Pinero, those manipulators of 'dead machinery' who were the Inge, Schary and Chayevsky of their day?"

Gilman asked this question in 1962, and here it is 1971 and Pinero's *Trelawney of the Wells* is flourishing off-Broadway at a time when Shaw's plays are nowhere to be seen on the horizon. The point is that Shaw's theater notices still enrich the reader's nights even if they do not carry the day with theatergoers. And thus 'tis a pity that Gilman should have renounced drama reviewing for the more formal didacticism of academe, and even more of a pity that he should have organized his book topically rather than chronologically so as to convert an inspired journalist (especially strong in particulars) into an indifferent essayist (especially weak in universals). What Gilman has not grasped throughout his restless career and in what he has chosen to reprint is that it is the critic that makes the subject and not the subject that makes the critic.

As it happens, *Common and Uncommon Masks* is so closely patterned in policy and structure to Robert Brustein's *Seasons of Discontent* that the casual reader of both volumes may lose track of where Brustein leaves off and Gilman begins. And backing up both Brustein and Gilman are the seminal essays of Francis Fergusson and Eric Bentley, comprising the academic artillery being fired (first from Columbia and now from Yale) at the Philistines in Sardi's and Shubert Alley, the entrenched Establishment of Lincoln Center and the Actors Studio, and the New Breed of Barbarians swarming south of 14th Street through the Living Theater and toward other assorted dead ends.

It is not too farfetched to suggest that Fergusson, Bentley, Brustein and Gilman represent an authentic revolution in the modern theater away from realism of both the poetic and prosaic variety toward a still undetermined fusion of the ironic and the absurd. With tragedy in tatters and comedy in confusion, these modern critics have turned to irony as the only link between the formality of theater and the flux of history. Chekhov, Pirandello, Brecht and Beckett are neither tragedians nor comedians but ironists, and a genuinely ironic sensibility is something unheard of on Broadway. Hence, even on the infrequent occasions of revivals of Chekhov, Pirandello, Brecht and Beckett, the ironies of the plays are swallowed up by the slobbering sentimentality of a realistic stage tradition.

In this constantly contentious period of cultural history, Fergusson functioned as a remote Hegelian influence on the revolutionaries, Bentley played Marx as he translated Brecht, Brustein was Lenin arriving at the Finland Station on the New Haven Railroad, and Gilman wound up playing Trotsky by succumbing to the tortured self-consciousness that prevented him from playing his historical role to the hilt. On the other side, Walter Kerr became the Kerensky of the revolution by betraying his academic origins to consort with the hatred bourgeoisie, and the drama critics of the *Village Voice* became the left-wing revisionists of Off-Off Broadway.

That I tend to agree with Gilman and his fellow revolutionaries more often than I do with the reactionaries on the right and the revisionists on the left may be attributed to the fact that I am interested more in dramatic literature than in ritualized theater. And I strongly suspect that Gilman and company gain their most fervent adherents from the ranks of those who would rather read a play than see it performed. Indeed, Gilman makes it clear on many occasions that he could live very happily in a world in which no theater was being performed, his primary obligations being to art and truth and all that.

But the very real charm of his pieces comes from the suggestion that he doesn't entirely believe all his doomsday declarations. After all, it was Beerbohm himself who wrote back in 1904: "A critic who wants the drama to be infinitely better than it is can hardly avoid the pitfall of supposing it to be rather worse than it is. Finding that it rises nowhere near to his standards, he imagines that it must be in a state of motionless prostration in the nethermost depths."

Gilman is ultimately strongest on the authors he loves iconoclastically and on the entertainments he discovers unexpectedly. Gilman on Ibsen, Büchner, Strindberg, Beckett and Ionesco is especially insightful—as is Gilman on Zero Mostel and Robert Redford and Bert Lahr. He is less appealing in his grudging toleration of *Barefoot in the Park* simply as a means of putting down Jean Kerr's *Mary, Mary*. And even his Ibsen piece is marred by his distortion of Mary McCarthy's comments on the subject, a distortion on Gilman's part that comes closer to in-fighting than insighting. Indeed, Gilman's evocation of Yeats to explain Jack Gelber's failure in *The Apple* could be applied to Gilman himself in his more polemical writings: "In this he represents the latest cautionary figure: the man who instead of making poetry out of his quarrel with himself, makes rhetoric out of his quarrel with others."

JACK KEROUAC

If the latest spiritual adventures of Jack Kerouac (*Satori in Paris*) lack the ebullience of earlier explorations, it may be because he is hunting down a pedigree rather than an identity. ("As in an earlier autobiographical book I'll use my real name here, full name in this case, Jean-Louis Lebris de Kerouac, because this story is about my search for this name in France.") By his own admission, Kerouac was forty-three years old when he braved Paris and Brittany. That's a bit old for a Dharma Bum drunk on Dante's Beatitude, a Rover Boy with a yen for Zen, a traveler of the Fifties who managed to bypass Marx and Freud on the road across the American continent.

Once upon a time it could be argued that the literary establishment was underestimating Kerouac's influence on a generation of vagrant visionaries, fellahin without fellowships. "Beat" was a movement and a mannerism, a dialect and a dialectic. Beat preceded Pop and Camp as a burp against liberal rhetoric and official culture.

Even in the beginning, however, Kerouac's Beatitude sounded as tinny as Henri Bergson's *élan vital*. Still, the evolution of a beat bohemian style did coincide with the collapse of liberal optimism in the Eisenhower era, and Kerouac lent the Beats their speech rhythms to the point that even Tennessee Williams could imitate them in Lois Smith's jukebox soliloquy in *Orpheus Descending*.

Kerouac still writes a blue streak, but his skyrocketing prose no longer illuminates the landscape. He now travels alone, out of his time and place, more like a Babbitt than a beatnik. He now seems to revel in a calculating callousness, particularly in his country-club put-down of "a half dozen eager or worried future writers with their manuscripts all of whom gave me a positively dirty look when they heard my name as tho they were muttering to themselves 'Kerouac?

I can write ten times better than that beatnik maniac and I'll prove it with this here manuscript called "Silence au Lips" all about how Renard walks into the foyer lighting a cigarette and refuses to acknowledge the sad formless smile of the plotless Lesbian heroine whose father just died trying to rape an elk in the Battle of Cuckamonga, and Phillipe the intellectual enters in the next chapter lighting a cigarette with an existential leap across the blank page I leave next, all ending in a monologue encompassing etc. all this Kerouac can do is write stories, ugh'"—Ugh, indeed. No there-but-for-the-grace-of-God-and-Grove-go-I feeling in Kerouac's credit-card sensibility.

At times his aggressive religiosity resembles Muhammad Ali's "Methinks women love me and then they realize I'm drunk for all the world and this makes them realize I can't concentrate on them alone, for long, makes them jealous, and I'm a fool in love With God. Yes." As for what a "Satori" actually is, he explicates in quasi-religious terms: "Somewhere during my ten days in Paris (and Brittany) I received an illumination of some kind that seems to've changed me again, towards what I suppose'll be my pattern for another seven years or more: in effect, a *satori*: the Japanese word for 'sudden illumination,' 'sudden awakening' or simply 'kick in the eye.'" Unfortunately, the illumination comes at the end of a shaggy-dog story by a saloon Sartre who manages to get gushy over the straightforwardness of a Paris cab driver.

The main trouble with Kerouac is that he is too obtrusive a character to be the kind of observer his travel book requires. Whereas Burroughs can sit down in a corner and record things as they are, Kerouac has to be the center of attention, drinking, brawling, singing, and then writing the next morning, the next month, the next year with an awful hangover and no sense of artistic continuity. It might be said that he is to Mailer as Chateaubriand is to Stendhal, but the drop in discipline through the ages is too depressing for words.

BOY GRAVELY

The triads and tribulations of a serious composer in a corrupt society would seem to be the stuff more of a parody of old when-are-you-going-to-finish-that-symphony-Franz movies than of a supposedly sophisticated novel. The point is I can't help feeling that Iris Dornfeld's unique combination of writing talent and musical background might have dwelled more on fact and less on fable. As it is, a considerable effort has been expended on *Boy Gravely*, a novel so disarmingly didactic, so austerely allegorical and so instructively inspirational that one is numbed by the hellish chill of good intentions.

Miss Dornfeld seems to enjoy starting off her creative characters by calling two strikes on them even before they get out of the dugout. Jeeney Ray, the eponymous protagonist of Miss Dornfeld's first novel, was a spastic. Boy Gravely is an epileptic. Otherwise the hero is born with perfect pitch in an imperfect environment. While he is composing vertically, his mother is consorting horizontally with a procession of truant officers and welfare investigators. If Boy Gravely's mother is a monster of acquiescence, his grandmother is a monster of acquisitiveness in such change-of-pace roles as a Pershing Park pickpocket, pop-music promoter, blackmailer and fortuneteller extraordinary.

H. T. Grythke, a bogusly Byronic Hollywood director, and Warden Ort, a sexually deprived and socially depraved McCarthyite, round out the gallery of grotesques. Unfortunately, Miss Dornfeld's gargoyles, like those of Mr. Dickens, are more effective in satiric repose than in any sort of narrative development. Not that Miss Dornfeld's shadowy world lends itself to any realistic interpretation. At its most lucid, her prose is like a flashlight stabbing the blackness of the murky cellar of the American subconscious.

There are also the good guys, mostly professional musicians and appreciative outcasts, to be found, bypassed by the bourgeoisie, along the tortuous route beginning at the terminus of a Los Angeles slum located with symbolic exactitude between the mass of Mexican-America in Chavez Ravine and the muse of classicism in the Hollywood Bowl.

The odyssey to obscurantism moves on to the jazz joints of New Orleans, to Chicago, to Spanish Harlem and stereophonic Cologne and back to the Hollywood Bowl for the climax and the crescendo. Miss Dornfeld certainly touches all bases even if it means imagining the evolution of a Bix Beiderbecke into a Milton Babbitt.

No novel since Thomas Mann's ill-fated Dr. Faustus has attempted such a conscientious translation of music into language. We are told flatly that Boy Gravely's electrifyingly electronic opus, percussively supplemented with high heels and vacuum cleaner, is a work of genius, but the composer seems to function in a complete vacuum as far as his contemporaries are concerned. Though Beethoven, Mozart and Chopin are invoked from the past, there are no mentions of such moderns as Stravinsky and Schoenberg, Berg and Barber, and hence no precise coordinates with which to chart the relative gravity of Gravely's genius. One might ask if Boy Gravely is really a blithe spirit trilling an original tune or merely a bird in a gilded Cage of noisemakers. In these times, particularly, mere prodigiousness is often confused with genius, and an idée fixe with genuine insight.

What is most fascinating about Miss Dornfeld's fable is her implicit assumption of the unity of art and politics in the liberal imagination. It is a bit like those liberal journals which weep over the travail of the masses in the front pages and then cater to the tastes of the mandarins in the back pages. To believe at one and the same time in bread for the many and art for the few is not exactly a contradiction, but it does imply a disconnected sensibility. Most American artists and intellectuals belong to the Left in some vague form or other, be it liberal, anarchist, socialist, Communist, etc. Yet the claims of the highest art seem incompatible with the mass causes to which the intelligentsia devote their energies. One does not have to be an acute observer of the social scene to realize that the Daily News has many more readers among the oppressed than does the

Partisan Review even though the *News* is basically hostile to the interests of the oppressed.

Consequently, I am not impressed by Miss Dornfeld's assertion that her hero's esoterically electronic music incorporates the sounds of the streets and the slums. I think Miss Dornfeld is indulging in back-page wishful thinking when she suggests that modern music is socially useful in any such programmatic way. With music, particularly, the ivory tower has never seemed so distant from the barricades as today when Axel's Castle is wired for stereo.

Aside from a near seduction by his own forgetful mother, Boy Gravely shuns all mature sexual activity. Our hero is maneuvered instead into the old Capote–McCullers pseudo-sibling syndrome, first with a little Negro boy too neatly wrapped up as the Negro Problem for the benefit of white liberals, and then with his ugly pop banshee of a sister, Mary Mozart Gonzales Gravely. Emotional retardation is too high a price to pay for the projection of an idealistic image even in an allegory. Perhaps that is why Miss Dornfeld's novel, like so much of modern music, never really ends. It just stops.

GEORGE ORWELL

The Collected Essays, Journalism, and Letters of George Orwell, edited by Sonia Orwell and Ian Angus. Vol. I: An Age Like This, 1920–1940, $8.95. Vol. II: My Country Right or Left, 1940–1943, $8.95. Vol. III: As I Please, 1943–1945, $7.95. Vol. IV: In Front of Your Nose, 1945–1950, $8.95. Harcourt, Brace & World.

My brother George discovered George Orwell back in the early Fifties in a beat-up copy of a book called *Animal Farm*, which he related to me in its vivid images of pigs, horses, donkeys, dogs and chickens, all expressive of the author's aching feelings of hopes too long deferred and then brutally betrayed. This slim volume became our political Bible, our *Mein Kampf* and *Das Kapital*, our vindication and justification as obscure bystanders in a world we never made and seemed destined never to influence. Our family's upward mobility had taken us merely from the tributaries of the Flatbush trolley line to the green shores of Queens Boulevard, in effect from one repository of middle-class impotence to another. But being neither Catholic nor Jewish, we felt cut off from the compensating group-sings of extremist rhetoric with which the powerless serenade the powerful in this fair city. We felt at home neither with the Thomists nor the Marxists, neither with the yogi nor the commissar. Orwell became our intellectual shield against both the hoggish complacency of the Right and the swinish connivance of the Left. Almost instantly, it seemed, we had recognized a kindred spirit in the spare literary style of a matter-of-fact fantasy. We felt we had always known Orwell, though, in fact, he had died shortly before we detected the slightest trace of his existence on this earth. We gobbled up everything we could find by him—books, novels, essays. Thus we came to know him much better than we knew ourselves, and yet knowing him enabled us to come to terms with our own self-deceiving personae, those self-righteously repressed banshees of outraged innocence and class paranoia. We were not particularly shocked or surprised when we discovered that George Orwell had begun life as Eric Blair, and had never completely disentangled his real identity from his literary-political fantasies. Getting Out From Under Yourself is the favorite game of losers and outsiders, and all his life Orwell was something of a loser and an outsider, and only other losers and outsiders could ever love Orwell as he deserved to be loved and as he could never love himself.

I'm sorry my brother George didn't live long enough to see the four volumes of *The Collected Essays, Journalism, and Letters of George Orwell*, edited by Sonia Orwell and Ian Angus. As a confirmed Orwellian, George undoubtedly would have shared my reservations about the studied selectivity of the editors, who state: "We have excluded much of the journalism and many letters. The letters which are not included are of the 'glad to meet you Saturday' or 'would you send the proofs to the following address' kind. The journalism we have not printed is purely ephemeral and the very few surviving pieces of his youthful work are not important. No one could have written as much journalism as he did and kept it all on the same level, certainly not someone who was so often tired and unwell."

Granting the editors the best intentions in the world, I still regret their decision not to include all of Orwell's "journalism," including his BBC broadcasts to India. As an editor, I have always sinned on the side of exhaustiveness for the sake of historical perspective. In Orwell's case, the editors may have sacrificed some of the author's political relevance to his time out of fear for his literary reputation. The decision between quantity and quality is always a difficult one to make, but I would lean to quantity in an ostensibly definitive, posthumous enterprise of this nature. As it is, the volumes are too lumpy for the casual reader, and not lumpy enough for the loving Orwellian. I was particularly disappointed at not finding any of the theater and movie reviews to which references are made in both the editors' notes and the Orwell essay entitled "Confessions of a Book Reviewer." Orwell's letters are something else again, and I am willing to take the word of the editors on the ones that were excluded. Unlike many literary men of leisure, Orwell did not correspond with posterity through a Bloomsbury postmark. None of Orwell's published letters can be mistaken for an epistolary essay, and many would be indecipherably cryptic without helpfully pertinent footnotes from the editors. Also, Orwell was unusually reticent about his personal life even for an age that had not yet progressed to the point of freely discussing the various methods of masturbation. Still, though the letters provide few new insights into Orwell, they never contradict the intellectual and emotional evidence of his more formal writings.

Orwell's life and art were shaped by the convulsions attending the British Empire, two world wars, the Depression, the Spanish Civil War and the rise of modern bully-boy totalitarianism, cosmic crimes to which Orwell bore witness, often eyewitness, with a degree of candor and clarity that distressed the more "responsible" intellectuals of his time. Indeed, Orwell managed to step on so many influential toes of the Right and the Left that he finally found himself on an ideological island of which he was the only inhabitant. It was a queer sort of island full of wood-lore and working-class virtue and yet heavily stocked with books. No one quite believed in Orwell's island; it was too personal and romantic in its humble English-sparrowish way. But it was ultimately respected and even revered as journey's end for one of the most quixotic adventurers of the twentieth century.

George Orwell was born Eric Arthur Blair on June 25, 1903, at Motihari, Bengal. His father was a sub-deputy agent in the Opium Department, no less, of the Indian Civil Service. The Blairs came to England on leave in 1907, and Orwell did not return again to the Orient until 1922 when he joined the Indian Imperial Police in Burma. The editors profess ignorance of Orwell's exact motives for his exotic choice of a profession, but it seems reasonable to assume that a sensitive young man might be curious about the imperial conditions that molded the genteel middle-class poverty and snobbery of the Anglo-Indian community in England to which his parents belonged, a community moreover that Orwell was later to describe with such savage derision in "Coming Up for Air" and "The Clergyman's Daughter."

"From a very early age, perhaps the age of five or six, I knew that

when I grew up I should be a writer," Orwell recalled in a 1946 essay
entitled "Why I Write." Orwell developed the biographical basis of
his decision as if he were a clinical example of all writers:

I was the middle child of three, but there was a gap of five years on
either side, and I barely saw my father before I was eight. For this and
other reasons I was somewhat lonely, and I soon developed disagreeable
mannerisms which made me unpopular throughout my schooldays. I
had the lonely child's habit of making up stories and holding conversa-
tions with imaginary persons, and I think from the very start my literary
ambitions were mixed up with the feeling of being isolated and under-
valued. I knew that I had a facility with words and a power of facing
unpleasant facts, and I felt that this created a sort of private world in
which I could get my own back for my failure in everyday life.

Orwell was more explicit about the failures of his everyday life in
the most painfully autobiographical of all his essays the one entitled
with bitter irony "Such, Such Were the Joys." This anti-school-tic
recollection of student life at St. Cyprian's took the author through
the traumatically formative years of eight to thirteen. But these were
also the years (1911–1916) in which European history suffered the
first of many convulsions with which Orwell was to associate his own
political personality. It was probably at St. Cyprian's that Orwell felt
the first pangs of class envy:

In effect there were three castes in the school. There was the minority
with an aristocratic or millionaire background, there were the children
of the ordinary suburban rich, who made up the bulk of the school, and
there were a few underlings like myself, the sons of clergymen, Indian
civil servants, struggling widows, and the like. These poorer ones were
discouraged from going in for "extras" such as shooting and carpentry,
and were humiliated over clothes and petty possessions.

As in all of Orwell's official recollections, the most personal suffering is seen in historical perspective:

There never was, I suppose, in the history of the world a time when the
sheer vulgar fatness of wealth, without any aristocratic elegance to redeem it, was so obtrusive as in those years before 1914. It was the age
when crazy millionaires in curly top-hats and lavender waistcoats gave
champagne parties in rococo house-boats on the Thames, the age of
diabolo and hobble skirts, the age of the "knut" in his grey bowler and

cutaway coat, the age of *The Merry Widow*, Saki's novels, *Peter Pan*, and *Where the Rainbow Ends*, the age when people talked about chocs and cigs and ripping and topping and heavenly, when they went for divvy week-ends at Brighton and had scrumptious teas at the Troc. From the whole decade before 1914 there seems to breathe forth a smell of the more vulgar, un-grown-up kinds of luxury, a smell of brilliantine and creme-de-menthe and soft-centred chocolates—an atmosphere, as it were, of eating everlasting strawberry ices on green lawns to the tune of the Eton Boating Song. The extraordinary thing was the way in which everyone took it for granted that this oozing, bulging wealth of the English upper and upper-middle classes would last forever, and was part of the order of things. After 1918 it was never quite the same again. Snobbishness and expensive habits came back, certainly, but they were self-conscious and on the defensive. Before the war the worship of money was entirely unreflecting and untroubled by any pang of conscience. The goodness of money was as unmistakable as the goodness of health or beauty, and a glittering car, a title, or a horde of servants was mixed up in people's minds with the idea of actual moral virtue.

Orwell writes time and again of his morbid outlook, his despairing anticipation of death, his self-fulfilling fear of failure, his almost Swiftian preoccupation with the pores and blemishes of what he presumed to be his own socially disabling physical ugliness. And yet he never seemed to succumb to the culturally fashionable sin of pessimism, not even during the darkest days of World War II when even the threat of defeat itself was insufficient to reduce social injustice and intellectual confusion. What sustained Orwell as a relatively affirmative political activist was a belief in a modest form of Socialism dissociated from Utopianism.

"Socialists," he wrote in December 1943, "don't claim to be able to make the world perfect; they claim to be able to make it better. And any thinking Socialist will concede to the Catholic that when economic injustice has been righted, the fundamental problem of man's place in the universe will still remain. But what the Socialist does claim is that that problem cannot be dealt with while the average human being's preoccupations are necessarily economic. It is all summed up in Marx's saying that after Socialism has arrived, human history can begin."

Seven years earlier Orwell had traveled that metaphorical road from Mandalay (British Imperialism) to Wigan Pier (British Capitalism) where he had plunged down into the coal mines, a literary Prospero among the proletarian Calibans, draining himself of all personal self-pity with this eloquent gut insight:

In a way it is even humiliating to watch coal-miners working. It raises in you a momentary doubt about your own status as an "intellectual" and a superior person generally. For it is brought home to you, at least while you are watching, that it is only because miners sweat their guts out that superior persons can remain superior. You and I and the editor of the *Times Lit. Supp.*, and the Nancy poets and the Archbishop of Canterbury and Comrade X, author of *Marxism for Infants*—all of us *really* owe the comparative decency of our lives to poor drudges underground, blackened to the eyes, with their throats full of coal dust, driving their shovels forward with arms and belly muscles of steel.

The preceding passage would hardly offend anyone of liberal or Left leaning. Further on in *The Road to Wigan Pier*, however, Orwell so offended the readership of the Left Book Club that publisher Victor Gollancz was prompted to write a partial disclaimer as a preface. It takes no great powers of projection to imagine what Orwell would have thought of today's Crazies if he had lived to be heckled by them. With far less provocation in the mid-Thirties, he made the following almost cruelly anti-eccentric observation:

One sometimes gets the impression that the mere words "Socialism" and "Communism" draw towards them with magnetic force every fruit juice drinker, nudist, sandal-wearer, sex maniac, Quaker, "Nature Cure" quack, pacifist, and feminist in England. One day this summer I was riding through Letchworth when the bus stopped and two dreadfully-looking old men got on to it. They were both about 60, both very short, pink, and chubby, and both hatless. One of them was obscenely bald, the other had long grey hair bobbed in the Lloyd George style. They were dressed in pistachio-coloured shirts and khaki shorts into which their huge bottoms were crammed so tightly that you could study every dimple. Their appearance created a mild stir of horror on top of the bus. The man next to me, a commercial traveller I should say, glanced at me, at them, and back again at me, and murmured, "Socialists," as who should say, "Red Indians." He was probably right—the I. L. P. (Independent Labour Party) were holding their summer school at Letchworth. But the point is that to him, as an ordinary man, a crank meant a Socialist and a Socialist meant a crank.

But then Orwell was staring across the channel at Hitler and Mussolini and the shadows of their steel tentacles spreading across Europe:

We have got to admit that if Fascism is everywhere advancing, this is largely the fault of Socialists themselves. Partly it is due to the mistaken Communist tactic of sabotaging democracy, i.e., sawing off the branch you are sitting on; but still more to the fact that Socialists have, so to speak, presented their case wrong side foremost. They have never made it sufficiently clear that the essential aims of Socialism are justice and liberty. With their eyes glued to economic facts, they have proceeded on the assumption that man has no soul, and explicitly or implicitly they have set up the goal of a materialistic Utopia. As a result Fascism has been able to play upon every instinct that revolts against hedonism and a cheap conception of "progress." It has been able to pose as the upholder of the European tradition, and to appeal to Christian belief, to patriotism, and to the military virtues. It is far worse than useless to write Fascism off as "mass sadism," or some easy phrase of that kind. If you pretend that it is merely an aberration which will presently pass off of its own accord, you are dreaming a dream from which you will awake when somebody coshes you with a rubber truncheon.

In the context of upward class mobility into the literary intelligentsia, Orwell took an unusually dim but still timely view of "making it" with the London mandarins:

The modern English literary world, at any rate the highbrow section of it, is a sort of poisonous jungle where only weeds can flourish. It is just possible to be a literary gent and to keep your decency if you are a definately *popular* writer—a writer of detective stories, for instance; but to be a highbrow, with a footing in the snootier magazines, means delivering yourself over to horrible campaigns of wire-pulling and backstairs-crawling. In the highbrow world you "get on," if you "get on" at all, not so much by your literary ability as being the life and soul of cocktail parties and kissing the bums of verminous little lions. This, then, is the world that most readily opens its doors to the proletarian who is climbing out of his own class. The "clever" boy of a working-class family, the sort of boy who wins scholarships and is obviously not fitted for a life of manual labour, may find other ways of rising into the class above—a slightly different type, for instance, rises via Labour Party politics—but the literary way is by far the most usual. Literary London now teems with young men who are of proletarian origin and have been educated by means of scholarships. Many of them are very disagreeable people, quite unrepresentative of their class, and it is most unfortunate that when a person of bourgeois origin does succeed in meeting a proletarian face to face on equal terms, this is the type he most commonly meets. For the result is to drive the bourgeois, who has idealized the proletariat so long as he knew nothing about them, back into frenzies of snobbishness.

That Orwell's perceptions of class and power relationships are accurate enough to be applied to other times and climes can be demonstrated by the substitution of "white" for "bourgeois" and "black" for "proletarian" as a posthumously Orwellian commentary on the recent confrontation at Cornell: "With loving though slightly patronizing smiles we set out to greet our proletarian brothers, and behold! our proletarian brothers—in so far as we understand them—are not asking for our greetings, they are asking us to commit suicide. When the bourgeois sees it in that form he takes to flight, and if his flight is rapid enough it may carry him to Fascism."

The outbreak of the Spanish Civil War (July 18, 1936) provided Orwell's generation with a concrete cause to which they could respond emotionally and even physically. According to the editors' invaluable Appendix II, "A few days before Christmas, having sent off the completed manuscript of The Road to Wigan Pier to Leonard Moore on 15 December, Orwell left for Spain. On 30 December at the Lenin Barracks in Barcelona he enlisted in the militia of the POUM (Workers' Party of Marxist Unification)."

In Spain, Orwell, eternal loser that he was, managed to align himself not merely with the losing side but with the losing faction of the losing side. The POUM and the other revolutionary parties were denounced by the Stalinist-dominated Spanish Republican government, and Orwell was caught literally between two fires. Shot in the throat by a Fascist sniper in May 1937, he was forced to flee a month later across the French border by the pursuing Communist police. By the middle of July 1937, Orwell had begun writing Homage to Catalonia, perhaps the most truthful and most perceptive book ever written on the Spanish Civil War. From that point on, Orwell was to attain a certain eminence as the scourge of the Stalinists and the toast of the Trotskyists, particularly in America in the friendly pages of the Partisan Review, the New Leader and Dwight Macdonald's

Politics. "The sin of nearly all left-wingers from 1933 onwards," Orwell observed in 1944, "is that they have wanted to be anti-Fascist without being anti-totalitarian."

The two prevailing critical lines on Orwell are that he was more than a writer (conscience, humanity, fairness, virtue, decency, etc.) and less than a writer (chronicler, sociologist, pamphleteer, propagandist, etc.). But what is most surprising in his total work is the emergence of an orderly, consistent, coherent view of world literature out of bits and pieces and fragments of his supposedly ephemeral journalism. Lacking the power and authority and influence and public eminence of a Shaw, an Eliot, or a Leavis, and lacking also the academic assurance that he would be read on his own terms and not on his readers', Orwell was forced to scatter his insights like buckshot over a wide range of routine targets. Hence we receive his judgment of Melville and nineteenth-century America in a brief critique of Lewis Mumford's *Herman Melville,* a critique moreover that establishes Orwell at twenty-seven as something of an art-for-art's-sake boy at least as far as the highest art is concerned. His joint review of Edith Sitwell's *Alexander Pope* and Sherard Vines's *The Course of English Classicism* is a sure-footed tour from the garden of classicism to the jungle of romanticism and back again. His brief notes on Osbert Burdett's *The Two Carlyles* serve as a masterfully concise definition of Carlyle as "that fairly subtilized form of egoist, an orator." And so it goes with Byron, Conrad, Stendhal (rendered with a very precise definition of "charm" as grown-up romanticism), Joyce, Yeats, Lawrence, Kipling, Wells, Wilde, Swift, Eliot, France, Twain, and on to the massive pieces on Dickens, Dali, Henry Miller ("Inside the Whale") and others.

Some of Orwell's short-cut insights—e.g., his likening of the end of Tolstoy's life to the end of Lear's as motivation for Tolstoy's moralistic attack on Shakespeare in general and *Lear* in particular—are worthy of the analytical genius of a Freud or a Marx. His BBC dissection of "Felix Randal" by Gerard Manley Hopkins educates and elevates the non-reader of poetry without vulgarizing the poem, a feat of critical elucidation difficult to this day. Orwell was unusually sympathetic to poetry and poets even though or perhaps because (to cite the Proustian paradox once more) his own poetry was uncommonly pallid and lifeless. He vehemently argued (against James

Agate) that poets deserved military deferment more than professional athletes and entertainers because, among many other reasons,
poetry would always outlive the ephemeral entertainments of sport
and spectacle. (Indeed, Orwell's aversion to professional sports
marks him today as the most old-fashioned, most specialized and
most limited of litterateurs inasmuch as a Philip Roth seems so
proud of knowing Pete Reiser's batting average that one wonders
how Marcel Proust got by without recording the results of the
French bicycle races of his time.)

Still, Orwell's critical generosity to the more magical talents of
other poets and novelists knew no bounds of morality or ideology.
Orwell could appreciate the casual amorality of a Smollett or a
Thackeray precisely because such amorality liberated the author's
thoughtlessly if not heartlessly cruel sense of humor. To be inhibited
by lucidity, clarity and morality as Orwell was inhibited was to be
denied the glazed lyricism of mystics, magicians and madmen. But
though Orwell could never follow Lawrence, Joyce, Yeats and the
whole pack of anti-social pessimists out of Axel's Castle into the
whale and the womb and the ivory tower of anguished alienation, he
was basically right as a critic on the art that would live and the art
that would die. His research into the language made him so aware of
the possibilities of literary expression that though he stripped his
own style down to the bare bones of persuasion, his gray sparrow
feathers were never ruffled by the colorfully poetic plumage that flew
above him. He could admire literary style almost to the door of the
death camps without sacrificing any of his moral resolution to his
muse.

Orwell was aware that the storyteller in him was too often subordinated to the essayist (indeed in all his novels except *Burmese
Days*) and the essayist was too often subordinated to the moralist.
"A Hanging," an early short story, begins suspensefully enough as a
pitiless account of a sloppy execution in Burma. The solemn ritual is
interrupted momentarily by the heart-stopping recognition of the
human factor when the prisoner steps around a puddle on his way to
the gallows. In a Kafkaesque penal colony, the execution would
move forward as if nothing had happened, and the reader would be
left to his own conclusions after emerging from the writer's nightmare. But Orwell must stop the projector to give a lecture on what it

all means, and the story never recovers its narrative flow.

All his life Orwell was plagued by publishers who wouldn't pub-
lish him, editors who edited him with a meat-ax, and libel laws that
by more permissive American standards are still the scandal of British journalism and letters. Indeed the mere threat of libel is often
sufficient to prevent the poor and the weak from getting anything
derogatory published about the rich and the powerful. Orwell's first
three novels—*Burmese Days, A Clergyman's Daughter,* and *Keep
the Aspidistra Flying*—all had to be altered before publication for
fear of libel. And, needless to say, Orwell's frankness and iconoclasm
soon earned him the kind of reputation that severely limited the
number of his journalistic outlets.

Although Orwell wrote especially brilliant essays on the sociological implications of the postcards of Donald McGill ("obscene but
not immoral"), Boys' Weeklies, and "No Orchids for Miss Blan-
dish" (the Americanoid thriller by James Hadley Chase), he could
not be considered as prematurely pop-art-oriented, much less a camp
counselor. Orwell despised most of what passed for mass culture,
particularly in its emphasis on mindless violence and power-
worshipping "realism," the latter concept, according to Orwell, used
to justify an orgasmic passivity to every outrage from Al Capone to
the concentration camps. Orwell didn't seem to be particularly attuned to movies or most other mythic manifestations. Hence, he
tends to dismiss too lightly the large, vague, loose but nonetheless
poetically provocative ideological configurations of George Bernard
Shaw and Jean-Paul Sartre.

Orwell can be snappish, inconsiderate and ill-tempered, but he is
never hysterical. Even when the Nazi death camps were discovered,
Orwell did not scream to high heaven. And why should he have? He
didn't have Hitler on his conscience. Unlike so many parlor pinks,
Orwell had not rationalized the Molotov–Ribbentrop pact; he had
not flirted with a pacifist's pose toward fascism, nor shrunk from
bombing Dresden and Hamburg and Berlin to shorten the war and
save a few more Jews from the gas chambers. It is hard to remember
today the on-again, off-again antics of left-wing intellectuals all
through the Thirties and Forties, but Orwell's essays, columns,
broadcasts and letters bring back this entire period of massive bad
faith in clear focus. Orwell never fell for the fashionable fund-raising

gambit of treating the bombing of poor, defenseless civilians in cities as more outrageous than the slaughter of young men on the front lines. The more civilians bombed, Orwell argued, the less popular would wars become with warlike jingoists. And it might be argued even today that the maddest madmen in the Kremlin and the Pentagon might be thinking twice about getting themselves blown up.

Once the war was over, Orwell visited a prisoner-of-war camp in south Germany. He was shown around the camp by

a little Viennese Jew who had been enlisted in the branch of the American army which deals with the interrogation of prisoners. He was an alert, fair-haired, rather good-looking youth of about 25, and politically so much more knowledgeable than the average American officer that it was a pleasure to be with him. The camp was on an airfield, and, after we had been round the cages, our guide led us to a hangar where various prisoners who were in a different category from the others were being "screened."

Up at one end of the hangar about a dozen men were lying in a row on the concrete floor. These, it was explained, were SS officers who had been segregated from the other prisoners. Among them was a man in dingy civilian clothes who was lying with his arm across his face and apparently asleep. He had strangely and horribly deformed feet. The two of them were quite symmetrical, but they were clubbed out into an extraordinary globular shape which made them more like a horse's hoof than anything human. As we approached the group the little Jew seemed to be working himself up into a state of excitement.

"That's the real swine!" he said, and suddenly he lashed out with his heavy army boot and caught the prostrate man a fearful kick right on the bulge of one of his deformed feet.

"Get up, you swine!" he shouted as the man started out of sleep, and then repeated something of the kind in German. The prisoner scrambled to his feet and stood clumsily to attention. With the same air of working himself up into a fury—indeed he was almost dancing up and down as he spoke—the Jew told us the prisoner's history. He was a "real" Nazi: his party number indicated that he had been a member since the very early days, and he had held a post corresponding to a general in the political branch of the SS. In short, he represented everything that we had been fighting against during the past five years.

Meanwhile, I was studying his appearance. Quite apart from the scrubby, unfed, unshaven look that a newly captured man generally has, he was a disgusting specimen. But he did not look brutal or in any way frightening: merely neurotic and, in a low way, intellectual. His pale, shifty eyes were deformed by powerful spectacles. He could have been an unfrocked clergyman, an actor ruined by drink, or a spiritualist medium. I have seen very similar people in London common lodging houses, and also in the Reading Room of the British Museum. Quite obviously he was mentally unbalanced—indeed, only doubtfully sane, though at this moment sufficiently in his right mind to be frightened of getting another kick. And yet everything that the Jew was telling me of the history could have been true, and probably was true! So the Nazi torturer of one's imagination, the monstrous figure against whom one had struggled for so many years, dwindled to this pitiful wretch, whose obvious need was not for punishment, but for some kind of psychological treatment. . . .

I wondered whether the Jew was getting any real kick out of this new found power that he was exercising. I concluded that he wasn't really enjoying it, and that he was merely—like a man in a brothel, or a boy smoking his first cigar, or a tourist traipsing round a picture gallery— telling himself that he was enjoying it, and behaving as he had planned to behave in the days when he was helpless.

It is absurd to blame any German or Austrian Jew for getting his own back on the Nazis. Heaven knows what scores this particular man may have had to wipe out; very likely his whole family had been murdered; and, after all, even a wanton kick to a prisoner is a very tiny thing compared with the outrages committed by the Hitler regime. But what this scene, and much else that I saw in Germany, brought home to me was that the whole idea of revenge and punishment is a childish day-dream. Properly speaking, there is no such thing as revenge. Revenge is an act which you want to commit when you are powerless and because you are powerless: as soon as the sense of impotence is removed, the desire evaporates also.

Who would not have jumped for joy, in 1940, at the thought of seeing SS officers kicked and humiliated? But when the thing becomes possible, it is merely pathetic and disgusting. It is said that when Mussolini's corpse was exhibited in public, an old woman drew a revolver and fired five shots into it, exclaiming, "Those are for my five sons!" It is the kind of story the newspapers make up, but it might be true. I wonder how much satisfaction she got out of those five shots, which, doubtless, she had dreamed years earlier of firing. The condition of her being able to get near enough to Mussolini to shoot at him was that he should be a corpse.

That Orwell eventually outlasted most of the leeches of the London Left is a tribute as much to his talent as to his tenacity. He has been rightly hailed for his virtue and his decency, but the dullest virtue and the most vapid decency might have impelled a middle-class intellectual to venture out to the colonies, down into the coal mines and off to Spain. But to come back with three personal testaments like *Burmese Days*, *The Road to Wigan Pier* and *Homage to Catalonia* required more than virtue and decency. It required a command of the English language and a passion for clarifying the most complex issues and resolving the most disturbing ambiguities. As it is, the praise of Orwell's sincerity too often obscures his extraordinary subtlety, the latter quality more apparent in his total oeuvre than in the one work for which he is unfortunately most noted, 1984, that neat little horror story of linguistic lunacy that has been conveniently misunderstood by its more vulgar American admirers as a cultural instrument of the Cold War. If Orwell had lived long enough, he might have enjoyed the good financial fortune of being lionized by the Luce publications to the extent of getting free passage to America, a mythical realm he could never afford to visit. But the general tone of his writing on American civilization makes Jean-Luc Godard sound like an agent for the CIA. And Orwell was complaining about the "Americanization" of Europe long before most Europeans were even remotely aware of this irreversible process.

Orwell, we must remember, was not simply English, but patriotically and even parochially English down to the cup of tea, without which, he confessed, he could never begin writing in the morning. And yet he managed expressions of universal compassion that put to shame most of his allegedly cosmopolitan contemporaries. What I remember most vividly from all Orwell's writing is that fantastic passage in *Homage to Catalonia* in which he describes the cold mountain air near Monflorite and how he and his ill-clad comrades shivered; and then, his heart skipping across the enemy lines, he concludes: "How the Moors must have suffered." To call such a man uncharitable, as Mary McCarthy did in her dull hatchet job in the *New York Review of Books*, is merely to spit on the grave of one of the most enlightened human beings this century has produced. Miss McCarthy even has the temerity to equate Orwell's ordeals with her own Catholic girlhood pranks. But then Miss McCarthy, the closest equivalent of a Lucrezia Borgia of letters, virtually admits taking it upon herself to revenge all the parlor-pink coupon-clippers Orwell spent his life ridiculing. Because the well-pampered and well-connected Miss McCarthy seems to feel there is something perverted about a writer without independent means, she practically accuses Orwell of causing the death of his first wife, Ellen, through neglect of her material and medical needs. But though Orwell was concerned about medical costs even as he himself lay dying, his main thought was for his son, Richard: "I am so afraid of his growing away from me, or getting to think of me as just a person who is always lying down and can't play. Of course children can't understand illness. He used to come and say 'Where have you hurt yourself?'—I suppose the only reason he could see for always being in bed."

During the last year of his life, Orwell expressed his feelings for Richard indirectly through his feelings for all children as he had expressed his feelings for all children indirectly through his feelings for Richard: "I read recently in the newspaper that in Shanghai (now full of refugees) abandoned children are becoming so common on the pavement that one no longer notices them. In the end, I suppose, the body of a dying child becomes simply a piece of refuse to be stepped over. Yet all these children started out with the expectation of being loved and protected and with the conviction which one can see even in a very young child that the world is a splendid place and there are plenty of good times ahead."

The last words in Orwell's notebook: "At 50 everyone has the face he deserves." George Orwell died of pulmonary tuberculosis on January 21, 1950. He was forty-six.

MAX JAMISON

Sheed constructs a bright, cutting prose from the dross of everyday slang. He wields that prose with a subtle ear for speech rhythms and a sardonic eye for the telltale gesture . . . he is justly rated as one of the nation's most gifted writers.

—Time

The foregoing blurb for *The Blacking Factory and Pennsylvania Gothic* may help explain why Wilfrid Sheed has been twice a bridesmaid at the National Book Awards (1967, *Office Politics*; 1970, *Max Jamison*) without catching a bouquet. It may be that adjectives like "bright," "cutting," "subtle" and "sardonic" set the literary lions to growling: "Sheed? Very clever writer. Harumph. Too clever. No heart. Good critic but no feeling for life. Funny but cruel, cold, smart, snobbish, etc., *vide* Nabokov, Updike, *et al.*" As it happens, Wilfrid Sheed is indeed one of the nation's most gifted writers, and he is simply paying the penalty democracy exacts from its most brilliant stylists. (See De Tocqueville.) To write well when society is in turmoil is to display a lack of tact bordering on sacrilege. But I haven't taken pen in hand to damn Sheed with pitying praise. Nor to castigate the National Book Awarders for prize-giving formulas even more cabalistic than the dark, devious rites of the occult Oscars. Sheed has been gathering points for years with such novels as *A Middle Class Education, The Hack, Square's Progress* and the non-award-winning works mentioned previously. One of these years he will suddenly blossom as an old dependable without ever having been a young hopeful. Then and only then will the guardians of the novel recognize that Sheed's work—fiction and non-fiction alike—is all of a piece in its moral and intellectual concerns. For the time being, however, I would like to relate to Sheed's *Max Jamison* not so much as a random reviewer than as a professionally interested party to the proceedings (like a whaling captain reviewing *Moby Dick*)—that is, as a member of that brawling brotherhood of critics to which *Max Jamison* addresses itself with such devastating wit and humor.

Max Jamison was originally brought to my attention more than a year ago by Dick Adler, then managing editor of *Show* magazine. It was rumored at the time that Jamison bore more than a passing resemblance to John Simon and that Sheed had taken the opportunity to tell tales out of school about the National Society of Film Critics, a stormy petrel of an organization to which we three—Sheed, Simon, Sarris—belonged. Adler's idea was that I would use Sheed's book as a springboard to give my own version of the society and its colorful members. To this end the book turned out to be a disappointment. Sheed records some of the chirps of critical egos without describing the dazzling varieties of emotional plumage, and how can he when he seems to despise the very process of assembly, at least through the glazed eyes of morally hungover Max:

The critics' circle was in session when he arrived. They met in the Asshole Room of the Hotel Asshole, as far as Max was concerned. His mind tasted quite foul now, and spewed little bits of garbage into his mouth. He had better not talk too much tonight. He had not written his review, and he felt guilty and hungover about that; not, as he had hoped, roguish and liberated. They sat at a long baize-covered table with various-colored potions in front of them, looking, to Max's yellow eye, like wizards, alchemists, dwarfs.

They were talking, his fatheaded circle, about the admission of new members. Jack Flashman, wise guy emeritus at the other news magazine, was on the agenda. "Frankly," said Isabel Nutley of *Women's Thoughts,* "I don't think he quite comes up to our standards." "If we had any standards at all, half of you wouldn't be here," growled the tireless Bruffin. "Gentlemen, gentlemen," said the chairman. "I don't know— who writes the stuff on that magazine anyway? How can you tell? Flashman may be dead, for all we know." "He's a gossip writer, for Christsake. What does he know about the theater?" "What do any of you know about the theater?" "Gentlemen, gentlemen." "Frankly, if Flashman gets in, I quit. I can't stand the guy." "That's too damn bad, we'll miss you, honey, but Flashman happens to write for a very important magazine. You can't just ignore it." "What's wrong with gossip writing? Most of you don't even reach *that* level." "Gentlemen."

As he looked at their small maniac faces round the table, fighting like cannibals over a dead missionary's pants, Max thought, What you need around here is nothing less than a spiritual rebirth. Let me bring it to you! Let me start the ball rolling. But their eyes were crazed, myopic, their voices high and fanatical; they operated out of little glass bowls, and no one could come in.

"What do you say, Max?"

"I say, why not?" Max said with staring eyes. "Why should any man carry through life the stain of being rejected by this damn fool society?"

"Well, that's true," conceded Bruffin.

"Let's hear it now for spiritual rebirth. You too, Bruffin! Down on your knees, you dog. Can't you see that we all have to change? I'm not the only one. You're all self-important asses. Or threadbare clowns. Or pretentious hacks. No exceptions, right? You all know that about each other, at least. Take a vote." The room was rimy with contempt; he had never seen such mutual loathing in any group.

"So let me lead you into the waters of salvation. My tattered little scout troop, my bee-keepers, my bank clerks. Good enough critics, at least, to know each other's worthlessness. Let us begin with that. Lord, they are not much, I know. But take them for what they are. What's that you say, Lord? You'll call us? I see. Yes, I quite understand."

These meetings always gave Max a sovereign headache. All that trade talk. He couldn't connect with it at all tonight. There were too many serious thoughts to be shuffled solemnly around his own showroom. Did these other critics have lives too? He supposed so. Cold sweats. Silent screaming in the night. Isabel Nutley crouched in a corner of her bathtub watching the water rise. Each must come in here sometimes clamoring for rebirth and deploring the triviality of the others; they probably took turns at it. Tonight was old Max's turn. Nothing important.

Sheed's vision of his erstwhile colleagues pertains more to a circle of hell on the *Hellzapoppin* level than to the Algonquin circle. ("Hotel Asshole" is an unduly harsh approximation of "Hotel Algonquin," where, in fact, our turbulent meetings transpired.) Oh, there are the usual defenses and disclaimers, like our movie group being disguised as a theater group and, elsewhere, John Simon being mentioned casually in the text the way George Jean Nathan is mentioned in *All About Eve* alongside Addison Dewitt, partly to throw the outsider off the scent and partly to underline the resemblance between the real and the made up for those who prefer gossip to fiction. Aside from a few nasty scenes in public, however, Max Jamison seems closer in spirit to Wilfrid Sheed (and possibly Richard Gilman) than to John Simon. Jamison resembles Simon mainly in his ambidextrous coverage of movies and theater as regular beats, a strain less on the intellect than on the calendar. Sheed and Gilman come closer to the other options Jamison toys with: Academe: Jamison, Winslow; Sheed, Princeton; Gilman, Yale; national magazines: Jamison, *Now*; Sheed, *Esquire*; Gilman, *Newsweek*; higher-brow-lower-pay alternatives: Jamison, *Rearview*; Sheed and Gilman, *Commonweal*. Over the years Sheed and Gilman have reviewed both movies and plays, but never with Simon's showy simultaneity. Both have been candid about the paradoxes (if not outright contradictions) involved in writing at one and the same time for money and immortality, for the bellies of one's children, the respect of one's peers and the memorial wreaths of posterity. The sell-out syndrome that figures so obsessively in *Max Jamison* is therefore understandable as moral rhetoric more for a Sheed or a Gilman than for a Simon. And just to keep us off biographical balance there is a soupçon of Walter Kerr and Jean (*Please Don't Eat the Daisies*) Kerr in Sheed's epilogue on Jamison's career. No matter. *Max Jamison* can be treated as fantasy and fable much more satisfactorily than as Sunday Supplement Sociology. The critic Sheed has created is a compost heap of every spiritual affliction known to the critical temperament except dullness, ineptness and mealy-mouthed kindness. Whatever else he is, Max Jamison is at least not a fool. Sheed clearly intends that Mean Old Max should tower intellectually over the cultural wasteland he surveys. Sheed himself in his old *Esquire* days once likened Godard to a fifth-rate Albanian novelist or some such literary groundling, and Jamison trots along dutifully behind his master on that issue like a pet poodle: "We've got some stuff on the New Film, the meaning of silence in Jerry Lewis, Godard's use of the tit . . ."—a joke directed at Jamison by one of his editors but one of Sheed's less deceptive sleights of hand in the context of Jamison's earlier encounter with a gorgeous blonde coed Godardophile whom he puts down even as he beds down. She: "But you make jokes about Jean-Luc Godard." He: "Exactly." Mr. Gallagher (and Mr. Simon), meet Mr. Sheed.

When Jamison is not beset by Godard and Godardophiles, he must endure Bonded splinters of plastic psychedelia masquerading as movies or waffled Kirk Douglas westerns with overly cutesy titles like *Wagonwheels*. Not that poor, versatile Max finds the theater any more scintillating than the silver screen. When he is not being bored by hysterically old-fashioned three-walled drama (*The Family Three*) and cocktail parties for Helen Hayes, he must contend with a new barbarian like Heinrich Fuller, author of *Theater Dynamics*, and "one of the new strippers: a fat little man who took off his clothes and rolled around the stage, jeering at the audience. 'Your bodies are dead,' Fuller would scream, his little penis flapping. 'Your souls are dead men's shit.' Very funny fellow." And so much for all the Theatrical Nights of the Living Dead.

Curiously, Max Jamison has been greeted by most book reviewers as a fair approximation of a critic but a foul caricature of a human being. Apparently, nothing is too bad for a critic, nor too good for a human being. My reaction to Jamison is quite the opposite in that I find him believable as a human being and unbelievable as a critic. I simply can't buy the utter joylessness and egregiousness of the scene he covers. But then, unlike Richard Rhodes of the New York *Times Book Review*, I have always thought of Sheed as more of a novelist than a critic even when he was writing criticism. Movies and plays do not exist as autonomous entities in his prose, thereby lump- ily distending it and blocking its marvelous flow. No, even old Anton Chekhov must be ground down into a joke, a vaudeville rou- tine, or, at most, a controlling metaphor in the ever-ripening process of a sensibility already too refined for most workaday critical func- tions. Max Jamison is therefore something of a fraud when he sets himself up as the definitive critic striving to be a human being. Most critics and artists and intellectuals come into being as critics and art- ists and intellectuals because of vague feelings of loss, waste, defeat or deficiency in their lives. Presumably even Heinrich Fuller might have been diverted from the theater if he had had a larger penis to flap offstage. (See *The Wound and the Bow*.) However, once the monstrousness of compensation (see Wilhelm Reich on Emotional Fascism) has been accepted as the condition of the critic, it is too late to worry about the wife and the kiddies and the state of the world. Sheed tries to have it both ways with Jamison by locking him into a ludicrously self-doubting power role and yet making him seem morally superior to everyone else playing that role. Worse still,

Sheed denies Jamison any of the emotional dividends accruing from being paid to watch movies and plays regularly and write about them. The pride of power is consumed in ironic jests about pick-up ploys with print-struck student lays. The pleasure of leisure is turned sour by nostalgia for home and hearth and long forgotten intimations of I-thou. The sheer atavistic enjoyment of sneaking off to movies in the afternoon and parading to the theater in the evening disappears under a wave of emotional guilt for a life (Sheed-Jamison's perhaps?) not really being lived. It is as if Life were Out There Somewhere far beyond the long shots and footlights.

Stuff and nonsense, I say, as a member of two critics' circles. I don't know all that much about the private lives of my colleagues, but from all accounts most of these lives partake of the messiness and instability of our age. It may be argued that the most monstrous among us have never been very seriously tempted to become full-fledged human beings. Still, what distinguishes and even ennobles us is the genuine passion aroused by something outside our admittedly petty personalities. And we are aroused by our métier. To that much I can testify with complete conviction. Besides, if we had not risen to prominence in the practice of our craft, we would be that much harder to get along with in our interpersonal relationships. It is not the so-called critic's temperament that is the corrosive agent in marital affairs so much as it is the acid generated by the scraping of any two egos.

What Sheed has isolated in Max Jamison's persona is merely the somewhat comical paradox that as much as the intellect wishes to treat existence as a gloomily speculative Samuel Beckett play, the emotions persist in reducing family life to a mushy Walt Disney movie. Sheed is especially good with children and their unprogrammed wants in conflict with the programmed wills of the adults. Indeed, Max Jamison's children begin by being obtrusive and end by being obsessive as if all the alleged intellectual passion of a critic had been completely displaced by the rampaging guilt of a failed father. Sheed's creative feat in *Max Jamison* is to make us aware of the dangerous tightrope between art and life, career and family, mind and heart we must all walk in order to fulfill our duties and possibilities on this earth. But he has made it too easy for the heart by not sufficiently taxing the mind of his protagonist. There is too much fat in Max Jamison, too many unused mental muscles, too few competitive stresses and not a trace of cultural challenge. Why? I suspect that along with a self-deprecating irony there is a decided lack of presumption in Sheed. It is no accident that by far the most perceptive epilogue to the curiously masochistic campaign of Eugene McCarthy was written by Sheed for *New American Review*. As I look back on the piece, I can't help feeling that McCarthy's campaign was the kind of campaign Sheed or Jamison might have conducted. With a mixture of arrogance toward the moral claims of others and humility in the face of one's own inescapable aspirations, the whole point of the McCarthy campaign seems to have been to fail with a certain snide grace, gaining little and conceding less. Similarly, the moral geometry of *Max Jamison* is circular rather than triangular in that the characters do not so much bounce off each other into new directions as follow each other around a preordained pattern. Sheed even switches point of view well past midstream from Jamison himself to the mother of his two sons, and, even more important, the only objective witness to Jamison's fairness. It seems that Jamison (and Sheed) could not go on if there seemed to be the slightest suspicion that they wielded their critic's scalpels with a ghoulish taste for the artist's blood. Sheed need not have bothered. His fairness is one of the glories of his rhetoric. At one point in the novel, Max Jamison is building up a head of forensic steam at the expense of a like-you-know student McLuhanite: "Suppose, sir, that you do have this particular mystic pipeline to today's youth, that you are truly in a position to speak for them, and not just for your lazy self—can you tell me why I should throw away a lifetime in the arts, a lifetime of hard-won appreciation and of the most intense pleasure, on the word of some child who has never been there at all? and whose method of persuasion is alternately to grunt and to wriggle?

"Don't misunderstand me, sir. I am not against youth as such. They are wonderfully teachable. But that they should be teaching us; that we should invest them with oracular powers, read into their shrugs and moans some great gnostic wisdom—this is an American superstition so crass that one scarcely knows where to begin with it."

But just as he is gathering strength out of the arsenal of his cultural righteousness, Jamison gets a glimpse of his confederates inside the Winter Palace: "The old men cheered for the first time, loudly and wildly, to the point of cardiac risk. Max felt green mold forming in the seams of his cheeks, as he led his old men's army over the barricades; hobbling and leering and brandishing their wooden limbs. He didn't want to go on with this argument, he was suddenly sick of it. But he had to conclude."

The ability to confront the invidious implications of one's own rhetoric at the peak of its persuasiveness is the mark of a fair-minded writer. That too many of his targets are propped-up straw men and sitting ducks attests not so much to Sheed's lack of fairness as to his lack of interest in the logic and nuance of cultural heresies. But that isn't the real problem with Max Jamison as far as certain portions of the literary establishment are concerned. Sheed's real offense against decorum is his minute examination of all the disagreeable details of being a middle-class intellectual in a society where only inherited money is truly admired. How gloriously grubby are Sheed and Jamison on the lecture circuit, in academe, in the corridors of the castrating news magazines, in the cluttered dungeons of avant-garde pretense, and, above all, at dinner with the breadwinning wife who must be kept in her place so that her husband is not as emasculated psychically as he will always be economically. What grubby book reviewer can forgive Sheed for exposing the grubbiness we all share as we lurch onward and upward with the arts?

INDEX

B 2/8